Clear Grammar **3**

2nd Edition

Clear Grammar **3**

2nd Edition

Keys to Grammar for
English Language Learners

Keith S. Folse

Ann Arbor
University of Michigan Press

Thanks to the readers and contributors of exercises—Katya Goussakova, Mary Ann Maynard, Deborah Mitchell, Laura Monroe, Shawn Pollgreen, Donna Tortorella, and Dorothy Zemach.

ISBN-13: 978-0-472-03243-3

2018   2017   2016   2015   4   3   2   1

Contents

10: Review of Units 1–9

To the Teacher

The purpose of a grammar book for English language learners (ELLs) is to help our students acquire the patterns of English. Simply put, grammar is nothing more than patterns. Some of these patterns are relatively easy (e.g., adjectives precede nouns), while others are more difficult (e.g., prepositions or articles). To help our students acquire these patterns, the four books in the *Clear Grammar* series feature a unique combination of useful grammar information written in simple language with activities that promote more accurate and fluent writing, speaking, reading, and vocabulary.

Clear Grammar 3 offers students and teachers solid presentations of grammar information and useful practice activities for intermediate to high-intermediate students. It is part of a four-volume corpus-informed series of grammar books for all levels of students of English as a second or foreign language. Book 3 covers grammar points for intermediate to high-intermediate non-native speakers of English, including phrasal verbs, infinitives and gerunds, passive voice, and adjective clauses.

Clear Grammar 1 begins the series with basic grammar points, such as simple present and simple past tenses, count and non-count nouns, and prepositions. *Clear Grammar 2* continues with grammar points such as irregular past, articles, and modals. *Clear Grammar 4* continues with grammar points such as word forms, conditionals, noun clauses, and past perfect tense.

Clear Grammar 3 contains exercises that provide relevant practice in basic grammar points for ELLs at the intermediate to high-intermediate level. It assumes that students have knowledge of basic English grammar, including simple sentence structure and verb tenses (past progressive, present perfect, future) and modals. It is designed to be used by adult learners—high school age and up. It is suitable for either intensive or non-intensive programs.

Important features of all four new editions of *Clear Grammar* include:

1. clear grammar explanations with user-friendly charts
2. a grammar discovery task using students' inductive learning skills
3. a large number of activities (about 190 in this book), as well as a wide variety of activities (fill in the blank, sentence completion, scrambled sentences, matching, error ID, editing, original writing, reading, and vocabulary)
4. many more grammar activities at the longer discourse level
5. corpus-informed vocabulary items connected to a unit's target grammar
6. reading skills: each unit includes a critical reading activity and a sentence-reading exercise in which the target grammar is featured
7. writing skills: each unit concludes with two writing activities, one on editing student writing and the other for original student writing
8. vocabulary quizzes: each unit includes at least two vocabulary reviews, one of which focuses on collocations

9. communication skills: each unit includes one to five speaking activities that require students to speak and listen to each other while using the target grammar

10. online extra practice activities that are indicated within each unit

The books in the *Clear Grammar* series have eight main goals:

1. to teach the basic grammar points necessary for ELL students
2. to expose students to a substantial amount of useful, high-frequency, corpus-informed vocabulary that is related to the grammar point being studied, including words, phrases, and idioms
3. to provide ample written practice in these structures at the multi-sentence and dialogue levels
4. to provide practice at varying cognitive levels (i.e., not just rote grammar knowledge and comprehension but also synthesis and evaluation)
5. to engage ELLs through a variety of activities and games
6. to improve students' writing, speaking, reading, and listening
7. to provide ample opportunities for students to check their progress while studying these structures
8. to serve as a grammar reference that is written with language and terms that an ELL at the upper-intermediate or advanced level can understand without teacher assistance

The units may be done in any order. However, it is recommended that the general sequencing of the units be followed whenever possible. An attempt has been made to recycle material from one unit into following units where appropriate.

Although a great deal of variety of material exists in the book, there is a general pattern within each unit.

If you see a key in the right margin in a grammar lesson, it means that this grammar point is featured as one of the 15 keys in *Keys to Teaching Grammar to English Language Learners* by Keith Folse (2009).

Unit Organization

1. **Discover Grammar Task**. In many grammar classes, the teacher simply presents the grammar lesson to the students. Another effective technique is to involve the students in an inductive grammar discovery task that begins each unit.

   Students work together to read a short passage or conversation of one to two paragraphs that are rich in examples of the target grammar and then answer a series of questions about the structures in the text. These questions focus on grammar and meaning.

   Students may or may not be able to actually figure out the grammar issue, but this creates a teachable moment in response to the learners' need to know. Your goal is to pique the students' curiosity about the lesson's grammar. After completing the task in their books, students should discuss their answers as a class before beginning the actual lesson. Some students are better able to remember information that they themselves have worked with, so involving students in this kind of discovery task may ultimately benefit their learning.

2. **Grammar Presentation Charts.** Simple, easy-to-follow charts explain the target grammar, which often features corpus-based vocabulary connected to the grammar point.

3. **List of Potential Errors with Corrections.** This section of the unit includes a list of several of the most common errors made by learners. Following each error is the corrected form so that students can see not only what they should avoid but how it should be corrected. Our students represent a wide range of linguistic groups, and every effort has been made to take this into account in selecting which kinds of errors to include here.

4. **Written (as opposed to Speaking) Exercises.** Teachers and students want a large number of written exercises to allow for ample practice of the newly learned structure. The exercises have been sequenced so that the early exercises require only passive knowledge of the grammar point. For example, students circle one of two answers or put a check mark by the correct word. These exercises are followed by others that are more cognitively demanding and require active production of the language structure. In this way, students can comfortably move from passive knowledge to active production of a structure.

   The written exercises in this book are short enough to be done in a small amount of time, yet they are thorough enough to provide sufficient practice for the structure in question. These exercises may be done in class or as homework. Furthermore, they may be checked quickly either by individual students or by the class.

5. **Grammar at the Discourse Level.** As often as possible, the written exercises in this book consist of connected sentences related to a single topic, with the title of the material indicated just before the grammar activity. This connected discourse helps ELLs improve their overall English fluency while focusing on the target grammar items.

6. **Extra Online Practice.** After students have practiced a structure, they are directed to do corresponding interactive activities on the website that accompanies this series (**www.press.umich.edu/elt/compsite/cleargrammar/**). Students record their scores for these activities in their books, which gives teachers who so desire an opportunity to see how students are doing on a particular grammar item.

7. **Mini-Conversations.** Instead of unconnected single-sentence exercises, this written exercise consists of dialogues that require students to recognize or use the target grammar in a broader context than single sentences.

8. **Editing.** Students need to become proficient at editing their own grammar. To that end, a special activity in each unit allows ELLs to be the judge of whether or not a given sentence does or does not contain an error with the target grammar items.

9. **Sentence Study for Critical Reading.** In this activity, students read a sentence that contains the target grammar and then must choose which of three sentences that follow are true based on the information in the original sentence. To improve

critical-thinking skills, one, two, or all three of the statements may be true, so students must read all three and carefully consider their veracity.

10. **Speaking Exercises.** Each unit has at least one interactive speaking activity that provides an opportunity for students to practice the grammar and build fluency.

11. **Two Review Tests.** Equally as important as the teaching of a given grammar point is the measurement of the learning that has taken place. Near the end of every unit are two review tests. These review tests have various kinds of questions to assess learners' ability in different ways.

    Review Test 1 contains multiple choice questions. It is important to discuss not only why the correct answers are correct but also why the distractors are not correct. Review Test 2 is Production and Evaluation. Part 1 of this review test requires production of the grammar, usually through a fill-in-the-blank activity. Because editing grammar is such an important student skill, Part 2 requires students to edit material that contains typical ELL errors.

12. **Reading Practice.** This longer reading activity generally consists of 200–400 words of text followed by several comprehension questions. The target grammar has been underlined to reinforce students' knowledge and awareness of the grammar.

13. **Two Vocabulary Practices.** Grammar knowledge without expanding vocabulary knowledge is useless, so vocabulary must be practiced and learned. The units overtly present new vocabulary to help students increase their vocabulary as much as possible. To this end, two vocabulary practice activities help solidify students' knowledge of vocabulary.

    Word Knowledge features 25–35 key words from the unit and two answer options. Students should select the one word that is clearly related to the target vocabulary word.

    Collocations features 25–40 key phrases or word combinations that are used frequently. Here students choose the one word that best completes the phrase. Examples include *a* _____ *menu* with *sauce* and *special* as answer choices, and *in* _____ with *fact* and *menu*.

14. **Writing Practice.** The writing practice at the end of each unit has two parts. Part 1 provides additional editing practice as students must edit a student writing sample according to a list of errors that have been identified. These errors represent the most typical ELL errors for this proficiency level and grammar point. In Part 2, students are to write a short assignment based on something similar to the passage written for Part 1. Teachers may elect to have their students write sentences or paragraphs depending on the curriculum in their program.

15. **One-Minute Lesson Notes.** A unique feature of this series is the inclusion of numerous student notes, which appear in two small shaded boxes in each unit. These notes contain important information on an array of language areas, including grammar, vocabulary, pronunciation, capitalization, punctuation, and learning strategies, which teachers may discuss with the whole class or just point out to students for additional information.

Keys to Using This Book for Students

 Grammar Lesson

These charts have useful grammar information. Learn this information. If you do not understand something, ask your teacher.

 BE CAREFUL!

These mistakes are common. Do you make these same mistakes? Study these mistakes and the corrections very carefully.

 Editing Practice

Editing practice is offered in several places within a unit. This exercise practices the grammar by asking you to recognize errors.

 Connecting Grammar and Vocabulary

This symbol indicates a box explaining how vocabulary is tied to a specific grammar text. Content is based on real language samples.

 One-Minute Lesson

These boxes have important information about grammar, vocabulary, spelling, or language usage.

 Online Exercise

This symbol means that there is an extra practice activity online. Be sure to write your score in your book.

 Speaking Practice

Doing exercises on paper is not enough. In these conversations and speaking activities, you must try to use your new grammar as much as possible. Listen to other students' grammar.

 Review Tests

Each unit has two review tests. The first one has multiple choice questions, and the second has other kinds of questions.

 Reading Practice

As you do this practice, be sure to notice the underlined grammar examples in the reading.

 Vocabulary Practice

Grammar is important, but you need to have a large vocabulary. Pay careful attention to the two vocabulary practices.

 Writing Practice

Part 1 works on editing. You need to be able to write correctly, so this part is very useful. In Part 2, you can write original work.

Unit 1

Phrasal Verbs

Discover the Grammar

Read the passage about one person's difficulty in waking up on time. Then answer the questions that follow.

Line	
1	For his whole life, Nick has never been able to **get up** early. When he
2	was in elementary school, his mother would set the alarm clock for 6:00 AM,
3	but it would not **wake** him **up**. When Nick was in high school, his alarm
4	clock would **go off**, but he simply **turned** it **off** and **went back** to sleep.
5	Every morning his father would shout, "**Come on**, Nick! You're going to
6	be late." The shouting did not help, however. On a few days, Nick would
7	**show up** two hours late! Nick knew that his school would not **put up with**
8	this situation much longer. His parents were frustrated, but they could not
9	**give up**.
10	One day Nick's mom **came across** a blog on the Internet where people
11	were sharing their stories about oversleeping and different solutions they had
12	**come up with** to solve their problems. After **going over** a few of these stories
13	and realizing there could be an underlying health issue, Nick's mother **made**

14	**up** her mind that the best advice was to **look for** a sleep specialist on the
15	Internet.
16	After **checking out** several websites, Nick's mom **found out** about a
17	specialist for her son's condition. She **called** him **up** and left a message. The
18	next day, the doctor **called** her **back** to **talk about** Nick's situation. Now the
19	family is **counting on** him to help solve Nick's problem.

1. The bold words are called phrasal verbs. Each phrasal verb has a meaning that is different from its verb and second word. Write the meaning for these phrasal verbs from Paragraph 1.

Line	Phrasal Verb	Meaning
1	get up	
3	wake up	
4	go off	
4	turn off	
4	go back	
5	come on	
7	show up	
7	put up with	
9	give up	

2. Sometimes a phrasal verb can have a word between its two parts. Write the four phrasal verbs that have a word separating the two parts.

Line	Separated Phrasal Verb	Line	Separated Phrasal Verb
3		17	
4		18	

3. Why do you think these are separated?

_____

_____

Grammar Lesson

Phrasal Verbs

A phrasal verb is a special kind of verb that consists of two (or three) parts. The first part is always a verb. The next part is a word such as **across, after, away, back, down, in, into, off, on, out, over,** or **up.** In a phrasal verb, this second part is called a **particle.**

Examples	Meaning
When I clean my sofa cushions, I sometimes **come across** lost coins.	find
Before an important exam, you should **look over** your notes.	review
Due to the bad weather, the coach **called off** the game.	canceled

<u>Rule 1</u>. A phrasal verb must have at least two parts: VERB + particle.

<u>Rule 2</u>. Phrasal verbs present a huge vocabulary challenge because most phrasal verbs are idioms. As such, the meaning of a phrasal verb as a unit is usually very different from the meanings of the individual verb and the particle: the meaning of **come across** is not equal to the meaning of *come* and *across.*

<u>Rule 3</u>. Like other common words, a phrasal verb can have more than one meaning: The airplane took off is not the same as Their business took off or I took off my shoes.

 BE CAREFUL!

Common Learner Errors	Explanation
1. Excuse me. How can I ~~ascertain~~ find out which bus goes to Jensen Stadium?	Do not avoid using phrasal verbs. The single-word alternatives found in a dictionary often sound more technical or formal than the equivalent phrasal verb.
2. My cousin ~~picked me~~ picked me up at the airport last night.	Do not forget to use the whole phrasal verb, not just the verb.

Connecting Grammar and Vocabulary

Phrasal verbs are a common component of the English language. Study this list of the 10 most common phrasal verbs.

| 10 Common Phrasal Verbs in Spoken and Written English ||
Phrasal Verb	Example Sentence
1. go on	What's **going on**?
2. carry out	They **carried out** the boss's plan.
3. set up	It is expensive to **set up** a new business.
4. pick up	Can you **pick** me **up** at the airport next Monday?
5. go back	When did Pierre **go back** to France?
6. come back	What time will you **come back**?
7. go out	The lights **went out** around ten.
8. point out	The teacher **pointed out** the most important pages.
9. find out	When did you **find out** about the accident?
10. come up	His divorce did not **come up** in our conversation.

Source: Gardner, D., & Davies, M. (2007). Pointing out frequent phrasal verbs: A corpus-based analysis. *TESOL Quarterly 41*, 339–359.

EXERCISE 1. Identifying Phrasal Verbs in Context

Underline the eight phrasal verbs in this short passage.

An Afternoon at the Library

Today I am going to the library because I need to take back a book I checked out two weeks ago and then pick out a new book to read. One of my

favorite things is to take off my shoes, sit down on the sofa, and hold a real book in my hands as I devour the pages. Of course I could look over a list of e-books and download one to my Kindle, but it's just not the same experience. I also like going to the library because there is always a chance I might run into an old friend there. Sometimes my best friend and I meet at the library for coffee and catch up on each other's news before we find new books to take home. I really enjoy my library visits.

EXERCISE 2. Identifying Specific Meanings of a Phrasal Verb

Match the meaning of **make up** with its definition by writing the correct number on the lines.

> Meaning 1. combine to equal:
> *These five cities make up more than half of the state's entire population.*

> Meaning 2. become friends again, apologize, reconcile:
> *I argue with my uncle a lot, but we make up pretty quickly.*

> Meaning 3. create (a story):
> *Some people are good at making up jokes, but I am not one of those people.*

> Meaning 4. put in order, prepare, arrange:
> *In a hotel, a maid makes up the beds.*

> Meaning 5. serve to compensate for something that was lost or missed:
> *I couldn't work on Monday, so I will make up the hours on Saturday.*

_____ a. My nephew is learning how to talk, but he can't **make up** a sentence on his own yet.

_____ b. One job of a chef is to **make up** the menu for the week.

_____ c. I was absent yesterday, so I will **make** the test **up** at the next class meeting.

_____ d. I love this salad. It is **made up** of kale, cashews, and blueberries.

_____ e. My husband and I have a rule. If we fight about something, we always **make up** before the sun goes down.

_____ f. I can't believe that story. Did you **make** it **up**?

_____ g. The digestive system is **made up** of several organs, including the stomach and intestines.

_____ h. My brother had a fight with his girlfriend, but I'm sure they'll **make up** again.

Grammar Lesson

Separable Phrasal Verbs

The phrasal verbs in this group can be separated when there is a noun as the object. If there is a pronoun as the object, the phrasal verb must be separated.

In informal English, the particle can sometimes be several words away from the verb. In more formal writing, it is best to keep the verb and the phrasal verb together. When the object is a pronoun, however, the verb and the particle <u>must</u> be separated. See the list on page 8.

	Noun Object	Pronoun Object
separable	Please **put on** your shoes.	Please put on ~~them~~.
	Please **put** your shoes **on.**	Please **put** them **on.**

	Noun Object	Pronoun Object
non-separable	The teacher **called on** Josh.	The teacher **called on** him.
	The teacher called ~~Josh on~~.	The teacher called ~~him on~~.

<u>Rule 1.</u> With separable phrasal verbs, it is possible to move the particle after a noun object. However, this movement is not common in formal writing.

<u>Rule 2.</u> With separable phrasal verbs, you must separate the verb and particle when a pronoun is used as the object.

<u>Rule 3.</u> Separable phrasal verbs often use these nine particles: **up, down, on, off, in, out, away, back, over.** (An easy way to remember the first six is that they are pairs of opposites: **up ≠ down, on ≠ off, in ≠ out.**)

<u>Rule 4.</u> Be careful with phrasal verbs using **on** because some are separable but others are non-separable. For example, **put on** is separable, but **call on** is non-separable. The only way to know which is which is to check a dictionary for every phrasal verb using **on.**

	Separable Phrasal Verbs			
Phrasal Verb	**No. 1 PHR. VERB + NOUN**	**No. 2 Separated by NOUN**	**No. 3 PHR. VERB + PRONOUN**	**No. 4 Separated by PRONOUN**
call back (return a call)	*call back John*	*call John back*	~~*call back him*~~	*call him back*
call off (cancel)	*call off the game*	*call the game off*	~~*call off it*~~	*call it off*
call up (telephone)	*call up the teacher*	*call the teacher up*	~~*call up her*~~	*call her up*
cross out (draw a line through)	*cross out the mistakes*	*cross the mistakes out*	~~*cross out them*~~	*cross them out*
figure out (find the answer to a problem)	*figure out the answer*	*figure the answer out*	~~*figure out it*~~	*figure it out*
fill in (write information)	*fill in the blank*	*fill the blank in*	~~*fill in it*~~	*fill it in*
fill out (complete a paper)	*fill out the form*	*fill the form out*	~~*fill out it*~~	*fill it out*
find out (get information)	*find out the price*	*find the price out*	~~*find out it*~~	*find it out*
give away (give something to someone)	*give away the prize*	*give the prize away*	~~*give away it*~~	*give it away*
give back (return something to someone)	*give back the reward*	*give the reward back*	~~*give back it*~~	*give it back*
hand in (submit)	*hand in my paper*	*hand my paper in*	~~*hand in it*~~	*hand it in*
hand out (give one to everyone)	*hand out the papers*	*hand the papers out*	~~*hand out them*~~	*hand them out*
leave out (omit)	*leave out the sentence*	*leave the sentence out*	~~*leave out it*~~	*leave it out*
look up (look for information)	*look up this word*	*look this word up*	~~*look up it*~~	*look it up*
make up (invent a story)	*make up a story*	*make a story up*	~~*make up one*~~	*make one up*

pick up (1. lift 2. go get someone)	pick up my son	pick my son up	~~pick up him~~	pick him up
put away (return to the correct place)	put away the clothes	put the clothes away	~~put away them~~	put them away
put back (return to the original place)	put back the boxes	put the boxes back	~~put back them~~	put them back
put off (postpone)	put off the test	put the test off	~~put off it~~	put it off
put on (wear)	put on your coat	put your coat on	~~put on it~~	put it on
put out (extinguish)	put out the fire	put the fire out	~~put out it~~	put it out
take off (remove)	take off your shoes	take your shoes off	~~take off them~~	take them off
tear up (rip into small pieces)	tear up the bill	tear the bill up	~~tear up it~~	tear it up
throw away (discard, put in the trash)	throw away the bag	throw the bag away	~~throw away it~~	throw it away
try on (check to see if clothing fits)	try on those shoes	try those shoes on	~~try on them~~	try them on
turn down (decrease)	turn down the radio	turn the radio down	~~turn down it~~	turn it down
turn on (start)	turn on the lights	turn the lights on	~~turn on them~~	turn them on
turn off (stop)	turn off the TV	turn the TV off	~~turn off it~~	turn it off
turn up (increase)	turn up the volume	turn the volume up	~~turn up it~~	turn it up
wake up (stop sleeping)	wake up the baby	wake the baby up	~~wake up her~~	wake her up
write down (make a note of something)	write down the name	write the name down	~~write down it~~	write it down

BE CAREFUL!

Common Learner Errors	Explanation
1. My new shoes hurt. I can't wait to ~~take off them~~ take them off when I get home tonight.	You must separate the verb and particle if the object is a pronoun.
2. I am ~~counting my father on~~ counting on my father to help me pay for my classes.	Be careful with phrasal verbs with **on**. Some are separable, but others are not.

EXERCISE 3. Vocabulary Practice with Separable Phrasal Verbs

Match the phrasal verb on the left with its meaning on the right by writing the letter of the meaning on the line by the number.

<u>Phrasal Verb</u>

<u>Meaning</u>

_____ 1. I <u>made</u> the story <u>up</u>.

a. found the solution

_____ 2. He <u>called off</u> the meeting.

b. started (some kind of machine)

_____ 3. She <u>crossed</u> her answer <u>out</u>.

c. discovered, learned

_____ 4. She <u>found out</u> the price.

d. took with my hand

_____ 5. I <u>put</u> it <u>off</u>.

e. returned to the original place

_____ 6. They <u>handed</u> their paper <u>in</u>.

f. checked to see if they fit

_____ 7. I <u>picked up</u> the coin.

g. invented, created

_____ 8. We <u>put</u> the boxes <u>back</u>.

h. canceled

_____ 9. I <u>tried on</u> the shirts.

i. submitted, gave

_____ 10. We finally <u>figured</u> it <u>out</u>.

j. drew a line through

_____ 11. She <u>turned</u> it <u>on</u>.

k. omitted, did not include

_____ 12. We <u>left out</u> number 8.

l. postponed

 ONE-MINUTE LESSON
When the object of a separable phrasal verb is a noun, you can separate the phrasal verb and particle (or not). In formal language, we usually keep the verb and particle together. However, we must separate the verb and particle when the object is a pronoun: *He* **called off** *the meeting* OR *He* **called** *the meeting* **off**.

EXERCISE 4. Vocabulary Practice with Separable Phrasal Verbs

Match the phrasal verb on the left with its meaning on the right by writing the letter of the meaning on the line by the number.

Phrasal Verb   Meaning

_____ 1. She <u>turned</u> it <u>off</u>.   a. return to the correct place

_____ 2. I <u>filled in</u> the blanks.   b. go get

_____ 3. Did you <u>throw away</u> the bag?   c. broke into small pieces

_____ 4. I <u>handed</u> them <u>out</u>.   d. stopped (a machine)

_____ 5. She <u>looked</u> the word <u>up</u>.   e. extinguished (a fire)

_____ 6. Can you <u>pick</u> me <u>up</u> after work? f. wore

_____ 7. Please <u>put</u> the milk <u>away</u>.   g. distributed to everyone

_____ 8. I <u>wrote</u> it <u>down</u>   h. increased the volume

_____ 9. He <u>put</u> his coat <u>on</u>.   i. completed, entered the information

_____ 10. They <u>put</u> it <u>out</u> right away.   j. discard, put in the trash

_____ 11. She <u>tore</u> it <u>up</u> immediately.   k. made a note

_____ 12. I <u>turned up</u> the TV.   l. looked for information about

Do Online Exercise 1.1. My score: _____ /10. _____ % correct.

EXERCISE 5. Mini-Conversations

Circle the correct words in these eight mini-conversations.

1. *Ella:*   Have you heard the weather report for tomorrow?

   Bob: No, I haven't, but I can turn the TV (in, on) now if you'd like.

   Ella: Ok, thanks. I'm planning to paint the porch, but if it rains I'll have to put it (off, up).

2. *Son:*   Dad, can I borrow your new snow boots?

   Dad: Uh . . . they're probably too big. Have you tried them (up, on)?

   Son: Yes. They'll fit perfectly if I put (away, on) two pairs of socks.

   Dad: All right. Just be sure to put them (out, back) where you found them.

3. *Hailey:* Mrs. Smith, I have a dental appointment tomorrow and my mom needs to pick (up me, me up) before school is out.

   Teacher: Thanks for telling me, Hailey. Here is the excuse form. Remember to ask your dentist to fill (out it, it out).

4. *Zoe:*   Another doughnut! Don't you know that eating food like that every morning is harmful to your health?

   Lucy: All right, all right. I'll put it (down, out).

5. *Yuka:*   In Japan, we always remove our shoes when we enter the house.

   Owen: Really? I only have to take mine (off, down) when they're muddy.

6. *Ryan:*   Hi, John. I missed math class this morning. What was the homework assignment?

   John: Oops. I forgot to write it (up, down)!

7. *Luis:*   How can I prevent someone from using my identification?

   Jack: One way is to tear (up, down) any old documents before you throw (away them, them away).

8. *Brody:*   Is our test really going to be tomorrow?

   Teacher: No, I've decided to put it (after, down, off, over) until next Tuesday.

EXERCISE 6. Practicing Pronoun Objects with Phrasal Verbs

Write each expression using a pronoun as the object of the phrasal verb. The first one has been done for you as an example.

1. Look up the new words. _____Look them up._____

2. She called off the wedding. _____

3. Please write down this number. _____

4. She tore up the letter. _____

5. Don't turn the TV on now. _____

6. He handed out the exams. _____

7. I left out two questions. _____

8. Did you fill out the form?_____

 # Grammar Lesson

KEY 11

Non-Separable Phrasal Verbs

The phrasal verbs in this group cannot be separated. Unlike the previous group of phrasal verbs, it does not matter whether the object is a noun or a pronoun. Some students find this group much easier because the word order is more straightforward with no variations. See the list on pages 14–15.

	Noun Object	Pronoun Object
non-separable	We are **counting on** the president.	We are **counting on** him.
	We are counting the ~~president~~ on.	We are counting ~~him~~ on.

<u>Rule 1.</u> With non-separable phrasal verbs, you can never separate the verb and the particle.

<u>Rule 2.</u> Common particles for non-separable phrasal verbs include: **across, after, into,** or **with.**

<u>Rule 3.</u> The best way to determine whether a phrasal verb is separable or non-separable is to consult a dictionary.

<u>Rule 4.</u> Phrasal verbs that consist of three words are always non-separable.

Phrasal Verb	No. 1 PHR. VERB + NOUN	No. 2 Separated by NOUN	No. 3 PHR. VERB + PRONOUN	No. 4 Separated by PRONOUN
call on (ask a question in class)	call on the student	~~call the student on~~	call on him	~~call him on~~
catch up (with) (reach the same level or position as)	catch up with the others	~~catch the others up with~~	catch up with them	~~catch them up with~~
check into (1. register at a hotel 2. investigate)	check into the hotel	~~check the hotel into~~	check into it	~~check it into~~
come across (find by chance)	come across a wallet	~~come a wallet across~~	come across it	~~come it across~~
count on (depend on)	count on your help	~~count your help on~~	count on it	~~count it on~~
get along (with) (be friends with)	get along with someone	~~get someone along with~~	get along with her	~~get her with along~~
get in (enter)	get in a car	~~get a car in~~	get in it	~~get it in~~
get off (1. exit 2. finish work)	get off a bus	~~get a bus off~~	get off it	~~get it off~~
get on (enter)	get on a plane	~~get a plane on~~	get on it	~~get it on~~
get out of (exit)	get out of a taxi	~~get a taxi out of~~	get out of it	~~get it out of~~
get over (recover from an illness or a problem)	get over a cold	~~get a cold over~~	get over it	~~get it over~~

get through (with) (complete)	*get through with the exam*	~~*get the exam through with*~~	*get through it*	~~*get it through with*~~
go over (review or check carefully)	*go over the test*	~~*go the test over*~~	*go over it*	~~*go it over*~~
look after (take care of)	*look after the baby*	~~*look the baby after*~~	*look after him*	~~*look him after*~~
look out (for) (be careful)	*look out for that car*	~~*look that car out for*~~	*look out for it*	~~*look it out for*~~
put up with (tolerate, stand)	*put up with that noise*	~~*put that noise up with*~~	*put up with it*	~~*put it up with*~~
run into (meet by chance)	*run into an old friend*	~~*run an old friend into*~~	*run into her*	~~*run her into*~~
run out (of) (not have any more)	*run out of gas*	~~*run gas out of*~~	*run out of it*	~~*run it out of*~~
watch out (for) (be careful)	*watch out for that dog*	~~*watch that dog out for*~~	*watch out for it*	~~*watch it out for*~~

 BE CAREFUL!

Common Learner Errors	Explanation
1. The detectives ~~came some new clues across~~ came across some new clues in their investigation.	You cannot separate the verb and particle if the phrasal verb is non-separable.
2. In yesterday's meeting, we ~~ran out time of~~ ran out of time.	You cannot separate the verb and particle in a three-word phrasal verb.

EXERCISE 7. Using Non-Separable Verbs in Context

Complete the sentences with the correct non-separable phrasal verbs.

1. When I get _____ work every day, I get _____ my car and drive straight home.

2. Every time the teacher calls _____ Boris, he is asleep. I don't know how she puts _____ _____ him.

3. Natalia got _____ a plane to Seattle last night to go look _____ her grandfather until he _____ _____ the flu. When she gets back to school, Natalia will have to _____ _____ on her homework.

4. Molly, look _____ _____ that car!

5. When I was cleaning my room, I _____ _____ some old papers from 1995.

EXERCISE 8. Using Non-Separable Verbs with Pronoun Objects in Context

Write each expression using a pronoun as the object of the phrasal verb. The first one has been done for you as an example.

1. We ran out of coffee.   _We ran out of it._

2. They're counting on Paul and me.   _____

3. I couldn't catch up with the other runners.   _____

4. The professor called on Jenny.   _____

5. We ran into Alana and Paulette.   _____

6. Before class, I went over my speech.   _____

 **Grammar Lesson**

KEY
11

Phrasal Verbs without an Object

There are some phrasal verbs that do not have an object because they are intransitive verbs. Verbs in this group consist of the verb and a particle. These two words express a complete meaning, and no object is possible. For example, **pass away** means "to die." It is possible to say, *Mr. Riley passed away*, but it is not possible to say, *Mr. Riley passed away him* or *Mr. Riley passed him away*. See the list on page 18.

Some students find this group the easiest because they do not have to worry about separating or not separating the phrasal verb. Because there is never an object, separating is not a problem.

Rule 1. Intransitive phrasal verbs cannot have an object.

Rule 2. The best way to determine whether a phrasal verb is intransitive is to consult a dictionary.

Rule 3. Some phrasal verbs can be **both** intransitive (no object) and transitive (object required). The meaning may be different.

make up = become friends again	After the argument, they made up.	no object
make up = invent, create	They made up that story.	object = *that story*

Intransitive Phrasal Verbs with Examples	
Phrasal Verb	**VERB + No Object**
break down (stop functioning)	My car **broke down**.
break up (end a relationship)	Susan and Jack **broke up** yesterday.
catch on (begin to understand)	It took me a long time to **catch on**.
come on (stop delaying)	**Come on**! We're going to be late.
eat out (eat at a restaurant)	It's expensive to **eat out** every day.
get up (leave bed)	What time do you usually **get up**?
give up (stop trying)	I was learning French, but I **gave up**.
go off (make a noise)	My alarm **went off** at 6:30.
grow up (become an adult)	I **grew up** in Canada.
hold on (wait)	**Hold on** a minute.
hurry up (go faster)	**Hurry up** or we'll be late.
keep on (continue)	Mike **kept on** talking.
show up (arrive, appear at a place)	Not many people **showed up**.
slow down (go more slowly)	Please **slow down**.
take off (leave the ground)	The plane didn't **take off** on time.
wake up (stop sleeping)	I **woke up** when I heard the noise.

 BE CAREFUL!

Common Learner Error	**Explanation**
1. The new employee finally ~~turned himself up~~ turned up at noon.	Intransitive verbs, including intransitive phrasal verbs, cannot have an object.

EXERCISE 9. Adding Particles to Complete Phrasal Verbs

Read the meaning of the phrasal verb, and then fill in the blank with the correct particle to complete each intransitive phrasal verb.

Phrasal Verb		Meaning
1. break _____	=	end a relationship
2. catch _____	=	begin to understand
3. keep _____	=	continue
4. take _____	=	leave the ground
5. give _____	=	stop trying
6. hurry _____	=	go faster
7. get _____	=	leave bed
8. show _____	=	arrive, appear at a place
9. grow _____	=	become an adult
10. hold _____	=	wait
11. slow _____	=	go more slowly
12. break _____	=	stop working

ONE-MINUTE LESSON

As with all vocabulary, phrasal verbs have multiple meanings. **Take off** can have different meanings: (1) leave the ground (*The plane* **took off** *late.*); (2) remove clothing (*I* **took off** *my socks.*); and (3) become successful (*Her career really* **took off** *in 2011.*).

Do Online Exercise 1.2. My score: _____ /10. _____ % correct.

EXERCISE 10. Adding Particles for Non-Separable Verbs in Context

Fill in each blank with the correct particle to complete the intransitive phrasal verb in each sentence.

1. *Ann:*   Paula, slow _____! You're driving too fast!

    Paul: A few minutes ago you told me to hurry _____. Make up your mind!

2. *Vicky:*   Why were you late for work this morning?

    Franco: I set my alarm clock for 7 AM and at 7 AM it went _____, but I didn't feel like getting _____, so I kept _____ sleeping.

3. *Tino:*   Tomas, come _____! We're going to be late, and you know Karina and Raquel are going to be really mad if we're late again.

    Tomas: I'm trying. You know I hate making plans to eat _____ with them. They never show _____ on time.

4. *Beth:*   How was your flight?

    Pam: As soon as the plane took _____, I fell asleep. I didn't wake _____ until we were just about to land here.

    Beth: You were able to sleep on the plane? I wish I could sleep on planes. I used to try to do that, but I gave _____ a long time ago. It seems there is almost always a crying baby near me on every flight.

5. *Carl:*   Jimmy, what do you want to be when you grow _____?

    Jimmy: I want to be a mechanic so I can fix our car when it breaks _____.

ONE-MINUTE LESSON

I wish I could sleep on planes means that "I cannot sleep on planes." When wishing for the opposite of a current situation, we use past tense after the verb **wish**: *I wish I had a million dollars* or *I wish I spoke Chinese.*

EXERCISE 11. Editing: Is It Correct?

If the sentence is correct, write a check mark (✔) on the line. If it is not correct, write an X on the line and circle the mistake. Then make the change above the sentence. (*Hint*: There are ten sentences. Two are correct, but eight have mistakes.)

Shopping Tips

_____ 1. The best sales are usually during a holiday weekend. It took years of paying higher prices before I caught it on.

_____ 2. If you're like me, then you don't have money to throw away it foolishly.

_____ 3. I usually go the ads over in the newspaper on Thursday.

_____ 4. On the Friday after Thanksgiving Day, I get up early, put my most comfortable walking shoes on, and drive to the mall for a full day of shopping.

_____ 5. Sometimes I come a great bargain across on the clearance rack.

_____ 6. However, you need to watch out damaged merchandise.

_____ 7. You should ask about the refund policy before leaving. Never count all stores to have the same policy.

_____ 8. After you try on a garment, you should be a good citizen and put the merchandise back where you found it.

_____ 9. Of course, it is usually the job of the store clerk to clear the fitting rooms and put the clothes off.

_____ 10. If you take someone with you when shopping for yourself, be certain that you get along for that person.

Do Online Exercise 1.3. My score: _____ /10. _____ % correct.

EXERCISE 12. Speaking Practice: Short Conversations with Phrasal Verbs

Step 1. Work in pairs. Look at the list of phrasal verbs pages 8–9, 14–15, and 18. With your partner, choose at least three phrasal verbs to use in a conversation.

Step 2. Choose one of the topics listed, or you may use your own idea. First, write a conversation using your three phrasal verbs, but of course you can use more if you like. When you have finished this step, then practice your conversation a few times until it sounds fluent.

Step 3. Perform your conversation for another pair. They will try to note which phrasal verbs you used. Then switch roles and listen to their conversation to identify their phrasal verbs. Can you catch all of them?

Step 4. After practicing your conversations out loud, make any final corrections to your paper. Underline all of the phrasal verbs before turning in your paper.

> Topic ideas:
> - Two friends talking about their plans for the weekend
> - A problem that you need to take care of
> - A teacher and student discussing a test
> - Two people planning a trip

EXERCISE 13: Sentence Study for Critical Reading

Read the numbered sentences. Then read the three answer choices and put a check mark (✔) in the yes or no box in front of each sentence to show if that answer is true based on the information in the original sentence. If there is not enough information to mark something as yes, then mark it as no. Remember that more than one true answer may be possible.

1. I asked my sister to give Jon a ride to the mechanic's shop because he needs to pick up his car at 4 o'clock.

   ☐ yes ☐ no a. Jon will select a car at the shop.

   ☐ yes ☐ no b. My sister will be a passenger in Jon's car.

   ☐ yes ☐ no c. Jon is in his car now.

2. Bob has a big surprise for his sister, so he asked his friends to be careful not to give it away.

   ☐ yes ☐ no a. Bob is worried his sister will give her surprise to his friends.

   ☐ yes ☐ no b. Bob wants his friends to be quiet about his planned surprise.

   ☐ yes ☐ no c. Bob has a surprise for his sister.

3. Before Cindy throws her old bills away, she almost always tears them up.

   ☐ yes ☐ no a. Cindy probably doesn't want anyone to read her bills.

   ☐ yes ☐ no b. Cindy begins to tear her bills from the bottom edge to the top.

   ☐ yes ☐ no c. When Cindy sees old bills, she puts them away as fast as possible.

4. Ahmed told his teacher Mrs. Smith that all classes would be called off due to the expected bad weather, but Mrs. Smith said she had to look into the situation more first.

   ☐ yes ☐ no a. Mrs. Smith is going to cancel classes.

   ☐ yes ☐ no b. Mrs. Smith will investigate the possibility of classes being canceled.

   ☐ yes ☐ no c. Mrs. Smith decided not to call off the classes.

5. Whenever Paul washes his car, he can count on it to rain soon.

   ☐ yes ☐ no a. It usually rains soon after Paul washes his car.

   ☐ yes ☐ no b. When Paul does not wash his car, he hopes it does not rain.

   ☐ yes ☐ no c. We can depend on Paul to wash his car after it rains.

6. Blanca is quite disrespectful to the customers, and her boss said he is not going to put up with it much longer.

   ☐ yes ☐ no a. Blanca's boss has been tolerating her bad behavior.

   ☐ yes ☐ no b. Blanca's boss may fire her soon if she doesn't begin to respect the customers.

   ☐ yes ☐ no c. The customers are probably not happy with Blanca.

7. While Gary and Linda vacation in Florida, Katrina will look after their pets.

   ☐ yes ☐ no a. Katrina will feed and water the pets and be certain they are safe.

   ☐ yes ☐ no b. Katrina will watch the animals during the day but not at night.

   ☐ yes ☐ no c. The animals belong to Gary and Linda.

8. June ran out of money on her trip, so she went to a bank machine and took more money out.

   ☐ yes ☐ no a. As a result of this action, June was able to get some money.

   ☐ yes ☐ no b. June was not able to go to the bank today.

   ☐ yes ☐ no c. June spent all her money on her trip.

REVIEW ▶ EXERCISE 14. Review Test 1: Multiple Choice

Circle the letter of the correct answer. Some are conversations.

1. "How is Janice?"

   "She's better now. It took her a long time to _____."

   a. get over the flu   c. get the flu over

   b. get over   d. get it over

2. "Your English is really good."

   "Thanks, but it took me many years to be able to catch _____ to American pronunciation."

   a. up   c. on

   b. off   d. with

3. "Did you complete both of the forms?"

   "Yes, I filled _____ before I left the office yesterday. Here you go."

   a. it out   c. out it

   b. them out   d. out them

4. They had to call the game off because _____.

   a. the weather was extremely bad

   b. the players were ready to play

   c. the tickets were printed on new paper

   d. the players were in good condition

5. Which one of these is correct?

   a. I counted him on.   c. I looked up them.

   b. I called him on.   d. I looked after them.

6. If you make a mistake in your handwritten essay, do not just _____. Instead, erase it completely.

   a. cross out it   c. turn down it

   b. cross it out   d. turn it down

7. In the end, the customer came up _____ enough money to purchase the car.

   a. on   c. with

   b. for   d. by

8. Our assignment for next week is to look all of the biology terms on pages 96 and _____.

   a. 97   c. 97 with

   b. 97 up   d. 97 out

EXERCISE 15. Review Test 2: Production and Evaluation

Part 1.

Read these short passages. Fill in the blanks with the correct particles.

1. I was so tired when I finally got home. I got _____ of my car and went inside my house. I put a pizza in the oven and set the timer for sixteen minutes. Then I sat on the sofa to watch the news. I used the remote control to turn _____ the TV. I couldn't hear it very well, so I turned

    _____ the sound. A few minutes later, the oven timer went _____, so I turned _____ the oven and put the pizza on a large plate. I was so hungry that I ate the whole pizza. When I got _____ from the sofa, I turned the lights _____ and went to bed.

2. The common cold is one of the most difficult illnesses to get _____ . Sometimes you just have to put _____ _____ the symptoms for a week or more. It is nice if you have someone to look _____ you, cook for you, and make certain you are resting and drinking plenty of fluids. If you are absent from several classes, you should contact the teacher to ask how you can catch _____ . If you miss written assignments, you should also ask if you can turn them _____ late. Your teacher may want a written note from your doctor.

Part 2.

Read each sentence carefully. Look at the underlined part. If the underlined part is correct, circle the word *correct*. If it is wrong, circle the word *wrong*. Then write the correction above.

correct   wrong   1.   *Anna:* Did you finish all the work?

Bob: Yes, I <u>got it through with</u> at noon.

correct   wrong   2.   I called the police when I couldn't <u>put up with</u> that noise any more.

correct   wrong   3.   *Sam:* Betina is a great friend.

Anna: Yes, I agree. You can always <u>count her on.</u>

correct   wrong   4.   *Dan:* Where are those old tennis shoes?

Javier: I <u>threw them away</u> last week. They were really old.

correct   wrong   5.   *Ricardo:* Is that a true story?

Wes: No, I <u>made it up</u>.

correct   wrong   6.   *Teacher:* Why didn't you answer Numbers 5 and 6?

Divya: I <u>left out them</u> because I didn't understand them.

correct   wrong   7.   *Will:* Some friends just heard that there won't be a baseball game today.

Zeke: That's right. We're <u>putting them off</u> until next Monday.

EXERCISE 16. Reading Practice: Solving a Mystery

Read this story, and then answer the comprehension questions that follow. Notice the use of phrasal verbs, both with and without pronouns. The grammar from this unit is underlined for you.

An Alaskan Mystery

It was another working day for the Alaska detective Mike O'Reilly. The police <u>called him up</u> and asked him to <u>find out</u> information about a suspicious December robbery. Myrna LaDame's jewelry had been stolen—but how?

"I read the report that you <u>filled out</u>," he said to Ms. LaDame. "But why don't you tell me what happened in your own words?"

"I <u>took off</u> my diamond necklace and <u>put it away</u> up there, on that high shelf, just as I always do," she explained tearfully. "The only way into this room is through this door. Last night I <u>woke up</u> after midnight sometime because I heard a noise from this room. I didn't know what it could be! But when I tried to <u>get into</u> the room, it was locked—from the inside! I could hear someone inside, so I <u>called up</u> the police on my cell phone, and waited here until they arrived. They broke the lock on the door, but no one was inside, and the necklace was gone. I just can't <u>figure it out</u>. How could the thief have <u>gotten away</u>?"

"What about that window?" asked one of the police officers.

"It's too high up," said Ms. LaDame. "And there's no furniture to <u>stand on</u> in here."

The detective walked around the room. "Hmmm," he said. "Look at this large pool of water in the middle of the room. And someone has <u>turned on</u> the heater. And <u>turned it up</u>, too. It is quite warm in here. I think your thief did <u>get away</u> through that little window way up there. And I think I know how."

1. Who is Mike O'Reilly?

   _____

2. What does Ms. LaDame mean when she says she "can't figure it out"?

   _____

3. How did Ms. LaDame contact the police?

   _____

4. What was stolen?

   _____

5. What happened when the heater was <u>turned up</u>?

   _____

6. What did the thief use to <u>get out of</u> the little window? After you guess, <u>look up</u> the answer on page 33.

   _____

   _____

EXERCISE 17. Vocabulary Practice: Word Knowledge

Circle the answer choice that is most closely related to the vocabulary on the left. Use a dictionary to check the meaning of words you do not know.

Vocabulary	Answer Choices	
1. frustrated	negative feeling	positive feeling
2. merchandise	you buy it	you eat it
3. distribute	hand in	pass out
4. the porch	part of a car	part of a house
5. come across a book	find a book	take a book
6. quite	peaceful	very
7. pass away	die	persuade
8. give up	postpone	surrender
9. muddy	dirty	friendly
10. discard	throw away	run out of
11. advice	requirements	suggestions
12. devour	eat	write
13. a maid	a person who cleans	a person who worries
14. leave out a letter	ABDEFG	ABCCDEFG
15. solve	argue about something	find an answer
16. take off	opposite of *put on*	opposite of *take on*
17. get rid of	make appear	make disappear
18. call on someone	ask a question	use a telephone
19. entire	0%	100%
20. a bargain	cooking	shopping
21. pick out	choose	disturb
22. suspicious	you trust	you do not trust
23. due to	because of	far from
24. run into someone	find someone	interview someone
25. call off	"There is no more time."	"There are no classes today."

EXERCISE 18. Vocabulary Practice: Collocations

Fill in each blank with the answer on the right that most naturally completes the phrase on the left. If necessary, use a dictionary to check the meaning of words you do not know.

Vocabulary	Answer Choices	
1. the _____ went off	driver	timer
2. show up _____	late	someone
3. an underlying _____	departure	problem
4. _____ a problem	measure	solve
5. leave a _____	mechanic	message
6. look over my _____	friends	notes
7. come across a _____	cloudy day	lost photo
8. catch up on _____	ideas	news
9. a _____ shelf	high	thin
10. get out of a _____	lion	taxi
11. fill out this _____	application	decision
12. get over _____	a cold	good news
13. _____ up a story	make	put
14. put on a _____	job	necklace
15. look after your _____	baby	onions
16. figure out the _____	answer	reply
17. put up with that _____ music	beautiful	loud
18. my _____ broke down	car	cup
19. you can count on _____	someone you know	someone you don't know
20. fill in the _____	blank	problem
21. exposure _____ the sun	for	to
22. get along with _____	a person	a store
23. tear up _____	a letter	a newspaper
24. extinguish a _____	fire	ticket
25. _____ the volume	make up	turn up

EXERCISE 19. Writing Practice: Narrating a First Experience

Part 1. Editing Student Writing

Read these sentences about someone's first airplane trip. Circle the 15 errors. Then write the number of the sentence with the error next to the type of error. (Some sentences have more than one error.)

_____ a. wrong verb tense   _____ d. missing subject

_____ b. phrasal verb error   _____ e. singular-plural of nouns

_____ c. article

My First Time Flying
1. Flying on an airplane may seem usual to most people, but my first time on a flights was just the last year.
2. I had always wanted to visit New York, so decided to go there.
3. It was also logical destination because I have a cousin there and was able to stay with him.
4. I now admit that I was nervous as got on the plane.
5. I picked off a seat and sat down.
6. Then the flight attendant explains to me that I had to sit in the seat number that was written on my boarding passes.
7. After the plane took up, I have finally been able to relax a little.
8. In fact, I fell asleep and woke up just before we land in New York.
9. Once the flight landed, stood up, got my luggages from the overhead bin, and walked off the plane.
10. I walked outside the airport to arrival area, and my cousin picked up me there.

Part 2. Original Student Writing

Write a short narrative paragraph in which you tell about the first time you did something new or difficult, such as flying on an airplane. Start with the beginning of your story. Tell the details of what you did. Make sure your story has a good beginning, detailed information about what happened, and a clear ending. Use at least three phrasal verbs in your narrative. Underline the grammar points that you have used so the teacher can see what you are trying to practice.

Solution to Exercise 16, page 29:

The thief stood on a large block of ice to reach the window. Before escaping, he turned up the heat so the ice would melt and leave no evidence.

Unit 2

Infinitives and Gerunds

Discover the Grammar

Read the passage about an interview. Then answer the questions that follow.

Line	
1	My workplace is having some problems right now because we do not have a
2	secretary. Our last secretary stopped working for the company more than a
3	month ago, and we desperately need to find a replacement for her. Our boss
4	has tried to get a new person, but this has been a difficult task.
5	We interviewed a great candidate last week. We all wanted to hire her. Our
6	boss agreed to offer the job to her, but before he could get in touch with her,
7	she had already accepted a job at another company. We cannot delay finding a
8	replacement any longer.
9	My boss has put together a hiring committee so we can find a replacement,
10	and I am on this committee. I enjoy meeting new people, but interviewing so
11	many candidates takes up a great deal of my time. I cannot finish my own work
12	if I stop to take part in the job interviews every week.

13	Perhaps we are being too picky. Perhaps the problem is that we expect
14	to find the perfect person. We hope to hire someone who likes being around
15	people and who is good at organizing files, schedules, and other documents.
16	The person should be someone who can help others do their jobs well and who
17	would like to work on extended projects.

1. Sometimes a verb is followed by **to + VERB**, which is called an **infinitive**. Put a box around the infinitives in Lines 3, 4, 5, 6, 12, 14, 14, 17. Which eight verbs comes before these infinitives? (You need to memorize which verbs are followed by infinitives.)

   _____   _____   _____   _____

   _____   _____   _____   _____

2. Sometimes a verb is followed by **VERB + –ing**, which is a **gerund**. Circle these gerunds in Lines 2, 7, 10, 14. Which four verbs come before these gerunds? (You need to memorize which verbs are followed by gerunds.)

   _____   _____   _____   _____

3. Gerunds function as nouns. Can you explain the use of *interviewing* in Line 10 (instead of an infinitive)? What about *organizing* in Line 15 (instead of an infinitive)?

   _____

   _____

   _____

4. The word *stop* should be in both 1 and 2. There is a difference in meaning, however, between using a gerund and using an infinitive after the verb *stop*. Can you figure out the difference?

   _____

   _____

   _____

Grammar Lesson

KEY 10

Infinitives

An **infinitive** consists of to and the base form of the verb. Examples are *to be, to eat,* and *to produce.*

An infinitive is not a verb. An infinitive can be a noun, an adjective, or an adverb.

Part of Speech	Function in a Sentence	Examples
Noun	subject	To win an election requires a great deal of money.
	subject complement (after **be**)	Her choice was to take the job in California.
	direct object	They want to wait.
Adjective	modify a noun	Her decision to quit her job shocked everyone.
Adverb	a shortened form of **in order to**; it gives a reason	To achieve their goals, the officials hired a new manager.

<u>Rule 1</u>. An infinitive is to plus the base form of a verb (**to + VERB** [*to sing*]) used as a noun, an adjective, or an adverb.

<u>Rule 2.</u> To make an infinitive negative, **not** is placed before the infinitive:

On a flight, I prefer **not to sit** by the window.

<u>Rule 3.</u> An infinitive can be used as the subject of a sentence, but this is relatively rare and sounds extremely formal. The same information is more often expressed by using the pronoun it as the subject:

To compete in the Olympics is an honor. (rare and very formal)

It is an honor to compete in the Olympics. (much more common)

<u>Rule 4</u>. An infinitive is not used as object of a preposition. Instead, we use a **gerund** (–ing form).

wrong: I am tired of to eat at that restaurant.

correct: **I am tired of eating at that restaurant.**

Rule 5. Adjectives come before nouns, but an infinitive used as an adjective comes after the noun it describes:

The flight (noun) **to take** (infinitive as adjective) medicine to the hurricane survivors will depart at noon.

Rule 6. An infinitive used as an adverb expresses **purpose or reason**. You can also say **in order to**:

The airline added a flight to Miami **in order to handle** the increased winter passenger volume.

The airline added a flight to Miami **to handle** the increased winter passenger volume.

BE CAREFUL!

Common Learner Errors	Explanation
1. ~~Educate~~ **To educate** as many people as possible is the president's top goal.	Do not use a base form of the verb for the subject. (However, a gerund is more common for subjects. See pages 39–40.)
2. We need ~~study~~ **to study** more.	Do not use a base form of the verb after a verb unless the first verb is a modal such as *can* or *will*. Many verbs, such as *need* and *want*, are followed by an infinitive.
3. ~~For learn~~ **To learn** a lot of new vocabulary, you should write new words in a notebook.	To express a reason or purpose, use an **infinitive**. Do not use *for* + VERB.
4. To complete the purchase of a product ~~online you~~ **online, you** usually need a credit card.	Remember to use a comma after an infinitive as adverb when it comes at the beginning of a sentence.

EXERCISE 1. Identifying Infinitives in Context

Underline the infinitives in each sentence. (*Hint*: The word **to** appears 24 times, but only 20 are part of an infinitive.)

A Family Trip to Kennedy Space Center

1. Last weekend our family decided to go to Kennedy Space Center to learn about the space program.

2. Because it is difficult to predict the weather at this time of year, we all packed umbrellas to be prepared in case it rained.

3. To get to the space center to take our tour, we had to drive through Merritt Island Wildlife Refuge.

4. To stand in the "Rocket Garden" next to the enormous rockets was amazing!

5. Just as we were ready to enter the IMAX Theater, my little brother spotted the Space Shop and wanted to explore it.

6. Due to a time constraint, he wouldn't be able to do much shopping, so we persuaded him to wait until the end of the day.

7. It was so fascinating to see the images of deep space from the Hubble Space Telescope.

8. Dad convinced us to experience a shuttle launch, so we all strapped in our rocket seats and pretended to be astronauts.

9. We had an opportunity to tour the gigantic Vehicle Assembly Building that was used to assemble rockets and space shuttles.

10. There was too much to explore in one day, so we opted to return the next day to complete our adventure.

 **Grammar Lesson**

KEY
10

Gerunds

A **gerund** consists of the base form of the verb plus –ing. Examples are *being, eating,* and *producing.* A gerund is always used as a noun.

Part of Speech	Function in a Sentence	Examples
Noun	subject	**Winning** an election requires a great deal of money.
	direct object	Some people enjoy **driving** long distances.
	object of a preposition	Are you interested in **going** to see a movie tonight?

<u>Rule 1</u>. A gerund is the base form of a **VERB + –ing** and is used as a noun. As a noun, it can function as a subject, direct object, or object of a preposition.

<u>Rule 2</u>. To make a gerund negative, place **not** before the gerund:

Not knowing the future is difficult for some people to accept.

<u>Rule 3</u>. To negate after **there + be**, use the negative adjective **no** before a gerund:

There is no eating or **drinking** in the computer lab.

<u>Rule 4</u>. **Go** is followed by a gerund to express certain sports or fun activities. Common examples are **go shopping, go swimming, go running, go bowling, go skiing,** and **go sightseeing:**

Maria and Jose never **go fishing** on Sundays.

<u>Rule 5</u>. When an action word comes after a preposition, we always use a gerund.

wrong: We are extremely interested in purchase a new car this year.

correct: **We are extremely interested in purchasing a new car this year.**

<u>Rule 6</u>. When a gerund is the subject of a sentence, the verb is singular even if the gerund has a plural object after it:

Visiting New Zealand is expensive. Visiting New Zealand and Australia is expensive.

BE CAREFUL!

Common Learner Errors	Explanation
1. ~~Educate~~ **Educating** as many people as possible is the president's top goal.	Do not use a base form of the verb for the subject. Although you can use an infinitive, a gerund is the more usual and preferred form in the subject position.
2. Most people dislike ~~go~~ **going** to the dentist.	Do not use a base form of the verb after a verb unless the first verb is a modal such as *can* or *will*. Certain verbs, such as *dislike* and *enjoy*, are followed by a gerund.
3. We are tired of ~~eat~~ **eating** sandwiches for lunch every day.	Do not use a base form after a preposition. Use a gerund.

EXERCISE 2. Identifying Gerunds in Context

Underline the 16 gerunds in this conversation. (*Hint*: There are 23 words that end in **–ing**, but only 16 are gerunds.)

Mom: Pete, I'm going running. Do you want to come?

Pete: Running sounds good, but can you wait until I finish playing this video game?

Mom: I can't believe you think those games are so entertaining.

Pete: To me, playing video games is really relaxing, but I understand if you don't agree with me.

Mom: Well, I find most of those games annoying.

Pete: You are entitled to your opinion, and I respect that, but right now I have to finish playing this game, ok?

Mom: Ok, let me know when you're ready to go. I'll be waiting for you in the kitchen.

Pete: Running isn't a pastime that I really enjoy doing. It's sad, but I prefer playing video games instead of doing any kind of running or exercising. I mean, playing video games is kind of like exercising, right?

Mom: No, it's not. I'm talking about exercising your whole body. Moving your thumbs isn't helping you stay in shape. I'll be in the kitchen.

Pete: I had no idea that running was so important to you. I'll be there in less than fifteen minutes, ok?

ONE-MINUTE LESSON

Playing video games is kind of like exercising, right? The idiom **kind of** is a synonym for *sort of.* Both mean "more or less" to "some degree." These are two very frequent idioms in spoken North American English.

Grammar Lesson

Infinitives and Gerunds after Verbs

When you want to express an action after a verb, the next word can be an infinitive, a gerund, or the simple (base) form. However, the choice of infinitive, gerund, or base form depends on the first verb. Some verbs are always followed by an infinitive, but others are always followed by a gerund. Modal verbs are always followed by the simple form of a verb.

I **intended** to study last night, but I carefully **avoided** opening my books.
intend + infinitive   *avoid* + gerund

I **should** study more.
 modal + simple verb

In English, we use an infinitive after the verb **intend**. (We cannot say, *I intended studying.) We use a gerund after **avoid**. (We cannot say, *I avoided to open my books.) We use a simple form of the verb after any modal. (We cannot say, *I should to study or *I should studying.)

It is important to learn which verbs are followed by infinitives and which verbs are followed by gerunds. There is no systematic explanation for the choice, so you have to memorize the correct forms. You can also practice example sentences again and again in order to become familiar with the correct combinations. To learn this important information, you should use a study method that works well for you.

<u>Rule 1.</u> There are certain verbs that **take an infinitive after them,** but not a gerund.

Group A. Verbs Followed by Infinitives				
afford	demand	hope	need	promise
agree	deserve	intend	offer	refuse
ask	expect	know (how)	plan	want
decide	hesitate	learn	pretend	would like

wrong: I intended studying last night, but I decided watching TV instead.
correct: I intended to study last night, but I decided to watch TV instead.

Rule 2. There are certain verbs that **take a gerund after them,** but not an infinitive.

Group B. Verbs Followed by Gerunds				
appreciate	detest	finish	look forward to	quit
avoid	discuss	get through	miss	recommend
can't help	dislike	go (shopping)	postpone	risk
consider	dread	insist on	practice	suggest
delay	enjoy	keep on	put off	think about

wrong: We may dread to pay a visit to the dentist's office, but we cannot avoid to go
there.

correct: We may **dread paying** a visit to the dentist's office, but we cannot **avoid
going** there.

Rule 3. Phrasal verbs are followed by a gerund.

wrong: We talked over buy the coach a gift.

correct: We **talked over buying** the coach a gift.

Rule 4. The verb **go** is usually followed by a gerund when it refers to certain sports or
a fun activity, including **go shopping, go swimming, go running, go bowling,
go skiing,** and **go sightseeing.**

 BE CAREFUL!

Common Learner Errors	Explanation
1. Many parents ~~avoid to give~~ avoid **giving** sweets to their kids, but most kids really ~~want eating~~ **want to eat** candy.	Do not use infinitives after verbs that take gerunds (and vice versa).
2. I didn't enjoy reading the book because I ~~couldn't to understand~~ **couldn't understand** the main character.	Remember that **modals always take a simple form of the verb.**

EXERCISE 3. Practicing Verbs Followed by a Gerund or Infinitive

Underline the correct verb form.

1. refuse   (doing, to do)

2. enjoy   (doing, to do)

3. hope   (doing, to do)

4. insist on   (doing, to do)

5. can't help   (doing, to do)

6. consider   (doing, to do)

7. promise   (doing, to do)

8. learn   (doing, to do)

9. finish   (doing, to do)

10. intend   (doing, to do)

EXERCISE 4. Practicing Verbs Followed by a Gerund or Infinitive

Write **to swim** or **swimming** on the lines.

1. think about   _____

2. need   _____

3. expect   _____

4. keep on   _____

5. avoid   _____

6. put off   _____

7. go   _____

8. decide   _____

9. get through   _____

10. persuade me   _____

11. know how   _____

12. went   _____

EXERCISE 5. Mini-Conversations

Circle the correct words in these eight mini-conversations.

1. *Jean:* Would you like (to go, going) to the mall tomorrow?

   Marta: I'm a little claustrophobic. I dread (to walk, walking) through the mall during the holidays.

2. *Ethan:* My family decided (to go, going) (to camp, camping) next weekend. Do you want (to come, coming)?

   Owen: I'll think about (to go, going). I'll let you know tomorrow.

3. *Eric:* Mom, the baby is refusing (to eat, eating) his peas.

   Mom: Don't worry. I'll handle it.

4. *Advisor:* Did you consider (to take, taking) the Organic Chemistry class next semester?

   Student: No, I want (to put off, putting off) (to take, taking) it until my last semester.

5. *Emma:* Everyone in class has a cold. How did you avoid (to catch, catching) one?

   Tina: I guess I'm just lucky.

6. *Talal:* I hope (to pass, passing) my driver's test tomorrow.

   Beatriz: I promise (to help, helping) you with the rules tonight.

7. *Clerk:* I finished (to inventory, inventorying) all the stock.

   Manager: Thanks, that's really helpful. I planned on (to meet, meeting) the owners tomorrow with that information. You saved me a lot of time.

8. *Lisa:* When we're at the lake, our dog goes (to swim, swimming) whenever we let him out.

   Sue: That's amazing! Our dog avoids (to get, getting) wet whenever possible.

 Do Online Exercise 2.1. My score: _____ /10. _____% correct.

EXERCISE 6. Speaking Practice: Playing Charades with Infinitives and Gerunds

Refer to the list of verbs that only take infinitives and the list of verbs that only take gerunds on pages 42–43.

The teacher creates 30 cards with one of the listed verbs on one side in small letters and an action verb on the other side written in capital letters (or a different color). The action verbs should be verbs that students can easily act out in class.

Student A chooses an index card and then acts out the action. In this game, students in the class will guess the action. The person guessing correctly then writes a phrase with the listed verb (from the other side of the card) and the target verb (*sing*) on the board.

If the card has **sing** and **refuse**, one student acts out **sing,** and the student who guesses it first writes a phrase on the board such as *refuse to sing*. (*Refuse singing* is incorrect.)

 # Grammar Lesson

**KEY
10**

Verbs Followed by Infinitives or Gerunds with Similar Meaning

Some verbs can be followed by either an infinitive or a gerund with no difference in meaning:

If you **start** **to cook** now, dinner will be ready by 7:30.

If you **start** **cooking** now, dinner will be ready by 7:30.

Group C. Verbs Followed by Infinitives or Gerunds: Similar Meaning			
begin can't stand	continue hate	like love	prefer start

<u>Rule 1.</u> There is a group of verbs that **can take either an infinitive or a gerund and have similar meanings:**

When I arrived, it **started** **to rain** hard.

When I arrived, it **started** **raining** hard.

<u>Rule 2.</u> When the main verb has an **–ing** form, it takes an infinitive, but not a gerund, even though it appears you can use either form. In general, we try to avoid putting two **–ing** forms back to back.

wrong: When I arrived, it was just starting raining.

correct: When I arrived, it was just **starting to rain**.

BE CAREFUL!

Common Learner Errors	Explanation
1. I ~~enjoy to drive~~ enjoy driving.	Do not use direct object infinitives and gerunds interchangeably and expect the same meaning with verbs not in this list.
2. I **am** ~~starting understanding~~ starting to understand this grammar.	If the main verb already has an –*ing*, it is best to avoid using an –*ing* form right after the main verb even if that verb can be followed by an –*ing* form. Instead, use an infinitive.

EXERCISE 7. Using Gerunds and Infinitives in Context

Read the sentences and circle the forms that are possible. (Sometimes more than one answer may be correct.)

Raining Cats and Dogs

1. Last night it began (rain, rains, rained, raining, to rain) around 7:30.

2. It continued (rain, rains, rained, raining, to rain) through the late night, and it seemed like it would never let up.

3. Our cat hates (hear, hears, heard, hearing, to hear) thunder, especially when it is dark outside.

4. She loves (hide, hides, hid, hiding, to hide) under the bed until the storm passes.

5. On the other hand, our dog loves (watch, watches, watched, watching, to watch) the lightning light up the darkness.

6. He prefers (sit, sits, sat, sitting, to sit) on the window sill, so he can (bark, barks, barked, barking, to bark) at the light show all night long.

7. Neither our cat nor our dog can stand (is, are, was, were, be, being, to be) outside in the rain.

8. Oh no! It's starting (raining, to rain) again, so our cat's not going to be very happy!

EXERCISE 8. Writing Original Sentences with Verbs Followed by Infinitives and Gerunds

Write five original sentences with five of the verbs in this group—*begin, can't stand, continue, hate, like, love, prefer, start*—followed by an infinitive or gerund.

1. _____

2. _____

3. _____

4. _____

5. _____

Grammar Lesson

KEY
10

Verbs Followed by Infinitives or Gerunds with Different Meanings

There are a few verbs that **can be followed by either an infinitive or a gerund, but the meaning of the sentence is different.** This group includes remember, forget, stop, and try.

Group D. Verbs Followed by Infinitives or Gerunds: Different Meanings			
remember	forget	stop	try

---

remember (forget is similar)

1. *Susan*: Here are the tomatoes that you asked me to buy.
   Sam: Thanks. I'm happy that you **remembered to buy** them.
   (First, she remembered them. Second, she bought them.)

2. *Chuck*: I found this old book with your name in it. Is it yours?
   Christy: Well, I don't **remember buying** it, but it must be mine, if it has my name in it.
   (First, she bought it. Second, she didn't remember it.)

stop

1. *Allie*: Why are you late?
   Peter: My car was almost on empty, so I **stopped to get** some gas.
   (**stop + to + VERB** tells why. **To** is the same as **in order to**. See page 37.)

2. *Robert*: Does Stan still smoke?
   Cindy: No, he doesn't. He **stopped smoking** last May.
   (**stop + VERB + –ing** tells what he stopped.)

try

1. *Anne*: Are you ready for today's test?
   Sally: I don't know. I **tried to learn** all the verbs, but it was difficult to do.
   (**try + to + VERB** = "make an effort to" do that action; it usually means the action failed to achieve its goal.)

2. *Philip*: Hey, this radio won't work.
   Jan: Why don't you **try turning** the switch to the right?
   (**try + VERB + –ing** = "use another method or way to do something"; it usually means you tried the verb/action.)

Rule 1. The verbs **remember**, **forget**, **stop**, and **try** can take either infinitives or gerunds, but the meanings are different.

Rule 2. When you use an infinitive after **remember**, **forget**, or **stop**, it refers to a subsequent time. In other words, you first **remember** (or **forget** or **stop**) and then you do the verb/action.

> **Joan remembered to turn off the stove.**
>
>   1   2
>
> (First, she remembered. Then she turned off the stove.)

> **Joan forgot to mail the letter.**
>
>   1   2
>
> (First, she forgot. As a result, she didn't mail the letter.)

> **Joan stopped to buy a newspaper.**
>
>   1   2
>
> (First, she stopped. Then, she bought a paper.)

<u>Rule 3.</u> When you use a gerund after **remember**, **forget**, or **stop**, it refers to a previous time. In other words, you first do the verb/action and then remember (or forget or stop) it.

> **Joan remembered turning off the stove.**
>
>   2   1
>
> (First she turned off the stove, and then she remembered.)

> **Joan forgot mailing the letter.**
>
>   2   1
>
> (The letter was mailed, and then she forgot.)

> **Joan stopped buying a newspaper.**
>
>   2   1
>
> (She bought papers, and then she stopped.)

<u>Rule 4.</u> Try + infinitive refers to making an effort. (It implies that it was not successful.)

He **tried to open** this jar of pickles, but the lid was stuck.

(He made an effort to open the jar, but he did not open it.)

<u>Rule 5.</u> Try + gerund refers to using another method/way.

Next, he **tried running** hot water over the jar.

(He ran water over the jar.)

 ## BE CAREFUL!

Common Learner Errors	Explanation
1. We were tired, so we ~~stopped to drive~~ stopped driving.	Using the wrong form can change the meaning of the sentence.
2a. I will **try** <u>to paint</u> the office tomorrow. (= If I have time, I'll do it.) 2b. I will **try** <u>painting</u> the office tomorrow. (= I have not done it before.)	Do not use infinitives and gerunds interchangeably after *remember, forget, and try*. Infinitives and gerunds will result in different meanings.

EXERCISE 9. Using Infinitives and Gerunds in Context

Fill in the infinitive or the gerund form of the given verb. Sometimes more than one answer is possible.

A Mother's Day Surprise

On Mother's Day morning, Steven woke up on his own about five minutes before the alarm was set to go off. He wanted his wife to be able to sleep in, so he remembered ❶ _____ (turn off) the alarm before it woke her up. Steven tried ❷ _____ (be) quiet when he was getting ready, but everything sounded extra loud. Downstairs, the children tried ❸ _____ (surprise) their mom by making breakfast for her. First, they tried ❹ _____ (make) coffee. Then, they tried ❺ _____ (cook) eggs in the microwave because they are not old enough to use the stove by themselves. What a surprise! They forgot ❻ _____ (put) a lid over the eggs and the result was quite messy. Luckily, Steven came to the kitchen before too much more damage was done and helped them make a great breakfast for mom. Mom was so happy to get a perfect breakfast in bed.

Do Online Exercise 2.2. My score: _____ /10. _____ % correct.

EXERCISE 10. Speaking Practice: Interviewing Classmates

Ask your partner these questions and write their answers as if you were a reporter. You must use the word in parentheses in your sentence and circle the word form (infinitive or gerund) that you put after it.

Example: You: What do you remember about last night?

Partner: (remember) I remember (hearing) noises in the parking lot.

1. As a child, what kinds of activities do you remember doing with your grandparents?

   (remember)_____

2. Do you have any memories you wish you could forget?

   (wish I could forget)_____

3. Do you tend to finish one book before you begin another, or do you like to read several books at the same time?

   (tend) _____

4. Are there any sports that you haven't participated in that you would like to try?

   (would like to try) _____

5. What have you forgotten to do that someone has had to remind you to do?

   (forget) _____

6. What have you reminded someone else to do that they have forgotten?

   (remind) _____

ONE-MINUTE LESSON

The verb **like** can be followed by an infinite or a gerund with no change in meaning. The expression **would like** is followed by an infinitive usually. The verb **dislike** is followed by a gerund.

Grammar Lesson

KEY
10

Verb + Noun/Pronoun + Infinitive

Some verbs are followed by an infinitive but with a noun or pronoun object between.

Group E. Verbs Followed by Noun/Pronoun + Infinitive						
advise allow ask	cause convince expect	forbid force get	invite need order	permit persuade remind	teach tell urge	want warn would like

I want to go to the post office.
I want Mike **to go** to the post office.

What is the difference between these two sentences? Both are correct, but the meanings are different. Both sentences have the verb **want** and an infinitive. In the first sentence, there is one subject (**I**) and two verb forms (**want** and **to go**). This means that **I want** and **I go**. In other words, one person is doing both actions.

In the second sentence, there are two people (**I** and **Mike**) and two verb forms (**want** and **to go**). In this sentence, one person is doing the first action (**I want**), and another person is doing the second action (**Mike goes**).

Now read these situations and the sentence that describes each situation.

Situation 1:   The teacher said, "Do the exercise on page 19."

Description 1: The teacher told the students to do the exercise on page 19.

Situation 2:   "Jean, please call Ahmed as soon as possible."

Description 2: I want Jean to call Ahmed as soon as possible.

The new sentences have two verb forms. The first word is a verb that asks or tells someone to do something. The second word is the action.

Example 1: The teacher **told** the students **to do** the exercise on page 19.
                          1   2

Example 2: I **want** Jean **to call** Ahmed as soon as possible.
                    1   2

Notice that the first verbs are often similar in meaning. These verbs often ask or tell someone to do an action. These verbs are followed by **noun/pronoun + infinitive**.

The basic pattern here looks like this:

Someone	+	Verb	+	someone	+	Infinitive.	
I		would like		you		to help	me tonight.
She		asked		Kevin		to open	The door.
The president		told		the soldiers		to do	their best.
The boss		would like		us		to attend	the meeting.

 BE CAREFUL!

Common Learner Errors	Explanation
1. I ~~want that you eat~~ want you to eat dinner with me tonight.	With these verbs, never use VERB + *that* + SUBJECT + VERB. This is common in some languages, but it is not correct in English.
2. Would you ~~ask Maggie let~~ ask Maggie to let us use her car?	Do not forget to use an infinitive. Do not use a simple form of the verb or a gerund.
3a. We want ~~Carol goes~~ Carol to go with us. 3b. In 1974, the government ordered ~~people to stopped~~ people to stop using leaded fuel.	Do not add –s, –ed, –ing, or any other endings on the second verb. The first verb can change (according to singular/ plural or tense), but the second verb form does not change. Remember that only the first verb can have –s for **he, she, it.**

EXERCISE 11. Editing: Is It Correct?

If the sentence is correct, write a check mark (✔) on the line. If the sentence is not correct, write an X on the line and circle the mistake. Then make the change above the sentence. (*Hint*: There are eight sentences. Two are correct, but six have mistakes.)

_____ 1. Maria's job at Senator Allen's campaign headquarters is gets people to vote.

_____ 2. She urges everyone vote.

_____ 3. In dozens of calls daily, Maria persuades that unregistered voters to register before the deadline.

_____ 4. Voters usually ask her where they should vote because they are not sure of their voting location.

_____ 5. After confirming their address, Maria tells they go to a specific voting location.

_____ 6. Maria reminds senior citizens to take advantage of free van rides to the polling places.

_____ 7. `Seniors don't expect that volunteers gives free rides, so they often offer to pay for gas.

_____ 8. Drivers often have to convince to them that the ride is free.

EXERCISE 12. Questions with Verb + Noun/Pronoun + Infinitive

Using the given verb, write a question with the pattern verb + noun/pronoun + infinitive. Then underline the infinitives. Follow the example.

Example: (allow) *When would you allow someone <u>to drive</u> your car?*

1. (ask) _____

2. (want) _____

3. (invite) _____

4. (expect) _____

5. (tell) _____

6. (order) _____

7. (teach) _____

8. (remind) _____

Grammar Lesson

Four Special Verbs: *make, let, have, help*

Four very common verbs do not use an infinitive or a gerund.

Group F. Four Special Verbs: *make, let, have, help*
make: She **made** the children **eat** their vegetables.*   **let:** She **let** the children **play** outside.   **have:** She **had** the children **do** their homework first.**   **help:** Can you **help** me **carry** these boxes to the basement?
<u>Note</u>: The verb **help** also allows an infinitive (with no change in meaning).   Can you **help** me **to carry** these boxes to the basement?

There are four verbs that are usually followed by a person and another verb. However, the verb that comes after the object with these four verbs follows a different pattern.

make, let, have: The second verb is the simple base form of the verb.

    make: She made the children **eat** their vegetables.

    let: She let the children **play** outside.

    have: She had the children **do** their homework first.

help: The second verb can be simple base form or an infinitive. Both are equally correct; there is no difference in meaning.

    help: Can you help me **carry** these boxes to the basement?

    help: Can you help me **to carry** these boxes to the basement?

---

* *to make someone do something* means "to force him or her to do the action."

** *to have someone do something* means that "someone else does the work for you because you paid that person, because you are in a power position (mother-child), or because you asked him or her."

EXERCISE 13. Writing Original Sentences with *make/let/have/help* + Action Word

Write two examples for each verb followed by the pattern practiced in this lesson. Write about real situations. The first one has been done for you as an example.

1. make *The teacher made us rewrite our essays.* _____
   _____

2. make _____
   _____

3. let _____
   _____

4. let _____
   _____

5. have _____
   _____

6. have _____
   _____

7. help _____
   _____

8. help _____
   _____

Do Online Exercise 2.3. My score: _____ /10. _____ % correct.

EXERCISE 14. Sentence Study for Critical Reading

Read the numbered sentences. Then read the three answer choices and put a check mark (✔) in the yes or no box in front of each sentence to show if that answer is true based on the information in the original sentence. If there is not enough information to mark something as yes, then mark it as no. Remember that more than one true answer may be possible.

1. Sophie has a very important position; she is in charge of organizing the sales meetings. This week, she has a scheduling conflict, so she hopes no one will object to her moving it to Thursday.

   ☐ yes ☐ no   a. Sophie is used to managing all the departments.

   ☐ yes ☐ no   b. Sophie wants the others to agree to meet on Thursday.

   ☐ yes ☐ no   c. Sophie is moving on Thursday.

2. Mia and Jill love to explore life in big cities. Whenever they travel, they go sightseeing, and they make note of the unique shops and boutiques along the way. Going window shopping is one of their favorite pastimes, and shoe shopping is another.

   ☐ yes ☐ no   a. A pastime is something that happened a long time ago, and you cannot look forward to seeing it again.

   ☐ yes ☐ no   b. Mia and Jill rarely go sightseeing.

   ☐ yes ☐ no   c. Mia and Jill are building a new house, and they are now shopping for windows for their house.

3. The professor remembered to tell his students to prepare for the upcoming quiz. After correcting the quizzes, he was surprised that everyone did so well.

   ☐ yes ☐ no   a. The professor forgot to tell his students to study.

   ☐ yes ☐ no   b. The professor reminded his students to study.

   ☐ yes ☐ no   c. The quiz covered the first part of the book and included some tough material.

4. Max and Nick were eager to climb Mt. McKinley, so they prepared themselves mentally and physically for a year before attempting the climb. Other climbers told them to train every day.

   ☐ yes ☐ no   a. Max and Nick were motivated to go mountain climbing.

   ☐ yes ☐ no   b. Max and Nick were determined to get into shape for the climb.

   ☐ yes ☐ no   c. Max and Nick traveled by train every day.

5. Nora's parents let her choose a puppy at the animal shelter. They make her follow a feeding schedule and help her prepare the puppy's food. They tell her to use the same bowl in the same location for each feeding.

   ☐ yes ☐ no a. Nora makes her parents help her.

   ☐ yes ☐ no b. Nora lets her puppy eat anywhere it wants to.

   ☐ yes ☐ no c. Nora's parents worked at the animal shelter.

6. Doug and Al were thinking about living together to save money. They expected to find an apartment close to campus so they could walk to classes. Since it is the beginning of October, all the apartments are occupied; therefore, they have to postpone rooming together until next semester.

   ☐ yes ☐ no a. Doug and Al dislike walking to class.

   ☐ yes ☐ no b. Doug and Al appreciate saving money.

   ☐ yes ☐ no c. Doug and Al would like to be roommates.

7. Carl invited Victoria to go to the prom. Victoria wanted her father to buy her a gown to wear to the prom, and Victoria's mother advised her to wait until after dinner to ask him to do that.

   ☐ yes ☐ no a. Victoria wanted her father to pay for her dress.

   ☐ yes ☐ no b. Victoria urged her mother to ask her father for a dress.

   ☐ yes ☐ no c. Victoria's father invited Carl to dinner to ask Victoria to the prom.

8. Steve bought a big-screen TV that his neighbor Chad helped him to carry into the family room. The cable company made Steve purchase a special box so that the TV and computer could have high-speed access.

   ☐ yes ☐ no a. Chad let Steve carry the TV by himself.

   ☐ yes ☐ no b. Steve had to buy a box from the cable company.

   ☐ yes ☐ no c. Chad lives near Steve.

EXERCISE 15. Review Test 1: Multiple Choice

Circle the letter of the correct answer.

1. Do you remember _____ to the beach every summer when we were kids?

   a. that we go   c. to go

   b. went   d. going

2. My grandfather is always complaining about _____ care of his dogs.

   a. to have to take   c. he has to take

   b. having to take   d. having taking

3. When standing in front of the judge today, the thief denied _____ the money, but the evidence presented from witnesses caused the jury _____ him guilty of the crime.

   a. taking, found   c. taking, to find

   b. to take, found   d. to take, to find

4. Stores often offer enticing sales because they want _____ into their stores so that shoppers will purchase even more.

   a. customers to come   c. that customers come

   b. customers come   d. to customers that come

5. This university has prerequisite courses for math majors, but it lets students _____ Pre-Calculus?

   a. to take   c. taking

   b. taken   d. take

6. I need _____ my father pay my rent this month because I'm broke.

   a. that   c. having

   b. to have   d. have

7. Last night I reminded _____ write an e-mail to the bank about our account.

   a. to wife   c. my wife to

   b. that my wife to   d. that my wife

8. I don't expect _____ to my education.

    a. that my parents contribute   c. my parents to contribute

    b. contributing parents   d. to contributing

9. I just got an email from my dentist this morning that advised _____ an appointment.

    a. me to make   c. me make

    b. me to making   d. that I am making

10. Are we allowed _____ in the parking garage without a parking permit?

    a. that we park   c. that we parking

    b. parking   d. to park

11. Last semester our teacher let _____ extra credit.

    a. that students do   c. students to do

    b. students do   d. students doing

12. I'm hungry. I want to go to the cafeteria, but I'd like _____ with us.

    a. that Miguel to goes   c. to invites Miguel to go

    b. inviting Miguel to go   d. to invite Miguel to go

EXERCISE 16. Review Test 2: Production and Evaluation

Part 1.
Read the short passage. Fill in the blank with the correct form of the given verb.

Going Shopping for Antiques

Tourists love to go ❶ _____ (antique) in the rural areas of the county. Whenever they see a Sale sign, they stop ❷ _____ (investigate). Sellers let them ❸ _____ (browse) as long as they want to. Store owners look forward to ❹ _____ (discuss) where their customers are traveling from and where they are going next. Some of the owners invite their customers ❺ _____ (sample) homemade local specialties, such as blueberry muffins. Many of the tourists are interested in ❻ _____ (hear) about the stories associated with the antiques. In order ❼ _____ (add) drama to local legends, the sellers frequently become animated storytellers. Many tourists purchases an antique they don't need ❽ _____ (buy), but they do so solely because of these stories. There is ❾ _____ ([negative] deny) the old adage: "One man's trash is another man's treasure." Everyone enjoys ❿ _____ (find) a good deal.

Part 2.

Read the short passage. There are seven mistakes. Circle the mistake, and write the correction above the mistake.

Pumpkin Picking

Have you ever been to a pumpkin patch? Because they grow on vines, pumpkins need a large area to spreading out. In the fall months, farmers let them to ripen on the vine until they turn a bright orange color. Toward the end of October, children enjoy to pick the pumpkin they want for Halloween. Use a knife can be dangerous, so parents don't want children carve their own pumpkins into jack-o-lanterns. In order to no waste the seeds, some parents bake them in the oven for a delicious and healthy snack. On the other hand, some parents plant the seeds for starting their own pumpkin patches.

EXERCISE 17. Reading Practice: Understanding a Job Ad

Read this ad, and then answer the comprehension questions that follow. The grammar from this unit is underlined for you. Use your dictionary for words that you do not understand.

Babysitter Wanted

If you need a job this summer, we would appreciate <u>hearing</u> from you. We are in desperate need of <u>finding</u> a babysitter. The babysitter must be ready <u>to come</u> over to our house at a minute's notice. My husband is a fireman who is on call and needs someone here so he is able <u>to leave</u> quickly when there is a fire. I am an EMT, and I am on call, too. A babysitter's tardiness cannot cause us <u>to be</u> late for emergencies. The babysitter has to be prepared <u>to step</u> into the role of surrogate parent to our five boys. The babysitter should be happy <u>to help</u> with homework and be glad <u>to play</u> with the younger boys. The babysitter should not be afraid <u>to change</u> diapers. With two-year-old twins, that is certainly a necessity. The babysitter should be confident enough <u>to ask</u> for a demonstration or <u>to seek</u> help. <u>Making</u> dinner and <u>putting</u> dirty dishes in the dishwasher are the chores of our older sons, so there is no need for the babysitter <u>to worry</u> about that. At bedtime, the babysitter must remind the older boys <u>to read</u> a book to their reading buddies. The babysitter should also suggest that the boys brush their teeth before story time. After the boys are in bed, the babysitter has our permission <u>to invite</u> a friend over <u>to keep</u> her or him company until one of us gets home. You will be amazed <u>to hear</u> how much this job pays! Please don't hesitate <u>to call</u>.

1. Make a list of six things the babysitter needs to be able to do.

   _____

   _____

   _____

2. What does the information say about changing diapers?

   _____

   _____

3. Do you think it will be easy for this family to hire a babysitter soon? Why or why not?

_____

_____

_____

4. This job requires many things. What are some tasks that you think a babysitter should refuse to do?

_____

_____

5. Would you be willing to take this job? Why or why not?

_____

_____

_____

EXERCISE 18: Vocabulary Practice: Word Knowledge

Circle the answer choice that is most closely related to the vocabulary on the left. Use a dictionary to check the meaning of words you do not know.

Vocabulary	Answer Choices	
1. a constraint	a limitation	an opinion
2. to assemble	to put together	to take apart
3. to refuse	say no	say yes
4. a sill	in an automobile	in a window
5. thunder	you hear it	you see it
6. to spot	to decide	to see
7. the headquarters	the main office	the main person
8. a basement	above the house	below the house
9. extend	decrease	increase
10. to opt	to choose	to wish
11. to let up	decrease	increase
12. tardy	expenseive	late
13. to inventory	to count for a company	to create new things for a company
14. shocked	confused	surprised
15. be on empty	almost no energy	too much energy
16. object to an idea	disagree with an idea	like an idea very much
17. to seek	look for	agree with
18. carve	cut	hold
19. a pastime	your family's history	a hobby
20. be determined to do something	100% effort	100% failure
21. a character	a person	a thing
22. postpone	put off	run out of
23. enormous	very big	very small
24. quite	every	very
25. an image	you hear it	you see it

EXERCISE 19. Vocabulary Practice: Collocations

Fill in each blank with the answer on the right that most naturally completes the phrase on the left. If necessary, use a dictionary to check the meaning of words you do not know.

Vocabulary	Answer Choices	
1. be good _____ doing something	at	on
2. my driver's _____	car	test
3. to launch something _____	into space	with food
4. interested _____	at	in
5. we desperately _____	need	take
6. to be _____ awake	very	wide
7. take up _____	bread	time
8. _____ running	go	take
9. to light _____ the sky at night	on	up
10. our _____ goal	above	top
11. a _____ citizen	candidate	senior
12. intended _____	studying	to study
13. a scheduling _____	agreement	conflict
14. find a _____ deal	good	jealous
15. to participate _____ sports	at	in
16. along the _____	human beings	way
17. to _____ somebody company	have	keep
18. be in _____ of	charge	demand
19. to seek _____	cents	help
20. we're in desperate _____ of	need	purchase
21. to _____ an appointment	do	make
22. a very rural _____	area	person
23. an upcoming _____	event	storm
24. to avoid _____ a cold	catching	taking
25. to be _____ call	on	with

EXERCISE 20. Writing Practice: Explaining Steps in a Process

Part 1. Editing Student Writing

Read these sentences about hot air ballooning. Circle the 15 errors. Then write the number of the sentence with the error next to the type of error. (Some sentences may have more than one error.)

_____ a. an infinitive is needed   _____ d. subject-verb agreement

_____ b. a gerund is needed   _____ e. article

_____ c. a base verb form is needed

Hot Air Ballooning	
1. Hot air ballooning is becoming popular sport and leisure activity.	
2. Soaring high into the air may look easy, but it takes a great deal of the time and effort.	
3. The crew has to find an open area from which to launch, and lay out the balloon is awkward because of its size.	
4. The workers have to attach the wicker basket that carries the passengers and need tether the balloon to their van so that it will not to fly away before the riders can get in.	
5. The pilot cannot steer the balloon, so knowing wind patterns and speed are important.	
6. The pilot can control vertical speed by opening and close the valves on the gas tanks.	
7. For make the balloon rise, the pilot opens the valve, the gas ignites and burns, and the balloon starts rising.	
8. To lower the balloon, the pilot opens a hatch at the top to let air to escape.	
9. Cars, houses, and onlookers seem shrink as the balloon rises above the trees.	
10. Land the balloon takes skill and perfect timing.	
11. Upon descend, the pilot has everyone to bend their knees to absorb the shock of the basket as it hits the ground.	
12. Once everyone is safely out of basket, packing up the balloon and equipment take a lot of time.	

Part 2. Original Student Writing

Write a paragraph in which you explain how to do something that is relatively complicated. You may consult an outside reference source if you need help with specific information. Use at least seven examples of infinitives and gerunds. Underline the grammar points that you have used so the teacher can see what you are trying to practice.

Unit **3**

Participial Adjectives:
–ing vs. *–ed*

Discover the Grammar

Read the passage about an amazing trip to New Zealand. Then answer the questions that follow.

Line	
1	New Zealand consists of two islands. The South Island is about one-third
2	bigger than the North Island, so it is therefore **surprising** that about three-
3	quarters of all New Zealanders live on the North Island.
4	The North Island is **fascinating** because it has a lot of volcanic activity.
5	There are active volcanoes, but there are also other kinds of **unexpected** vol-
6	canic activity that I had never experienced before. In the city of Rotorua, for
7	example, I saw puddles of **boiling** water on the side of the streets. At first, I
8	was a bit **shocked** to see steam on the side of the street, but once I was no
9	longer **surprised**, I thought it was kind of **exciting**.
10	I am **convinced** that the South Island is perhaps the most beautiful place I
11	have seen anywhere. The scenery with mountains and incredible blue lakes was
12	absolutely **amazing**. In fact, I saw so many beautiful areas that I was
13	**overwhelmed** at times and did not know what to take a picture of.

14	Visiting New Zealand was one of the best experiences of my entire life, but
15	getting there was **complicated**. It took me five hours to fly from my home in
16	Florida to California and then twelve hours to New Zealand. The trip was
17	certainly **tiring**, but New Zealand is such an **interesting** country.

1. There are 13 adjectives in bold: seven end in *–ing* and six end in *–ed*. Can you think of a rule for when we use these two endings?

   _____

   _____

2. Why do we say *surprising* in Line 2, but *surprised* in Line 9?

   _____

   _____

3. Look at *overwhelmed* in Line 13. Is it also possible to use *overwhelming* here? Explain.

   _____

   _____

4. Not all *–ing* words are adjectives. For example, what is the function of *visiting* in Line 14?

   _____

   _____

Grammar Lesson

Usages of Past Participles

English verbs have three basic forms: **present**, **past**, and **past participle**.

	Present	Past	Past Participle
regular verbs	use	used	used
irregular verbs	choose	chose	chosen

A *past participle* of a regular verb ends in **–ed** (*shocked*). In contrast, a past participle of an irregular verb often ends in **–en** (*broken*), **–ne** (*done*), or **–n** (*torn*). In some cases, the verb has no change at all (*put – put –put*) or the past and past participle forms are the same (*lose – lost – lost*).

A past participle can be used three different ways: (1) it can be a verb form in a perfect tense such as **present perfect tense** or **past perfect tense**; (2) it can be used in **passive voice** (explained in Unit 5); and (3) it can be used as an **adjective**.

Usage	Examples
Present perfect tense	After you have sliced the onions, then you add the mayonnaise.
Passive voice	First, the onions must be sliced very thinly.
Adjective	I like salads that come with sliced onions.

<u>Rule 1</u>. A past participle can be part of a perfect verb tense. In this case, it follows a form of the auxiliary verb **have**: The news **has shocked** people greatly.

<u>Rule 2</u>. A past participle can be part of passive voice. In this case, it follows a form of the auxiliary verb **be**: People **were very** shocked by the news of the president's death.

<u>Rule 3</u>. A past participle can be a descriptive adjective. In this case, it can precede a noun or come after the verb **be**: I will always remember the shocked faces of the witnesses.

 BE CAREFUL!

Common Learner Errors	Explanation
1. This isn't Sue's first trip to Italy. She has already ~~went~~ gone twice before.	Be sure to use a **past participle**, not a past tense form, **for present perfect**.
2. The injured driver was ~~took~~ taken to the hospital immediately.	Be sure to use a **past participle**, not a past tense form, **for passive voice**.
3. My new shirt ~~shrunk~~ shrank because I put it in the dryer for an hour.	Never use a past participle to express simple past tense.

Connecting Grammar and Vocabulary

The 20 Most Common Past Participles as Adjectives	
1. unidentified	If you see a UFO, you've seen an **unidentified** flying object.
2. concerned	We're very **concerned** about our grandmother's health.
3. involved	Bryce was **involved** in a car accident yesterday.
4. supposed	I'm **supposed** to be at work right now.
5. interested	Are you **interested** in going to the zoo tomorrow?
6. united	The workers are **united** in their desire for a higher salary.
7. married	**Married** couples usually pay a slightly lower tax rate than two single adults.
8. used	I'd like to buy a **used** car.
9. increased	People who smoke have an **increased** risk of heart disease.
10. surprised	I was **surprised** to hear that Richard took a job at a different company.
11. limited	This offer is **limited** to residents of Texas and Oklahoma.
12. tired	We were so **tired** after the hike up and down the mountain.
13. so-called	The **so-called** sale lasted only for one day.
14. unknown	The identity of the bank robber remains **unknown**.
15. armed	Three **armed** soldiers rescued the children.
16. broken	One small **broken** pipe flooded my apartment over the weekend.
17. lost	The bumper sticker said, "I'm **lost**, but I'm ahead of you!"
18. advanced	My **advanced** grammar class is at noon.
19. complicated	The final exam was more **complicated** than any of the previous exams.
20. scared	I'm **scared** of spiders and snakes.

Source: Reilly, N. (2013). *A Comparative Analysis of Present and Past Participial Adjectives and Their Collocations in the Corpus of Contemporary American English.* Thesis, University of Central Florida.

EXERCISE 1. Identifying Past Participles in Context

Underline the past participle in each sentence. Then write V or ADJ above to indicate if it is being used as a part of a verb (present perfect or past perfect tenses) or as an adjective.

Switching to a New Cell Phone Plan

1. I have used the same cell phone company for the past six years.

2. I was concerned about signing a long contract, so I chose a six-month plan.

3. When I had my first chance to switch, I thought changing to a different company might be complicated, so I just stayed with my original phone company.

4. When my cell phone was broken, the service I got from my company was good, so I was not unhappy with my company.

5. Today, however, I received an email explaining that the company has increased its monthly rates.

6. Because rates went up in each of the last three years, I was really surprised to receive this email with this news today.

7. When I called the company to ask about these new rates, I found that they have limited their business hours to 9 AM to 4 PM.

8. These increased rates are not good for attracting new business.

9. In fact, these new rates have probably scared away many new customers.

10. My company has a TV commercial in which it calls itself "the thrifty caller's best friend," but with higher rates and less service, this so-called "friend" is not much of a friend to anyone.

EXERCISE 2. Using Past Participles in Different Grammatical Contexts

Fill in the blank with the correct past participle as part of a verb or as an adjective.

Verb	Past Participle in Present Perfect	Past Participle as Adjective
break	1. Anna Weston has _____ the world record in the 100 meters.	2. After the accident, the street corner was covered with _____ glass.
lose	3. I've _____ my place in this book again.	4. Unfortunately, certain _____ data can never be recovered.
use	5. People have _____ computers for only a few decades.	6. A new computer is more expensive than a _____ one, but is it so much better?
limit	7. Dr. Saunders has _____ the amount of time we have for the next exam.	8. The special sale on lightweight laptops is for a very _____ time only.
advance	9. Our team has _____ to the next round of the tournament.	10. This game is for _____ students with extremely good vocabulary.

Do Online Exercise 3.1. My score: ____ /10. ____ % correct.

Grammar Lesson

Usages of Present Participles

A present participle of a verb ends in **–ing** (*annoying*).

A **present participle** can be used in at least two different ways: (1) it can be a verb form in a progressive tense such as **present progressive tense** or **past progressive tense**; and (2) it can be used as an **adjective**.

Usage	Examples
Present progressive tense	The students are surprising their teacher with a birthday gift today.
Adjective	The major imports and exports between the U.S. and Canada are surprising.

Rule 1. A present participle can be part of a progressive verb tense. In this case, it follows a form of the auxiliary verb **be**:

My neighbors' dog's constant noise is annoying me.

Rule 2. A present participle can be a descriptive adjective. In this case, it can precede a noun or come after the verb **be**:

I don't like that annoying noise. (before the noun *noise*)

The dog's constant noise is annoying. (after the verb *be* [*is*])

 BE CAREFUL!

Common Learner Errors	Explanation
1. The announcement that the factory will close and we will all lose our jobs was ~~surprised~~ surprising to say the least.	Use a **present participle** to describe the thing or person **that causes or does the action** of the verb.
2. The audience seemed completely ~~boring~~ bored during most of the speaker's lecture.	Use a **past participle** for a person (or thing) **that receives the action** of the verb.

Connecting Grammar and Vocabulary

The 20 Most Common Present Participles as Adjectives	
1. interesting	"The Orange River" is one of the most **interesting** movies I have ever seen.
2. willing	A taxi driver's job is difficult because most people are not **willing** to work such long hours.
3. growing	There is **growing** interest in Chinese and Arabic as foreign languages.
4. following	The **following** words begin with vowels: *apple, egg, ice, orange,* and *ugly.*
5. living	Even though it does not move, coral is a **living** creature.
6. existing	The last **existing** speaker of that language died last year.
7. remaining	The only **remaining** dates for a meeting are the 29th and the 30th.
8. amazing	These potatoes taste **amazing**.
9. leading	A **leading** cause of car accidents is road rage.
10. increasing	An **increasing** number of people have serious allergies.
11. developing	This is a **developing** story, and we will update you as soon as we have more information.
12. surprising	A **surprising** number of students failed the final exam.
13. working	I do not have a **working** computer right now, but I hope to remedy this situation by tomorrow.
14. ongoing	There is an **ongoing** dispute between those two countries.
15. exciting	That is very **exciting** news.
16. running	About 25% of the houses in this region do not have **running** water.
17. changing	The politician lost the election because of his constantly **changing** positions.
18. missing	The **missing** child was found around noon yesterday.
19. overwhelming	My work this week has been **overwhelming**.
20. continuing	High unemployment is a **continuing** problem in Spain.

Source: Reilly, N. (2013). *A Comparative Analysis of Present and Past Participial Adjectives and Their Collocations in the Corpus of Contemporary American English.* Thesis, University of Central Florida.

EXERCISE 3. Identifying Present Participles in Context

Underline the present participle in each sentence. Then write V or ADJ above to indicate if it is being used as a part of a verb or as an adjective.

In Search of Volunteers for a Beneficial Experiment

1. I saw a very interesting sign at the post office today.

2. It said that a hospital is looking for volunteers for an experiment.

3. It said, "If you are willing to take part in a health experiment, you can earn up to $500."

4. The information at the bottom of the sign had the following notes.

5. The number of people with allergies is increasing rapidly.

6. In fact, allergic reactions are now one of the leading causes of hospital emergency room visits.

7. A group of doctors at Miami Regional Medical Hospital is running an experiment to find out more about allergies.

8. The doctors are developing a possible solution to this problem.

9. They want to know if people's changing diets have any impact on new allergies.

10. The time commitment is eight months, but this is part of a larger ongoing scientific study.

11. When doctors conducted a similar study two years ago, they had an overwhelming response from the public.

12. My best friend is working at the same hospital, so I have asked her for more information.

EXERCISE 4. Using Present Participles in Different Grammatical Contexts

Fill in the blank with the correct present participle as part of a verb or as an adjective.

VERB	Present Participle in Present Progressive Tense	Present Participle as Adjective
remain	1. We are _____ in London for a week.	2. Please take advantage of the _____ items on sale.
surprise	3. Our son is _____ us with his good grades in math.	4. A _____ number of people have applied for the director's job.
live	5. My sister is _____ in New York now.	6. There are no _____ creatures on the moon.
grow	7. I am _____ corn and beans in a garden in my backyard.	8. There is a _____ demand in the U.S. for Chinese goods.
lead	9. Russia has one of the world's _____ basketball teams.	10. Right now Canada is _____ Russia in the basketball game.

ONE-MINUTE LESSON
The expression **up to + a number** means "that number or less (fewer)." Therefore, if *an employee can work* **up to** *16 hours a week*, that means he or she cannot work more than 15 hours per week. A parallel expression is **at least + a number**, which means "that number or more." In the sentence **At least** *five accidents took place right at 6:00*, it means that there were five or more accidents that happened at that time.

Grammar Lesson

Interesting vs. *Interested*: A Comparison of –*ing* and –*ed* Adjectives

Both present participles and past participles can be used as adjectives.

–**ing** is for the person or thing **that makes or causes the action**.
–**ed** (or any past participle ending) is for the person or thing **that receives the action**.

	The news surprised me.	Joe disappointed us.
Action	surprise	disappoint
Person or thing that causes the action	the news	Joe
	= The news was surprising.	= Joe was disappointing.
Person or thing that receives the action	me	us
	= I was surprised.	= We were disappointed.

Rule 1. An –ing adjective usually describes a **person or thing that causes the action**. The person or thing (the noun) that the adjective is describing is actually doing something.

Rule 2. An –ed adjective (past participle) usually describes **the person who receives the action**. It can also be used for things, but it is more common for people or living creatures. The noun that is being described is not doing anything.

 BE CAREFUL!

Common Learner Errors	Explanation
1. What is that ~~annoyed~~ annoying sound?	Do not use past participles to describe a noun that is causing the action.
2. The students are ~~boring~~ bored in that class.	Do not use present participles to describe a noun that is not causing the action.
3. The ~~surprise~~ surprising election results were on the front page of the paper.	Do not forget to use an ending. Do not use just the simple verb form as an adjective.

Connecting Grammar and Vocabulary

Potentially Confusing *–ing* / *–ed* Adjective Pairs	
Present Participle Adjectives	**Past Participle Adjectives**
1. That noise is really **annoying**.	2. I was so **annoyed** by what he said.
3. This is the most **amazing** dinner!	4. The audience was **amazed**.
5. It is an **amusing** book, and I hope you enjoy reading it.	6. My parents were not **amused** by my bad grades.
7. His gold medal was **astonishing** because of all his previous injuries.	8. We were **astonished** to read that the voting age may be lowered to 16.
9. That class is so **boring**.	10. I was so **bored** in that class.
11. These instructions are so **confusing**.	12. I'm **confused**. What do I do next?
13. That is one of the most **convincing** arguments I've ever heard for higher taxes.	14. Jan is still not **convinced** that selling her house is the best plan.
15. It's the most **depressing** story I've ever heard.	16. Rainy weather makes people **depressed**.
17. What a **disappointing** result!	18. When I saw my grade, I was so **disappointed**.
19. I think the language in that movie is **disgusting**.	20. By the time the movie was over, I was so **disgusted** with it.
21. That's the most **embarrassing** moment of my entire life.	22. I was so **embarrassed**.
23. My first dive was **exciting**.	24. The kids were **excited** to see the clown.
25. Teaching kindergarten all day must be very **exhausting**.	26. At the end of the day, a kindergarten teacher is **exhausted**.
27. Military history is a **fascinating** subject to me.	28. The baby was **fascinated** by the music.
29. It was one of the most **frightening** experiences of my life.	30. What are you **frightened** of?
31. It was a **horrifying** experience.	32. We were **horrified** to hear the news.

Potentially Confusing *–ing* / *–ed* Adjective Pairs	
Present Participle Adjectives	**Past Participle Adjectives**
33. This book is so incredibly **interesting**.	34. We're not very **interested** in seeing that movie.
35. I found her e-mail **puzzling**.	36. I was **puzzled** by her e-mail.
37. I like to eat ramen, but it's not very **satisfying**.	38. Are you **satisfied** with your car repair shop?
39. The police have made a **shocking** discovery in the murder case.	40. We were all **shocked** by the news.
41. The **startling** rise in car accidents is a mystery.	42. I was **startled** by the noise.
43. The news was **terrifying**.	44. Many children are **terrified** of large dogs.
45. Driving for more than five hours is very **tiring**.	46. At the end of the day, we were **tired**.

Source: Reilly, N. (2013). *A Comparative Analysis of Present and Past Participial Adjectives and Their Collocations in the Corpus of Contemporary American English*. Thesis, University of Central Florida.

EXERCISE 5. Using Participial Adjectives in Context

Write the correct adjective form of the bold word on the lines. The first two have been done for you as examples.

1. The movie that Jill saw last night **shocked** her.

    a. Jill was _____shocked_____.

    b. The movie was really _____shocking_____.

    c. Some of the scenes at the end of the movie were especially _____.

2. Patty's decision **surprised** everyone in the room.

    a. Her decision was _____.

    b. Everyone in the room was _____.

    c. I was especially _____.

3. Question 5 on the test **perplexed** Bob.

    a. Bob had a _____ look on his face.

    b. Question 5 was _____.

    c. Bob was _____.

4. That was the most **frightening** movie I've ever seen.

    a. I was _____.

    b. The whole movie was _____.

    c. I'm sure that other people in the audience were _____, too.

    d. The opening scene in which the ghost flew out of the closet was definitely really _____.

    e. At the end of the movie, I heard one audience member say, "What a _____ movie!"

5. Today's lesson was **confusing** to all of the students.

    a. The lesson was _____.

    b. The teacher's explanations were _____.

    c. The students were _____.

    d. The _____ students are angry about the teacher's _____ explanations.

EXERCISE 6. Identifying Participial Adjectives in Context

Underline the correct participial adjective in each sentence.

My Uncle's Car

1. After driving my car for a few years, I was (disgusted, disgusting) by having to spend so much on gas each month that I finally decided to sell it.

2. My uncle had just bought two new cars, so it was (challenged, challenging) to find a place to park his old car and his new cars at his house.

3. After talking to his wife, he was (convinced, convincing) that he should give me his old car.

4. When he called me and told me about it, his news was (shocked, shocking).

5. I really needed a car, and I was (concerned, concerning) about what I was going to do after selling my gas-guzzling car.

6. When I got my uncle's car, I was (surprised, surprising) to find out that the gas mileage rate is 36 miles per gallon!

7. That was very (thrilled, thrilling) news, and I will be saving at least $60 per week in gas costs.

8. My uncle and his wife were also (pleased, pleasing) to know that they now have room in their driveway and that I am saving money.

 ONE-MINUTE LESSON
In general, an inanimate thing (such as a book, the news, or the weather) uses an **–ing** form, while an animate thing (such as a cat or a human) can be either **–ing** or **–ed**.

 Do Online Exercise 3.2. My score: ____ /10. ____ % correct.

EXERCISE 7. Identifying the Participial Adjectives in Context

Underline the correct answers in each sentence.

1. *Ann:*   I don't know what to do now. I'm so **a** (confused, confusing).

   Jack: Maybe you should talk to your mom. She knows you're having some problems, and I'm sure she's very **b** (interested, interesting) in hearing your problems.

2. *Zina:*   That book sounds **c** (interested, interesting).

   Carol: I like the part when the people were trapped in the car in the river. They were **d** (terrified, terrifying).

   Zina: Well, it sounds like a **e** (fascinated, fascinating) book. I'll get a copy as soon as I can.

3. *Paul:*   What are you doing this weekend?

   Alan: I'm driving to Miami.

   Paul: What do you mean?

   Alan: Why do you look so **f** (puzzled, puzzling)?

   Paul: Well, that's a really **g** (tired, tiring) trip. Why are you going there?

   Alan: I've been feeling sort of **h** (depressed, depressing) lately, so I've decided to do something totally different this weekend. One of my old college friends lives there, so I'm going to go visit him and his family. It'll be something different.

   Paul: Hey, if you need anyone to talk to, just let me know. Some people are **i** (embarrassed, embarrassing) to talk to their friends about things, but please just let me know if there's anything I can do for you.

EXERCISE 8. Using Participial Adjectives in a Longer Context

Write the correct form of the adjective. Use the root of the adjective in parentheses.

A Difficult Job

Sammi: Hey, Gina! It's great to see you! We haven't talked for so long. Have you been doing anything (interest) ❶ _____ lately?

Gina: Not really. I'm really not (excite) ❷ _____ about anything in my life right now.

Sammi: Are you serious? Gina, you were always the girl with the most (inspire) ❸ _____ career goals in college! What happened?

Gina: Well, I am so (bore) ❹ _____ at my job. I thought that going into law would be (reward) ❺ _____, but it always seems like I'm doing paperwork.

Sammi: Are you not (satisfy) ❻ _____ with the trials that you take part in?

Gina: My case load is so big that I am just (overwhelm) ❼ _____ by all of the things I have to remember.

Sammi: That is very (upset) ❽ _____. What are you going to do?

Gina: Well, even though my work is (disappoint) ❾ _____ right now, I am going to hire a new paralegal next week. At least with some help, I won't be so (exhaust) ❿ _____.

Do Online Exercise 3.3. My score: _____ /10. _____ % correct.

EXERCISE 9. Mini-Conversations

Circle the correct words in these eight mini-conversations.

1. A: Did you see that (interested/interesting) new drama on cable last night?

   B: No, I wasn't (interested/interesting) in watching it.

2. A: I tried to knit once. It was too (frustrated/frustrating).

   B: Yes, I am much less (frustrated/frustrating) when I crochet. I like using one needle better.

3. A: Do you hear that loud noise? It's non-stop and so (irritated/irritating)!

   B: No, I don't hear anything, but now I know why you are really (irritated/irritating).

4. A: I got a D on my last test because the verb forms were too (confused/confusing).

   B: Really? To me, grammar is not (confused/confusing) at all.

5. A: Deena is so (exhausted/exhausting) this evening because she took a class of 4th-graders on a field trip.

   B: I don't blame her. That sounds terribly (exhausted/exhausting).

6. A: I was (astonished/astonishing) to hear that gas prices were going up again.

   B: Yes, that is definitely (astonished/astonishing) news.

7. A: I'm so (excited/exciting). It's my birthday next week.

   B: Well, I hope that you go out and do something fun and (excited/exciting).

8. A: Jim did not look very (surprised/surprising) that his favorite team lost the game.

   B: Well, considering that they are ranked the lowest in their division, it is not at all (surprised/surprising).

EXERCISE 10. Editing: Is It Correct?

If the sentence is correct, write a check mark (✓) on the line. If it is not correct, write an X on the line and circle the mistake. Then make the change above the sentence. (*Hint:* There are eight sentences. Two are correct, but six have mistakes.)

The Baby Squirrel

_____ 1. My sister has always been very interesting in squirrels.

_____ 2. Last week her next-door neighbor heard a very puzzled noise coming from his backyard.

_____ 3. When the neighbor checked on the noise, he found a very frightened baby squirrel under a tree.

_____ 4. The neighbor was confusing and didn't know what to do with the baby, so he took it to my sister.

_____ 5. At first, she was astonishing because she had not seen a squirrel that small before.

_____ 6. Then she inspected the squirrel and was concerning because although it was not injured, it was shivering.

_____ 7. She got the squirrel warm and gave it a little water, and she was pleasing because it took a nap. She placed it in a box under the tree and waited.

_____ 8. Eventually, the baby squirrel's mother came down the tree and took him back to the nest, which was very encouraging.

EXERCISE 11. Sentence Study for Critical Reading

Read the numbered sentences. Then read the three answer choices and put a check mark (✔) in the yes or no box in front of each sentence to show if that answer is true based on the information in the original sentence. If there is not enough information to mark something as yes, then mark it as no. Remember that more than one true answer may be possible.

1. My brother is two years younger than I am. He has an interesting job. He travels all over the world to find out if people are interested in giving money to charities.

   ☐ yes ☐ no   a. People are interested in getting my brother's money.

   ☐ yes ☐ no   b. My brother is interested in receiving money for charities.

   ☐ yes ☐ no   c. I am two years older than my brother is.

2. He travels to rich countries and talks to them about devastated regions. He finds out if people living in the wealthy countries are concerned about these alarming living conditions.

   ☐ yes ☐ no   a. My brother's job is alarming rich countries.

   ☐ yes ☐ no   b. We need an alarm clock about the living conditions.

   ☐ yes ☐ no   c. The goal of all of this is to help people who are wealthy.

3. My brother says that his job is challenging. Many times, the people he talks with are not concerned about helping others. Sometimes he says that talking about people starving and being sick is very depressing.

   ☐ yes ☐ no   a. My brother's job is not so easy.

   ☐ yes ☐ no   b. The people he talks with sometimes do not want to give money to charity.

   ☐ yes ☐ no   c. My brother talks to people who are depressed.

4. He says that many people are already convinced that giving money to charity is always the right thing to do. This is very encouraging. He sometimes gets inspired by the amount of money people are willing to give to unknown people.

   ☐ yes ☐ no   a. My brother finds people who are very giving.

   ☐ yes ☐ no   b. These people are very inspiring for their generosity.

   ☐ yes ☐ no   c. My brother always has to convince people to give to charities.

5. Even though my brother loves to travel, he is always very pleased to return home. He has an amazing little cat named Dewey that misses him when he is gone. Although someone takes care of Dewey while my brother is away, it is not the same. Dewey is very comforting to my brother when he returns home from a long trip overseas.

   ☐ yes ☐ no   a. Dewey is missing.

   ☐ yes ☐ no   b. My brother is missing.

   ☐ yes ☐ no   c. My brother is glad he has a cat.

EXERCISE 12. Speaking Practice: Interviewing a Classmate

Step 1. Work with a partner. Interview your partner using *–ing* and *–ed* participial adjectives in these questions. Take notes on the answers as you will use them for Step 2.

1. Name one action that you are terrified of.

   _____

2. When you are bored, what do you do?

   _____

3. What has been the most satisfying book that you have ever read?

   _____

4. What is one thing that makes you very frustrated?

   _____

Step 2. Based on the notes that you took from your partner's answers, write four sentences. You should have one sentence for each of their answers.

1. _____

   _____

2. _____

   _____

3. _____

   _____

4. _____

   _____

EXERCISE 13. Review Test 1: Multiple Choice

Circle the letter of the correct answer.

1. The thought of raw broccoli for dinner tonight is _____.

       a. disgust   c. disgusting

       b. disgusted   d. disgusts

2. Dylan hasn't been answering our calls since his grandfather died. I think he might
   be _____.

       a. depress   c. depressing

       b. depressed   d. depresses

3. Although I am not into modern art, there are a few pieces that I find
   _____.

       a. interest   c. interesting

       b. interested   d. interests

4. Reports on the loss of life from the monsoon were _____.

       a. devastate   c. devastating

       b. devastated   d. devastates

5. No matter how many times I watch an opera, I am always _____.

       a. bore   c. boring

       b. bored   d. bores

6. Wow! Those dark clouds really look _____.

       a. threaten   c. threatening

       b. threatened   d. threatens

7. We need to take a trip to the beach. It's been a very long time since either of us
   felt _____.

       a. relax   c. relaxing

       b. relaxed   d. relaxes

8. Jenna's news about her volleyball team is extremely _____!

       a. exciting   c. excite

       b. excited   d. excites

EXERCISE 14. Review Test 2: Production and Evaluation

Part 1.
Read this short passage. Fill in the blank with the correct form of the verb in parentheses.

A Vacation Getaway

Chloe and Tim live in Miami. They are ❶ (bore)

_____ with their normal vacations, and they

want a change. They were ❷ (confuse) _____

about where to go on their next trip until they

found an ❸ (excite) _____ coupon in the

local paper.

The ❹ (fascinate) _____ travel package included a short cruise to the

Bahamas. Chloe had never been on a cruise, and she thought that it sounded

❺ (intrigue) _____. Tim gets seasick, so he was ❻ (concern) _____

about the cruise even though it was short. The cruise might be very

❼ (challenge) _____ for Tim, but Chloe was ❽ (tempt) _____ by

the idea of sailing on the open sea on a huge ship.

When they took their vacation, Chloe was ❾ (thrill) _____, but Tim

was ❿ (terrify) _____. As he predicted, his stomach was very ⓫ (disturb)

_____ by the rocking of the ship and he got extremely seasick. Chloe

relaxed on the ⓬ (unsettle) _____ ride while Tim stayed below deck and

tried to sleep. When they got off the boat, Chloe asked, "Isn't this the most

⓭ (satisfy) _____ and ⓮ (fulfill) _____ trip we've ever been on?"

Part 2.

Read this short passage. There are six mistakes. Circle the mistakes, and write the correction above the mistake.

The City of Light

Paris is also known as "The City of Light" and has enchanted sidestreets, intriguing buildings, and historic works of art. The people there have interested fashion styles, too. There are entertained tours of the city where you can experience European culture. Prepare to be

amusing by the local street performers. If you have time, make sure to visit the tree-lined Avenue des Champs-Élysées as well as the captivated Arc de Triomphe. The language may be challenged if you do not know French, but many people in Paris speak a variety of different languages.

EXERCISE 15. Reading Practice: Identifying a Problem

Read this short conversation between two friends, and then answer the comprehension questions that follow. The grammar from this unit is underlined for you.

There's Something in the Attic!

Amy: Hi, Leslie. I noticed you weren't at work yesterday. Were you feeling sick?

Leslie: No, I was too <u>tired</u> to come in. We have an <u>interesting</u> problem at our house these days.

Amy: Oh, no. A problem? That sounds rather <u>distressing</u>!

Leslie: It was at first. There was an <u>annoying</u> sound coming from our attic every night.

Amy: Oh, wow. I would be really <u>frightened</u> if I heard that at night.

Leslie: Well, you're right. I was <u>terrified</u> the first night because I thought someone was in the house.

Amy: A person in your attic would be very <u>alarming</u>! But it wasn't a person?

Leslie: No. We checked, and the noises continued. We were so <u>exhausted</u> every morning from the lack of sleep. Then we called a <u>recommended</u> professional and they found bats.

Amy: Bats? Real, live, <u>horrifying</u> bats? Like the ones in the horror movies?

Leslie: Yes! We were really <u>disgusted</u>. I almost wish that it had been a person in the attic instead.

1. What is an attic?

   _____

2. Why was Leslie absent from work yesterday?

   _____

3. Have you ever seen a bat? If so, where?

   _____

4. Which of these words describe your attitude toward bats? Circle all the answers that are true.

   a. scared   b. terrified   c. excited   d. undisturbed

   e. interested   f. satisfied   g. infuriated   h. intrigued

5. How did Leslie get the bats out of the attic?

   _____

6. How many people were hiding in the attic?

   _____

7. Fill in the blank with the name of a living creature. Use a plural count nount such as *cats*.

   Although most people are afraid of _____, I am not

   bothered by them at all.

8. Fill in the blank with the name of a thing (non-living). Use a gerund such as *swimming*.

   Although most people are terrified of _____, I do not

   find it terrifying at all.

EXERCISE 16. Vocabulary Practice: Word Knowledge

Circle the answer choice that is most closely related to the vocabulary on the left. Use a dictionary to check the meaning of words you do not know.

Vocabulary	Answer Choices	
1. overwhelming	too little	too much
2. ordinary	common	uncommon
3. lately	earlier	recently
4. irritated	negative	positive
5. not hungry at all	a little hungry	not hungry
6. injured	angry	hurt
7. a squirrel	a type of animal	a type of place
8. up to $100	$85, $90, or $95	$100, $105, $110
9. to flood	a lot of pain	a lot of water
10. puzzling	confusing	disgusting
11. a decade	10 years	100 years
12. a resident	a person	a thing
13. starving	needs to eat	needs to work
14. to update	to cancel	to renew
15. wealthy	rich	tired
16. an attic	a person	a place
17. a bumper sticker	on a car	on a house
18. thrifty	earn money	save money
19. to switch	to begin	to change
20. slightly	a great deal	a little
21. shivering	shaking	shining
22. to slice	cut	depend
23. disgusted	negative	positive
24. to annoy	bother	disappoint
25. to switch	change	scare

EXERCISE 17. Vocabulary Practice: Collocations

Fill in each blank with the answer on the right that most naturally completes the phrase on the left. If necessary, use a dictionary to check the meaning of words you do not know.

Vocabulary	Answer Choices	
1. an allergic _____	answer	reaction
2. the opening _____	climate	scene
3. my entire _____	life	name
4. a next-door _____	neighbor	resident
5. willing _____	for	to
6. trapped _____ a place	inside	outside
7. _____ an experiment	run	take
8. an embarrassing _____	moment	schedule
9. _____ a nap	make	take
10. that idea might catch _____	on	up
11. I'm not _____ modern art	about	into
12. _____ of	consist	include
13. _____ a budget	in	on
14. _____ seasick	get	take
15. put _____ until tomorrow	it off	off it
16. a _____ store	crowded	purchased
17. an overwhelming _____	response	storm
18. a _____ job	challenging	concerning
19. an _____ bus driver	exhausted	exhausting
20. a _____ commitment	time	trip
21. _____ of ten parts	consist	include
22. boiling _____	volcanoes	water
23. my _____ shrank	pet	shirt
24. _____ went up	rates	times
25. _____ a solution	develop	overwhelm

EXERCISE 18. Writing Practice: Describing a New Technology

Part 1. Editing Student Writing

Read these sentences about digital books. Circle the 15 errors. Then write the number of the sentence with the error next to the type of error. (Some sentences may have more than one error.)

_____ a. a past participle is needed   _____ d. an infinitive is needed

_____ b. a present participle is needed   _____ e. a gerund is needed

_____ c. articles   _____ f. phrasal verb error

E-Books
1. For several centuries, people have loved books because readers know they can count with books to take them out of their usual lives. 
2. Traditional books are comforted, but digital books are also captivating to read.
3. Usually referred to simply as e-books, digital books are an intrigued and modern way of accessing books.
4. Instead of going to a crowding bookstore, you can simply browse huge selection of e-books online.
5. Are you the type of person who is frustrated when you have wait in long line?
6. Are you irritating when you cannot find a parking place at the bookstore?
7. If this sounds like you, then shopping for books online will certainly be soothing experience for you.
8. Some readers on a budget may find they need purchase e-books because printed books are generally more expensive than their online counterparts.
9. Some traditional books can be quite large and exhausted to carry.
10. After read all this information, are you convincing to download an e-book now?
11. Don't put off it another day!
12. Because of all the advantages that e-books offer, read e-books is catching on extremely quickly.

Part 2. Original Student Writing

Write one or two paragraphs about a new technology. Define what it is and discuss its advantages and disadvantages. Underline all of the present and past participles used as adjectives so your teacher can see what you are trying to practice.

Unit 4

Prepositions after Adjectives, Verbs, and Nouns

 ## Discover the Grammar

Read the passage about weather differences in two places. Then answer the questions that follow.

Line	
1	The weather in Maine is **different** from the weather in Florida. Due to the
2	cold winter weather in Maine, college students there dream about warm
3	temperatures in Florida. They would love to take a break from their cold winters
4	in Maine. Winters in Florida, on the other hand, are mild in comparison.
5	Spring sees many changes. In Florida, people are **used** to thunderstorms
6	that may occur almost daily in late spring. When spring finally arrives in Maine,
7	there is an abundance of water, and Mainers call springtime "mud season."
8	They are always **concerned** about flooding from the rain and melting snow;
9	however, that increase in water is also **responsible** for spring's new plants.
10	In summer, with a rise in temperature and humidity, Floridians quickly
11	become **accustomed** to mugginess, which is the primary reason for air
12	conditioning. From June to November, the right combination of temperature,
13	wind, and water currents results in "hurricane season." Some Floridians worry
14	about these storms, but early weather predictions help people prepare for these

15	severe storms. Summer in Maine is usually very nice. Air conditioning is seldom
16	used because the temperatures are pleasant.
17	Fall in these two states is very different. Florida does not experience
18	<u>changes</u> in leaf colors in fall, but Maine is **famous** for its beautiful fall colors.
19	In fact, thousands of tourists travel to Maine in late September and early
20	October to see the dramatic colors that nature presents.

1. The six **bold** words are adjectives. What preposition follows each?

   different _____   used _____   concerned _____

   responsible _____   accustomed _____   famous _____

2. The four words in a box are verbs. What preposition follows each?

   dream _____   result _____   worry _____   prepare _____

3. The six <u>underlined</u> words are nouns. What preposition follows each?

   a break _____   an abundance _____   that increase _____

   the reason _____   the combination _____   changes _____

4. We cannot predict which preposition comes after a noun, a verb, or an adjective, so these combinations must be memorized. Which of the 16 combinations in Items 1, 2, and 3 are easy for you? Which are difficult? Why?

   _____

   _____

Grammar Lesson

Adjective + Preposition Combinations

KEY 6   KEY 14

Adjectives can come before a noun or after the verb **be** (or linking verbs such as **seem** and **look**).

a **full** room	the room is **full**
adj noun	be adj

However, if you want to explain the word **full** by adding a noun (or pronoun), you need to include a preposition between the adjective and the noun.

the room is **full of** children
adj   prep   noun

<u>Rule 1</u>. Adjectives require a preposition if you want to give more information that includes a noun or pronoun object.

<u>Rule 2</u>. There is no way to predict this preposition. You must memorize the correct combination.

<u>Rule 3</u>. If the object is an action word, use a gerund (**–ing**):

I'm interested in **reading** that book.

⚠ BE CAREFUL!

Common Learner Errors	Explanation
1. Susan is married ~~with~~ to William.	Do not use the wrong preposition with an adjective.
2. ~~She disappointed~~ She was disappointed with the results of her test.	Don't forget to use a form of **to be** or a linking verb (*seem, appear, look,* etc.) with these adjectives.
3. Alice is good at ~~write~~ writing paragraphs.	If the object of the preposition is an action word, it must be a gerund (**–ing**).
4. We never ate hot dogs before coming here, but now ~~we used to eat~~ we are used to eating them.	Don't confuse **used to + VERB** (past repeated actions) with **be + used to** (a habit or custom). **Be + used to + VERB + –ing** is the same as **be + accustomed to + VERB + –ing**.

Connecting Grammar and Vocabulary

This list consists of frequently used adjectives and words functioning as adjectives and their corresponding prepositions. Sometimes other prepositions are possible, too.

Common Adjective + Preposition Combinations	
be + Adjective + Preposition	**Examples**
1. be accustomed to	I'm **accustomed** to working long hours.
2. be afraid of	He's **afraid of** spiders.
3. be angry at	Why are you so **angry at** her?
4. be ashamed of	He's **ashamed of** what he did.
5. be aware of	We were not **aware of** any problems with the car.
6. be bad at	She's **bad at** spelling.
7. be bored with/by	I was **bored with** the play, so I left.
8. be composed of	Water is **composed of** hydrogen and oxygen.
9. be confused about/by	I'm so **confused about** this situation.
10. be curious about	I'm **curious about** why you chose this school.
11. be dedicated to	She is **dedicated to** her family.
12. be different from	How is this paint **different from** that paint?
13. be disappointed in/with	We were **disappointed with** the food.
14. be done with	Are you **done with** the homework?
15. be envious of	I'm **envious of** your ability to sing.
16. be excited about	He's **excited about** going on vacation next week.
17. be familiar with	Are you **familiar with** this road?
18. be famous for	Switzerland is **famous for** its watches.
19. be fed up with	I was **fed up with** the service at my bank.
20. be finished with	Are you **finished with** the computer?
21. be frustrated by/with	Mr. Wilson is **frustrated** with his old car.
22. be full of	The car was **full of** suitcases.
23. be good at	Are you **good at** sports?
24. be guilty of	I think he is **guilty of** taking the money.

Common Adjective + Preposition Combinations	
be + Adjective + Preposition	**Examples**
25. be harmful to	Smoking is **harmful to** everyone's health.
26. be important for/to	Water is **important for** all living creatures.
27. be impressed by/with	We were **impressed with** the service at the restaurant
28. be innocent of	Do you think he is **innocent of** the crime?
29. be interested in	Are you **interested in** going to the beach with me?
30. be jealous of	I'm **jealous of** her! She's so lucky!
31. be known for	Korea is **known for** its spicy kim chee.
32. be made of/from	Mayonnaise is **made of** egg yolks and vegetable oil.
33. be married to	He was **married to** someone else when I first met him.
34. be opposed to	I'm **opposed to** eating at a vegetarian restaurant.
35. be proud of	I'm so **proud of** my son's accomplishments.
36. be ready for	Are you **ready for** some dessert now?
37. be related to	Are you **related to** Donald Sibber?
38. be relevant to	That is not **relevant to** this topic.
39. be responsible for	You are **responsible for** your children's actions.
40. be satisfied with	Are you **satisfied with** the president's work so far?
41. be scared of	We aren't **scared of** anyone or anything.
42. be sick of	I'm **sick of** eating tuna fish sandwiches every day.
43. be similar to	Italian is **similar to** Spanish.
44. be sorry about	I'm **sorry about** spilling coffee on your shirt.
45. be successful in	He was very **successful in** the carpet industry.
46. be surprised at/by	No one was **surprised at** the election results.
47. be tired from	We are **tired from** working in the yard today.
48. be tired of	We are **tired of** eating chicken every day.
49. be used to	Kim and Hank are **used to** waking up early.
50. be worried about	We are not **worried about** arriving late.

EXERCISE 1. Using Adjective + Preposition Combinations in Context

Read the sentences. Underline the adjective, and then write in the preposition.

Tina's Promotion at Work

1. Tina is dedicated _____ her job.

2. She is known _____ working more than eight hours a day.

3. Sometimes she gets frustrated _____ her boss because he keeps piling on more work.

4. Tina is used _____ helping her coworkers whenever they become confused _____ procedures.

5. Tina is never bored _____ the variety of jobs she handles.

6. Her coworkers were not surprised _____ the promotion Tina received.

EXERCISE 2. Writing Grammar in Original Sentences

Write two adjectives for each preposition, and then write a sentence using the adjective + preposition combination. The first one has been done for you as an example.

1. _proud_____ of

   _Owen is proud of his high school diploma._____

2. _____ of

   _____

3. _____ to

   _____

4. _____ to

   _____

5. _____ with

   _____

6. _____ with

   _____

EXERCISE 3. Editing: Is It Correct?

If the sentence is correct, write a check mark (✔) on the line. If it is not correct, write an X on the line and circle the mistake. Then make the change above the sentence. (*Hint*: There are eight sentences. Two are correct, but six have mistakes.)

Healthier Food Options

_____ 1. Exercising and eating healthy foods are important with your health.

_____ 2. Some people are willing for pay extra in order to purchase organically grown vegetables.

_____ 3. People used to eating vegetables grown with a lot of chemicals until organic farming became popular.

_____ 4. It is important to wash vegetables before eat them.

_____ 5. Eating vegetables every day is necessary for strong bones, energy, and weight control.

_____ 6. Doctors were used to tell new mothers to feed babies creamed vegetables when they reach three months old, but now they tell mothers to wait until the baby is six months old.

_____ 7. Some mothers are satisfied with baby food in jars, while others make their own.

_____ 8. Don't be afraid from cooking many different kinds of vegetables for one meal.

ONE-MINUTE LESSON

The connector **while** has two very different meanings. One meaning deals with **time**: *I had an interesting conversation* **while** *I was flying to New York.* A second meaning is similar to **although**: *After college, I took a job in California,* **while** *my twin sister decided to work in Texas.* Note that the second meaning usually uses a comma before the connector **while**.

 **Grammar Lesson**

KEY
6

Verb + Preposition Combinations

Most verbs in English can be followed by a noun (or pronoun). Examples include **eat, write,** and **expect.** These are called **transitive verbs**.

subject +	verb +	object
The children	have eaten	all the candy.
I	did not write	a thank-you note.
Nobody	expected	such a hard test.

Other verbs cannot be followed by an object. The verbs require a preposition between the verb and the object. Three common examples include **look, listen,** and **wait.** To make a sentence with **look** followed by an object, it is necessary to include the preposition **at.** In English, you cannot *look something. In English, you can only **look at** something. The verbs **listen** and **wait** are similar, but they require different prepositions. These verbs are called **intransitive verbs**.

subject +	verb +	preposition +	object
The teacher	has already looked	at	our exams.
I	did not listen	to	the announcement.
Jonathan	will wait	for	the next flight.

<u>Rule 1</u>. Some verbs require a preposition if you want to give more information that includes a noun or pronoun object.

<u>Rule 2</u>. There is no way to predict this preposition. You must memorize the correct combination.

<u>Rule 3</u>. If the object is an action word, use a gerund (**–ing**):

Several guests complained about not having hot water in their rooms.

BE CAREFUL!

Common Learner Errors	Explanation
1. They ~~apologized to~~ apologized for their harsh words.	Do not use the wrong preposition with a verb.
2. Only two people on the committee did not ~~agree our plan~~ agree with our plan.	Don't forget to use a preposition with certain verbs.

Connecting Grammar and Vocabulary

This list consists of frequently used verbs and their corresponding prepositions. Sometimes other prepositions are possible, too.

Common Verb + Preposition Combinations	
Verb + Preposition	**Examples**
1. agree with	I **agree with** Bill.
2. approve of	Do you **approve of** the idea?
3. argue about/with	Let's not **argue about** the check; we'll each pay an equal amount.
4. ask (someone) for	They **asked** me **for** my credit card expiration date.
5. belong to	The green car **belongs to** Amy.
6. complain about	Where can I **complain about** the cost of these tickets?
7. concentrate on	I couldn't **concentrate on** my homework.
8. consist of	The lunch special **consists of** a salad and two vegetables.
9. count on	If she's your friend, then you can **count on** her.
10. depend on	For the past two years, I've **depended on** my dad for money.
11. disagree about/with	It is not polite to **disagree with** your parents in public.
12. forget about	Did you **forget about** the meeting tomorrow night?
13. give (something) to	When you are done with the calculator, please **give** it **to** José.

Common Verbs + Preposition Combinations	
Verb + Preposition	**Examples**
14. happen to	What **happened to** Pablo?
15. introduce (someone) to	Let me **introduce** you **to** my professor.
16. keep on	**Keep on** trying; you are almost there.
17. listen to	He never **listens to** the teacher.
18. look at	Can you type without **looking at** the keyboard?
19. look for	I waste a lot of time just **looking for** my keys.
20. look forward to	Fran is really **looking forward to** the trip.
21. pay attention to	You need to **pay attention to** the road signs as well as your GPS.
22. remind (someone) of	That song **reminds** me **of** my university days.
23. thank (someone) for	She **thanked** her **for** the money.
24. think about/of (=opinion)	What do you **think of** the new boss?
25. think of (=envision)	I'm trying to **think of** the best way to fix this broken pipe.
26. wait for	How long do you usually **wait for** the bus in the morning?
27. work on	Henry stayed late so he could **work on** his chemistry problem.
28. worry about	Parents **worry about** their children even after they have grown.

Source: Folse, Keith S. (2009). *Keys to Teaching Grammar to English Language Learners.* Ann Arbor: University of Michigan Press.

EXERCISE 4. Identifying Verb + Preposition Combinations in Context

Underline the correct preposition in each sentence.

Phones Past and Present

1. In the late 1800s the first telephone was introduced (on, about, to) the public.

2. The telephone users counted (with, on, in) operators to connect them with their person they wanted to talk to.

3. Many customers shared a party line, which belonged (for, to, with) multiple callers.

4. When neighbors listened (on, about, to) other neighbors' conversations, rumors and gossip spread.

5. People complained (about, by, for) the lack of privacy, but party lines used to be very common.

6. From rotary to push button, telephones kept (on, to, with) evolving.

7. Inventors constantly worked (by, in, on) new ideas.

8. What do you think we can look forward (about, for, to) in the next decade?

  Do Online Exercise 4.1. My score: _____ /10. _____ % correct.

EXERCISE 5. Verb + Preposition Combinations in Conversations

Fill in the blanks with verbs from the box, and then add their prepositions. The first one has been done for you as an example. (*Hint*: Some verbs may be used more than once.)

word bank	belong	introduce	think
	complain	look	work
	disagree	thank	worry

Visiting a New Restaurant

1. *Jack:*   What do you _think_ _about_ your food?

   Ashley: Honestly, I hate to _____ _____ it, but I'm not impressed.

2. *Jack:*   I haven't tried my food yet, but as I _____ _____ it, it looks pretty inviting.

   Ashley: I _____ _____ you. There should be more color and texture.

3. *Jack:*   You know what? The chef is a friend of mine. Do you want me to

   _____ you _____ him?

   Ashley: OK.

   Jack: Please don't argue with him.

   Ashley: You don't have to _____ _____ that.

4. *Jack:*   Chef Fritz, this is Ashley. Ashley, this is Chef Fritz.

   Chef: Pleased to meet you.

   Ashley: Pleased to meet you, too.

   Chef: How do you like your dinner? I _____ _____ it for over two hours.

   Ashley: Delightful!

5. *Jack:*   Isn't he great?

   Ashley: He _____ _____ a special group of chefs!

6. *Ashley:*   _____ you _____ inviting me to dinner.

   Jack: You're welcome.

Grammar Lesson

Noun + Preposition Combinations

If you want to explain a particular noun by giving more information about it, you need to include a preposition between the noun and that information. Just as with adjectives and verbs, there is no way to predict this preposition. You must learn the correct combination.

We decided to submit a **request**.
noun

We decided to submit a **request** for additional funds.
noun with more information

Rule 1. Nouns require a preposition if you want to give more information that includes an additional noun or object pronoun.

Rule 2. There is no way to predict this preposition. You must memorize the correct combination.

Rule 3. If the object is an action word, use a gerund (**–ing**):

One advantage of having a car is that you do not have to pay bus fare.

BE CAREFUL!

Common Learner Errors	Explanation
1. Frankfurt is located in the ~~center for~~ center of Europe.	Do not use the wrong preposition with a noun.
2. What is your opinion of ~~work~~ working at night?	If the object of the preposition is an action word, it must be a gerund (**–ing**).

Connecting Grammar and Vocabulary

This list consists of frequently used noiuns and their corresponding prepositions. Sometimes other prepositions are possible, too.

Common Noun + Preposition Combinations	
Noun + Preposition	**Examples**
1. an advantage of	One **advantage of** this plan is the low cost.
2. advice on	Most people need **advice on** negotiating a salary.
3. the answer to	What is the **answer to** question number 7?
4. an application for	Please fill out an **application for** a scholarship.
5. a benefit of	One **benefit of** working here is the great insurance.
6. a cause of	What were the main **causes of** World War 2?
7. the center of	United Bank is located in the **center of** town.
8. confusion about	There is some **confusion about** his cause of death.
9. the cost of	The **cost of** living in Singapore can be high.
10. a decision to	Her **decision to** quit her job is final.
11. a decrease by/in/of	We have seen a **decrease in** the number of jobs.
12. the demand for	The **demand for** coffee is growing yearly.
13. the difference in/between/of	The **difference in** today's weather is amazing.
14. an example of	Can you give me an **example of** a landlocked nation?
15. experience in/with	Do you have **experience with** Excel?
16. an excuse for	What is your **excuse for** arriving late again today?
17. an increase in/of	Have you noticed an **increase in** your water bill?
18. information about	Where can I get **information about** going to Egypt?
19. an invitation to	We received an **invitation to** Ben and Sara's wedding.
20. interest in	Do you have any **interest in** buying a new car?

| Common Noun + Preposition Combinations ||
Noun + Preposition	Examples
21. a lack of	This building has a **lack of** proper smoke detectors.
22. the matter with	What is the **matter with** you today?
23. the middle of	Nicaragua is in the **middle of** Central America.
24. a need for/of	There is a **need for** economic reform in our country.
25. an opinion of/about	What is your **opinion about** this music?
26. the price of	What is the current **price of** a barrel of oil?
27. a problem with	They have a **problem with** their new car.
28. a question about	Does anyone have a **question about** today's lesson?
29. a reason for	What was your **reason for** quitting the bowling team?
30. a reply to	Did you read Maria's **reply to** my email?
31. a request for	A **request for** a higher salary now will be denied.
32. a rise in/of	A **rise in** fuel prices results in higher airline tickets.
33. a solution to	Joshua offered the best **solution to** our problem.
34. a source of	Her children are a **source of** great pride.
35. a tax on	Why is there such a high **tax on** cigarettes?
36. trouble with	My colleagues had **trouble with** their new computers.

Source: Folse, Keith S. (2009). *Keys to Teaching Grammar to English Language Learners*. Ann Arbor: University of Michigan Press.

EXERCISE 6. Using Noun + Preposition Combinations in Context

Read the paragraph about two countries. Fill in the blanks with the preposition that comes after the given noun.

Malaysia and Thailand

Because Malaysia and Thailand are neighboring countries, it is natural to assume that these two countries are very similar. In fact, there are many important differences ❶ _____ these two nations. One example ❷ _____ these differences is language. People in Thailand speak Thai, but people in Malaysia speak Malaysian. These two languages are not similar ❸ _____ each other at all. Another difference is in the number ❹ _____ tourists who visit each year. In Thailand, tourism is a major source ❺ _____ revenue for the nation. Although Malaysia has experienced an increase ❻ _____ international visitors in recent years, tourism does not contribute to the Malaysian economy to the extent that it does in Thailand. Why do so many tourists visit Thailand? One answer ❼ _____ this question is that Bangkok is a major international business center, so there are more flights to Bangkok than to Kuala Lumpur. Another reason ❽ _____ this disparity in tourist figures is that Thailand has many more beaches, which are a major attraction for European tourists seeking to escape from the cold winter weather. Finally, there is a slight difference ❾ _____ the cost ❿ _____ living. Many sources state that life in Malaysia is somewhat more expensive than in Thailand.

EXERCISE 7. Editing: Is It Correct?

If the sentence is correct, write a check mark (✔) on the line. If it is not correct, write an X on the line and circle the mistake. Then make the changes above the sentence. (*Hint:* There are eight sentences. Two are correct, but six have mistakes.)

Stacey's Car Problem

_____ 1. Stacey's excuse of being late today was that she had a flat tire.

_____ 2. While driving to work, Stacey realized that there was something the mattered with her tire.

_____ 3. After a few minutes, she knew the reason to the problem.

_____ 4. Stacey have trouble with that same tire two months ago.

_____ 5. At that time, the tires was under warranty, so the tire store fixed it at no charge. However, the warranty has run out.

_____ 6. On the advice of her father, Stacey made the decision of buy a whole new set of tires.

_____ 7. The alternative solution to her problem would be to purchase only one tire.

_____ 8. Luckily, Stacey was able to take advantage of a sale on tires at a competitor's store.

Do Online Exercise 4.2. My score: ____ /10. ____ % correct.

EXERCISE 8. Mini-Conversations

Circle the correct preposition combination in these eight mini-conversations.

1. *Dan:*   Have you ever been involved (about, for, **in**) an accident?

   Chris: No, but I'm certainly guilty (about, **of**, for) speeding.

2. *Sam:*   There is a lot of confusion (**about**, of, without) whether there is class today. I heard it was canceled due to bad weather last night.

   Anna: Yes, I'm worried (**about**, on, with) the possibility of worse weather later today.

3. *Liz:*   The chef's enchiladas are absolutely delicious!

   Gary: Yes, she really pays attention (for, in, **to**) every ingredient.

4. *Mom:*   I'm concerned (**about**, for, on) the baby not getting enough sleep.

   Dad: Don't think (**about**, for, on) that. I'm sure he'll fall asleep when he gets so tired he can't keep his eyes open.

5. *Carol:*   Hi, Kate! I just read in the newspaper that you got married (from, **to**, with) Dave last week. Congratulations!

   Kate: Thank you, but I sent an invitation (of, **to**, with) you.

6. *Teacher:*   Are you familiar (for, on, **with**) the Pythagorean Theorem? That's a hint.

   Student: Are you sure (**about**, for, with) that?

7. *Babysitter:* Joey, take your medicine. It's good (about, at, **for**) you.

   Joey: I'll do it, but I'm not happy (**about**, of, on) it.

   Babysitter: I think you aren't used (for, in, **to**) the taste.

8. *Mike:*   Jeff, are you related (about, **to**, with) Harry?

   Jeff: No, but I am acquainted (of, to, **with**) him. He's my neighbor. Why do you ask?

   Mike: I'm just surprised (**at**, for, on) the resemblance. You could easily belong (at, **to**, with) the same family.

EXERCISE 9. Speaking Practice: Presenting Class Surveys

You and your partner are going to write three survey questions using verb + preposition, noun + preposition, and adjective + preposition combinations.

Example: What kind of music do you <u>listen to</u>?
Who gives you <u>answers to</u> school problems?
What chores are you <u>responsible for</u> at your home?

When you are finished writing the set of three questions, each of you will ask ten different people the questions, and write down their answers. Discuss your answers with your partner, consolidate your findings, and then present them to the class using preposition combinations in compare/contrast sentences. Prepare a visual to illustrate your findings.

Example: Jan: I found that seven out of ten people that I surveyed listen to rock music.
Barb: However, only five of the ten people I asked listen to rock music.

ONE-MINUTE LESSON
The noun **difference** can be followed by three different prepositions: **between, in, of.**

We use **difference between** before the two nouns that are being compared: *One* **difference between** *you and me is that I am afraid of flying.*

We use **difference of** for **an amount or number:** *There is a time* **difference of** *six hours between Florida and Alaska.* (Also, there is the a common expression: a **difference of opinion.**)

We use **difference in** to identify what is different: *There is a huge* **difference in** *the price of economy and first class air tickets.*

EXERCISE 10. Sentence Study for Critical Reading

Read the numbered sentences. Then read the three answer choices and put a check mark (✓) in the yes or no box in front of each sentence to show if that answer is true based on the information in the original sentence. If there is not enough information to mark something as yes, then mark it as no. Remember that more than one true answer may be possible.

1. The city wants to replace the four-way stop sign at the intersection of Oak Street and First Avenue with a traffic light, but people have different opinions about this move. What is the matter with this plan? One issue is the cost of installing a traffic light.

   ☐ yes ☐ no a. There is a question about who will take care of the road.

   ☐ yes ☐ no b. Most people are against the traffic light because of its cost.

   ☐ yes ☐ no c. The intersection has been the site of several car accidents.

2. Our nephew belongs to the Bear Scouts. He has received a number of awards for different things he has done, but he is confused about how many he needs to move to the next level.

   ☐ yes ☐ no a. Our nephew is making progress toward the next level in the Bear Scouts.

   ☐ yes ☐ no b. The Bear Scouts are known for moving to the next level.

   ☐ yes ☐ no c. The Bear Scouts are confused about the boy's level.

3. The price of gasoline often fluctuates vastly, as there is a rise in cost when the supply is less than the demand. On the other hand, there is a decrease in cost when the supply is more than the demand.

   ☐ yes ☐ no a. The question about change in price may depend on how many people want the product.

   ☐ yes ☐ no b. The reason for a higher price is that more people want more gas than is available.

   ☐ yes ☐ no c. The source of the problem is certainly the country where oil is produced.

4. Susan and Dennis are looking for information about a vacation destination. So far, they favor a trip to Mexico because the airfare is cheap, but they are still considering a trip to Hawaii.

☐ yes ☐ no   a. Susan prefers Mexico, but Dennis prefers Hawaii.

☐ yes ☐ no   b. Dennis prefers Mexico, but Susan prefers Hawaii.

☐ yes ☐ no   c. Lack of funds will probably be the reason Susan and Dennis don't go to Mexico.

5. The passengers were angry at the airport officials, but according to our pilot, the decision to cancel the flight was his alone.

☐ yes ☐ no   a. The pilot was angry at the passengers and the airport officials.

☐ yes ☐ no   b. Our flight might be canceled by our pilot.

☐ yes ☐ no   c. The pilot decided to cancel our flight.

REVIEW ▷ **EXERCISE 11. Review Test 1: Multiple Choice**

Circle the letter of the correct answer.

1. Simon isn't very happy _____ his boss for giving him all that extra work.

    a. at   b. for   c. on   d. with

2. You need to give the cashier more money; there's a difference _____ 35 cents.

    a. between   b. from   c. in   d. of

3. Since we bought a hybrid, there has been a drastic decrease _____ the amount of gas that we need each month.

    a. between   b. by   c. in   d. on

4. Are you sure _____ that answer? It doesn't look right to me.

    a. for   b. in   c. of   d. with

5. Can you think _____ another reason why I shouldn't quit my job?

    a. at   b. of   c. on   d. to

6. Why are you complaining _____ such an insignificant detail?

    a. about   b. for   c. in   d. with

7. The principal had to speak _____ Jerry about his inappropriate behavior.

    a. about   b. for   c. of   d. to

8. Can you name one advantage _____ leaving at night instead of in the morning?

    a. about   b. at   c. in   d. of

REVIEW | **EXERCISE 12. Review Test 2: Production and Evaluation**

Part 1.

Read this paragraph. Fill in the blanks with the correct prepositions.

Have you ever thought ❶ _____ writing a book? That question is

what got my friend excited and involved ❷ _____ writing. Long ago, we

looked ❸ _____ his "bucket list," which was full ❹ _____ some

great and some not so great ideas. I was most interested ❺ _____ the

idea that mentioned writing about his travels and experiences ❻ _____

life. As the years passed, I thought he forgot ❼ _____ our conversation.

Then, a little over a month ago, I saw him in a bookstore, in the middle

❽ _____ a group of people, and he was autographing books. When he

saw me, he smiled, held up a book, and said, "This is what I've been dreaming

❾ _____!" He said that the book was important ❿ _____ him

for many reasons, but he was especially looking forward ⓫ _____

reading it to his grandchildren one day. They could listen ⓬ _____

stories of his adventures and laugh ⓭ _____ his misadventures. Through

this book, he could introduce them ⓮ _____ different cultures. He

smiled again and said that my question was responsible ⓯ _____ this

outcome and that's why he dedicated the book to me. I am so proud

⓰ _____ my friend.

Part 2.

Read each sentence carefully. Look at the underlined part. If the underlined part is correct, circle the word *correct*. If it is wrong, circle the word *wrong*. Then write the correction above.

correct   wrong   1. Colleen <u>looks worried about</u> something.

correct   wrong   2. Johnny <u>was used to</u> hate onions when he was a child.

correct   wrong   3. Now Johnny is <u>used to eating</u> onions without any problems.

correct   wrong   4. Manuela felt bullied in school when two girls <u>laughed at</u> her red shoes.

correct   wrong   5. The professor <u>explained the theory for the class</u> twice.

correct   wrong   6. You need to have <u>confidence on yourself</u> before you give a presentation.

correct   wrong   7. What is the <u>solution in this problem</u> that we are facing?

correct   wrong   8. Hector must <u>reply the court</u> before the court date or he will pay a huge fine.

ONE-MINUTE LESSON

Many **verbs of oral communication**, such as **reply**, use the preposition **to**. Other examples include:

The president **explained** *his plan* **to** *the American public.*
The manager **announced** *the news* **to** *everyone.*
She **described** *her new apartment* **to** *us.*

EXERCISE 13. Reading Practice: Comparing Destinations

Read this article from a U.S. travel magazine, and then answer the comprehension questions that follow. The grammar from this unit is underlined for you.

Exploring National Parks

Would you like to travel to a unique group of places <u>known for</u> their beauty, wildlife, and historical artifacts? Then look no further than the states around you. The United States is <u>proud of</u> its national parks. These are the people's parks, and as such, the U.S. government (with taxpayer funds and individual donations) is <u>responsible for</u> their upkeep and financial support. The government is <u>committed to</u> conserving the parks for future generations.

From north to south and east to west, you have more than 50 choices from A (Acadia) to Z (Zion). Maine, for example, is home to Acadia National Park. Acadia is <u>composed of</u> more than 20 mountains and many islands. The top of Cadillac Mountain, the tallest on the east coast, is <u>important to</u> early rising visitors because they can be the first to see the sun rise over the United States. The pink granite cliffs and finger-like waterways <u>belong to</u> breathtaking views of the Mount Desert Island coastline.

Traveling southward, stop in Virginia and hike along the Shenandoah River to <u>look at</u> the peaceful waterfalls. Have you ever <u>thought about</u> visiting the Great Smoky Mountains of North Carolina or Tennessee? You had better take your hiking boots because there are miles and miles of trails. Or what about horseback riding or fishing? Traveling further south, you could go fishing in the Everglades in Florida or take an airboat ride. The mangroves are a beautiful sight as you drive right through Everglades National Park on Alligator Alley.

Heading west, take a trip to Big Bend National Park along the Rio Grande in Texas. The states of Utah, New Mexico, Arizona, and Colorado are the <u>sources of</u> numerous national parks. Arches made of sandstone in the <u>middle of</u> desert are the <u>answer to</u> why the park was named Arches National Park. There are many canyons and parks in Utah worth seeing. Would you like to see something entirely <u>different from</u> the rest of the parks? How about stalactites and stalagmites in Carlsbad Caverns? Going west, you could <u>look at</u> the lowest and hottest place in the United States—Death Valley, California.

Perhaps you'd like to head toward California and the Channel Islands. Part of this park is under water. While in California, you could visit Yosemite National Park and its giant sequoias and waterfalls. From there, head north to Crater Lake in Oregon—it's so clear and blue! Mount Rainier in Washington is actually an active volcano, and the top is covered by glaciers. Then if you travel east along the northern border, you can visit Glacier National Park or see the Grand Tetons in Wyoming. Don't <u>forget about</u> Yellowstone National Park, which is <u>famous for</u> its hot springs and the geyser named Old Faithful.

If you <u>keep on</u> heading north to Alaska, visit Denali National Park, where you can <u>look forward to</u> seeing the tallest mountain in North America, Mt. McKinley.

Are you <u>excited about</u> visiting a national park? Go online to book a trip now.

1. Why do you think they are called the Great Smoky Mountains?

   _____

   _____

2. What is a sequoia? Have you ever seen one in person?

   _____

   _____

3. Why do you think they named the road Alligator Alley?

_____

_____

4. How do you think Crater Lake was formed?

_____

_____

5. Which national park would you like to visit? Why?

_____

_____

_____

_____

_____

_____

EXERCISE 14. Vocabulary Practice: Word Knowledge

Circle the answer choice on the right that is most closely related to the vocabulary on the left. Use a dictionary to check the meaning of words you do not know.

Vocabulary	Answer Choices	
1. mud	dirt and water	flour and oil
2. harmful	dangerous	silly
3. the source	the beginning	the ending
4. count on	depend on	know about
5. evolve	accustom	develop
6. curious	need to discuss	want to know
7. a fine	you did something correct	you did something wrong
8. a site	a person	a place
9. disappointed	you are happy	you are not happy
10. a meal	food	information
11. impressed	you are happy	you are not happy
12. related	2 cousins	2 friends
13. aware	you don't know about it	you know about it
14. muggy	cool, dry weather	warm, wet weather
15. exhausted	very expensive	very tired
16. a warranty	a guarantee	a lesson
17. willing to do something	agree to do something	agree not to do something
18. severe	very bad	very good
19. pleasant	nice	silly
20. a set of car tires	two tires	four tires
21. predictions	the future	the past
22. disappointed	not happy	not on time
23. harmful	dangerous	luxurious
24. a jar	glass	paper
25. envision	final	imagine

EXERCISE 15. Vocabulary Practice: Collocations

Fill in each blank with the answer on the right that most naturally completes the phrase on the left. If necessary, use a dictionary to check the meaning of words you do not know.

Vocabulary	Answer Choices	
1. _____ of	consist	insist
2. _____ happened to you?	What	Who
3. not at _____	all	more
4. in recent _____	people	years
5. similar _____	like	to
6. _____ colors	dramatic	responsible
7. jealous _____	in	of
8. more expensive _____	than	that
9. _____ attention to	pay	receive
10. the primary _____	money	reason
11. involved in _____	an accident	an early lunch
12. _____ warranty	under	with
13. _____ two hours	on	over
14. _____ of	proud	surrounded
15. have a flat _____	tire	wheel
16. _____ on	count	persuade
17. submit a _____	request	rumor
18. _____ frustrated	feel	take
19. envious _____	by	of
20. breathtaking _____	population	views
21. _____ about	concerned	responsible
22. a slight _____	difference	number
23. _____ warranty	across	under
24. _____ with	acquainted	responsible
25. supply and _____	decrease	demand

EXERCISE 16. Writing Practice: Writing a Biography

Part 1. Editing Student Writing

Read these sentences about a famous athlete. Circle the 15 errors. Then write the number of the sentence with the error next to the type of error. (Some sentences may have more than one error.)

_____ a. wrong verb tense   _____ d. pronoun error

_____ b. wrong preposition   _____ e. singular-plural of nouns

_____ c. missing article   _____ f. an infinitive is needed

A Famous Tennis Player and Sports Hero
1. One of most important people in the history of the sport of tennis is Billie Jean King.
2. Some might argue that she is one of the most important people in the history of all sports because she is responsible in the increased prize money now paid to women in many sport.
3. As a child, Billie Jean King has learned to play tennis in her home state of California.
4. She was a natural athlete who played a lot of sports, but her parents encouraged them to play tennis.
5. At the age of 18, King defeated world's best woman tennis player, Margaret Court Smith, at Wimbledon.
6. During her career, King won Wimbledon, the French Open, the Australian Open, and the U.S. Open, which were the biggest tennis tournaments in the world, many time in both singles and doubles matches.
7. In addition to her excellence as an athlete, Billie Jean King is known about her dedication to improving the treatment and pay of women in sports
8. King has worked hard establish the first successful women's professional tennis tour, the WTP.
9. Due to her efforts, women receive same prize money as men in the U.S. Open.
10. Some people know King's name because of the famous tennis match against Bobby Riggs on 1973 in the Houston Astrodome.
11. Riggs had been the top tennis player in world, and he came out of retirement play the match.
12. This "battle of the sexes" match, as it was called, not only helped bring national attention to the sport of tennis, but it was proving that a woman could beat a man, thus helping to advance the cause of the women's equal rights movement.

Part 2. Original Student Writing

Write a paragraph or a short essay about a famous person (living or dead). Tell why this person is famous. Include the early history of this person as well as three or four of the person's major accomplishments.

Use at least two adjective + preposition combinations, one verb + preposition combination, and one noun + preposition combination. Underline these combinations and circle the preposition so the teacher can see what you are trying to practice.

 Unit 5

Passive Voice

Discover the Grammar

Read this passage about corn, and then answer the questions that follow.

Line	
1	Corn is one of the most popular vegetables in terms of the total amount
2	that is consumed each year. Corn is eaten in its usual form and as an ingredient
3	in many other products, including cereal and corn oil.
4	Corn has been a popular food for a long time. It is believed that corn was
5	first cultivated by the Mayans in Central America about 4,500 years ago.
6	Around the 15th century, corn seeds were taken by Spanish explorers from
7	Central America to Europe, where this food eventually gained popularity.
8	Did you know that corn is one of the few crops that must be cultivated
9	because it does not grow in the wild? Approximately 40 percent of the world's
10	corn is grown in the United States. In fact, the states of Iowa, Indiana, Illinois,
11	and Ohio are known as the Corn Belt because such good climate and soil
12	conditions for cultivating corn can be found there.

1. Copy the four examples of **is + past participle** here. This form is called **passive voice.** The first one has been done for you as an example.

Line	Passive Voice Verb	Possible Original Meaning
2	is consumed	people consume corn each year
		people eat corn
		people believe that corn was first cultivated by the Mayans
		farmers grow 40 percent of the world's corn in the U.S.

2. The verb form in the middle column is called **passive voice.** The verb form in the right column is called **active voice.** Both verb forms refer to the same action. Why do you think one form might be preferred instead of the other?

_____

_____

_____

3. Write the active voice (original meaning) for these passive voice examples.

Line	Passive Voice Verb	Possible Original Meaning
4–5	was cultivated	
6	were taken	
8	must be cultivated	

4. Do an Internet search and copy a sentence with these phrases in the left column. Why do you think passive voice is used in your examples?

is used	
have been used	
should be used	

Grammar Lesson

Active Voice and Passive Voice

Verbs can be either transitive or intransitive. Transitive verbs can have a direct object. Intransitive verbs can never have a direct object.

Common **transitive** verbs are **give** and **make** because they must have a direct object after them. We cannot say only *They gave or *She made. We have to **give something** and **make something**. Common **intransitive** verbs are **belong** and **happen**. We cannot say *It happened John or *The leaves fell me.

Transitive Verb		Intransitive Verb
Active Voice	**Passive Voice**	
They **use** Euros in Italy.	Euros **are used** in Italy.	This paper **belongs** to me.
Ava **wrote** that email.	That email **was written** by Ava.	The accident **happened** at noon.

Study these seven examples of active and passive voice.

	Active Voice	Passive Voice
simple present tense	We **elect** a new president every four years.	A new president **is elected** every four years.
simple past tense	Shakespeare **wrote** *Romeo and Juliet*.	*Romeo and Juliet* **was written** by Shakespeare.
present progressive tense	Apple **is developing** a new kind of communication device.	A new kind of communication device **is being developed** by Apple.
present perfect tense	A group of Russian astronomers **has discovered** a new planet.	A new planet **has been discovered** by a group of Russian astronomers.
past progressive tense	When I arrived at the shop, the clerk **was stapling** my copies.	When I arrived at the shop, my copies **were being stapled** by the clerk.
be going to	The police **are going to arrest** Josh Teague for stealing the money.	Josh Teague **is going to be arrested** for stealing the money.
modals	You **may purchase** a cheaper ticket online.	A cheaper ticket **may be purchased** online.

<u>Rule 1</u>. The **passive voice** is composed of the verb **be** and the **past participle**.

<u>Rule 2</u>. The verb **be** in passive voice must have the correct tense to indicate the time of the action.

<u>Rule 3</u>. The verb **be** in passive voice should be singular or plural according to the subject.

<u>Rule 4</u>. In general, we use passive voice when the doer of the action is unknown or is not the most important thing. In passive voice, the subject of the sentence is the receiver of the action. The subject can be either a person or a thing.

<u>Rule 5</u>. **Active voice** is common in both formal and informal English. **Passive voice** occurs much more frequently in academic or formal written English than in spoken English.

<u>Rule 6</u>. When you change a verb from active voice to passive voice, a helpful hint is to count the number of verb parts in the active sentence and then add one. The number of verb parts in the passive sentence is always one more due to the addition of a form of the verb **be** in the passive sentence.

Number of Verb Parts	Active	Passive
1 → 2	People **write** Arabic from right to left.	Arabic **is written** from right to left.
2 → 3	The vice president **will lead** the meeting	The meeting **will be led** by the vice president.
4 → 5	Local artists **are going to do** the paintings.	The paintings **are going to be done** by local artists.

Rule 7. If you want to name the doer in a passive voice sentence, you can use a **by + doer** phrase. However, we only name the doer when that information is new or important.

Active Voice	Passive Voice
A. Leonardo da Vinci painted the famous *Mona Lisa*.	B. The famous *Mona Lisa* was painted by **Leonardo da Vinci**. Note: Without the **by**-phrase, the sentence does not make sense.
C. The people reelected George Washington for a second term in 1792.	D. George Washington was reelected ~~by the people~~ for a second term in 1792. Note: The **by**-phrase is not new information. Everyone knows that people elect presidents.

Rule 8. To form a question with passive voice, invert the subject and the form of **be** (**am, is, are, was, were**) or **have** (**have, has, had**) or the modal (**will, can, should**, etc.).

 BE CAREFUL!

Common Learner Errors	Explanation
1. The final exam will ~~give~~ be given next week.	Do not use active voice when you should use passive voice.
2. This letter ~~sent~~ was sent to the wrong address.	Do not forget to use a form of *be* in the passive voice.
3. Arabic is written from right to left ~~by Arabic speakers~~.	Do not use the *by* + doer phrase of the information is not new or important.
4. The accident ~~was happened~~ happened around midnight.	Intransitive verbs can never be in the passive voice. Intransitive verbs cannot have a direct object, so they cannot be changed to passive voice. Common intransitive verbs include **happen, die, arrive, exit**, and **depart**.

Connecting Grammar and Vocabulary

Thousands of verbs can be used in passive voice, but you should focus your time on the verbs most commonly used in passive voice. Study this list of verbs frequently used in passive voice.

15 Past Participles Frequently Used in Passive Voice		
1. be used	6. be taken	11. be given
2. be made	7. be expected	12. be based
3. be done	8. be seen	13. be killed
4. be found	9. be considered	14. be told
5. be called	10. be born	15. be designed

Source: Corpus of Contemporary American English, www.americancorpus.org.

EXERCISE 1. Passive Voice in Different Tenses

Write the correct passive voice forms for the active voice phrase using the verb **do**. The first one has been done for you as an example.

		Active Voice		Passive Voice
1.	present tense	People do X.	X	_is done_.
2.	present progressive tense	People are doing X.	X	_____.
3.	past tense	People did X.	X	_____.
4.	modal : **should**	People should do X.	X	_____.
5.	modal : **might**	People might do X.	X	_____.
6.	**have to**	People have to do X.	X	_____.
7.	**be + going to**	People are going to do X.	X	_____.
8.	past progressive tense	People were doing X.	X	_____.
9.	present perfect tense	People have done X.	X	_____.

ONE-MINUTE LESSON

The verb **happen** is a very frequent verb. Because we often use it to talk about a specific event in the past, this verb usually occurs in simple past tense: **happened**. For some reason, many students make this common mistake: *it was happened*. The verb **happen** never occurs in passive voice, so *was happened* is never correct.

EXERCISE 2. Identifying Active and Passive Voice Verbs

Underline the entire verb each sentence. Then write *active* or *passive* on the line to the left to indicate which voice is used. The first one has been done for you as an example.

The Story of Mount Rushmore

passive   1. Mt. Rushmore <u>is visited</u> by more than two million visitors each year.

_____   2. The sculpture was carved into the granite face of Mt. Rushmore in South Dakota.

_____   3. Doane Robinson, a historian from South Dakota, is credited with coming up with the original idea for this incredible work.

_____   4. Gutzon Borglum, a famous sculptor, was invited to carve this giant monument.

_____   5. At the time of the invitation, Borglum was sculpting Stone Mountain in Georgia.

_____   6. From the planning in 1925, Borglum was constantly battling opposition to the monument.

_____   7. The faces of four U.S. Presidents, Washington, Jefferson, Roosevelt, and Lincoln, were chosen for the 60-foot-high monument.

_____   8. In the original plan for this sculpture, Robinson had envisioned the faces of early U.S. explorers such as Lewis and Clark.

_____   9. By order of President Calvin Coolidge, the U.S. President during the early planning, Washington plus two Republicans and a Democrat were selected for this huge sculpture.

_____   10. Since opening in 1941, this monument has attracted a great deal of attention as one the most popular tourist destinations in the United States.

EXERCISE 3. Identifying Passive Voice in Context

Underline the 12 verb phrases that have any form of the verb **be**. Then circle the three passive voice verb phrases among those verb phrases.

---

300 Jefferson Avenue
Orlando, FL 32806
October 1, 2015

United Mileage Plus Service Center
PO Box 6120
Rapid City, SD 57709-6120

To Whom It May Concern:

I am writing to request credit in my frequent flyer account for two trips that I recently took on Air New Zealand, which is one of your partner affiliates. I filled out the online form, but I did not receive any kind of reply. I then filled the forms out online again, and today I received a message that informs me that one flight is not eligible for my mileage program and that there was no person with my name on the second flight. I do not think this information is correct, so I am writing you this letter to see if these flights can be credited to my United Mileage Plus account.

Copies of both of my boarding cards are being sent with the letter so you can see that I did in fact take these two flights. I have written the ticket numbers and my mileage plus number on both of the boarding cards. The flights in question are two Air New Zealand flights from Sydney to Auckland and then from Christchurch to Sydney. These flights were on September 1 and September 15.

These flights took place more than a month ago, and I have attempted to resolve this matter several times. As of today, however, no credit has been received for either of these two Air New Zealand flights.

Many thanks in advance for whatever information you can give me about the status of these two flights. I have been a loyal customer for many years, and I do not understand why solving this situation has taken so long.

Sincerely,

Jorge Romero

EXERCISE 4. Identifying Passive Voice in an Academic Context

Circle the 10 of the 25 underlined verb phrases that include passive voice.

Using a Dictionary in a Different Language

Using an English-English dictionary ❶ may seem relatively straightforward. Skills that ❷ are needed to look up the correct meaning of a word ❸ include alphabetizing, using guide words, understanding the part of speech, interpreting pronunciation guides, and determining the most appropriate meaning. However, when I ❹ was learning Japanese, I ❺ came across very different problems when I ❻ attempted to look up a word in the dictionary.

In a class I ❼ was taking in a Japanese as a Second Language program in Tokyo, the teacher gave us a small writing assignment. We ❽ had to write approximately ten sentences about ourselves. Having had many years of second language learning and teaching experience, I thought this task seemed quite normal. In fact, I ❾ thought it ❿ was quite easy. Almost immediately, the students in the class ⓫ got up and left the room. They ⓬ were complaining about how hard this assignment was. I soon learned that their complaints ⓭ were actually justified.

Japanese ⓮ is written with three writing systems: hiragana, katakana, and kanji. Hiragana and katakana are syllabaries. In a syllabary, one symbol ⓯ is used for what we in English ⓰ would consider a whole syllable. For example, in these two systems, there are five different symbols for *ka*, for *ki*, for *ku*, for *ke*, and for *ko*. There is no symbol for just *k*. The kanji are from the Chinese characters that Japanese borrowed centuries ago.

All three of these systems **17** <u>are included</u> in the same sentence. In general, kanji **18** <u>are used</u> for most words, hiragana **19** <u>is needed</u> for word endings and grammar functions, and katakana **20** <u>is required</u> for foreign words. It is easy to learn and then read and write the symbols in hiragana and katana. However, there **21** <u>are</u> thousands of kanji, and each character **22** <u>is made</u> in a certain stroke order and **23** <u>may be pronounced</u> in a number of different ways. With three writing systems that a learner can hardly pronounce, how can I look up the meaning of a word? I do not know how to pronounce a kanji that I do not know, and there is no way to sound it out.

Using a dictionary in any language **24** <u>can be</u> challenging. What may seem so simple to us as speakers of one language **25** <u>is</u> not necessarily so easy to speakers of a very different language.

Source: Adapted from Folse, K.S. (2004). *Vocabulary Myths: Applying Second Language Research to Classroom Teaching*. Ann Arbor: University of Michigan Press.

ONE-MINUTE LESSON
When we use the verb **know** to talk about a skill or ability that we can do, we use the word **how** followed by an **infinitive**: *Do you* **know how to** *drive?* A common error is to omit the word **how**, but you must include it: *I* **know how to** *speak English*.

Do Online Exercise 5.1. My score: _____ /10. _____% correct.

EXERCISE 5. Editing: Is It Correct?

If the sentence is correct, write a check mark (✓) on the line. If it is not correct, write an X on the line and circle the mistake. Then make the change above the sentence. (*Hint*: There are eight sentences. Two are correct, but six have mistakes.)

A Mini Crime Spree

_____ 1. Over the weekend, three golf carts stole from the university campus.

_____ 2. A student reported to police that he was found the golf carts several blocks from the campus.

_____ 3. Despite the theft of the carts, no damage was reported.

_____ 4. Police believe more than one individual involved in the crime.

_____ 5. Including this incident, a total of 12 golf carts have taken from the campus so far this year.

_____ 6. The maintenance supervisor said, "We must be done something about these thefts."

_____ 7. It has been suggested that the university should install more security cameras.

_____ 8. Anyone with knowledge of these crimes is asking to call the campus police immediately.

EXERCISE 6. Changing Sentences with Active Voice to Passive Voice

Rewrite each sentence to include passive voice.

1. People use chopsticks in China.

   _____

2. The workers have made many improvements in the air conditioning system.

   _____

3. We did the work as fast as possible.

   _____

4. You can find canned soup on aisle seven.

   _____

5. His name is Robert, but people usually call him Bob.

   _____

6. An ambulance took the injured driver to the hospital.

   _____

7. Do people expect us to finish this job by tomorrow?

   _____

8. We could see Mercury and Venus without a telescope.

   _____

Do Online Exercise 5.2. My score: _____ /10. _____ % correct.

EXERCISE 7. Editing: Is It Correct?

If the sentence is correct, write a check mark (✓) on the line. If it is not correct, write an X on the line and circle the mistake. Then make the change above the sentence. (*Hint*: There are ten sentences. Two are correct, but eight have mistakes.)

Cars Without Drivers?

_____ 1. Self-driving cars are currently be designed by German companies.

_____ 2. Semi-automated cars are going to seen on the highways in the very near future.

_____ 3. A human sitting behind the wheel of a semi-automated car will be required for partial operation.

_____ 4. The driver of a semi-automated car may be call a "pilot" or an "operator."

_____ 5. Semi-automated cars is expected to be much safer because sensors will react quickly to avoid collisions.

_____ 6. The generation of cars following the semi-automated will be fully automated, where a driver's attention will rarely needed, leaving the driver free to drink a latte and read email.

_____ 7. The insurance industry is concern about self-driving cars because of system breakdowns that could cause accidents.

_____ 8. Wireless connectivity to other cars for safety and various traffic monitoring systems are considered essential for fully automated cars.

_____ 9. Car engines have based on the internal-combustion engine for a long time, and that part is not going away anytime soon.

_____ 10. However, manufacturers are still working on improvements to hybrid engines where both gasoline and electricity can used.

Grammar Lesson

Past Participles Used as Adjectives

Examples	Meaning
A. Two windows **are broken**.	There is no action. These sentences describe the condition of the window now.
B. Can you repair the two **broken** windows?	
C. The carrots are whole, but the onions **are chopped**.	There is no action. These sentences describe the condition of the onions now.
D. The **chopped** onions smell strong.	

Rule 1. Sometimes it is possible to use a passive verb form as an adjective to describe a condition or state instead of an action, as in A and C. This common structure may look like passive voice, but it is not true passive voice.

Rule 2. As an adjective, a past participle may come after the verb **be**, as in A and C, or before a noun, as in B and D.

 BE CAREFUL!

Common Learner Errors	Explanation
1. The windows are ~~close~~ closed now.	Be sure to use the correct adjective form.
2. Many readers found the story to be ~~confused~~ confusing.	Do not confuse the past participle (*–ed*, *–en*) and present participle (*–ing*) forms.

 ONE-MINUTE LESSON
Do not confuse the adjectives **broken** and **broke**. **Broken** means "not repaired, having a problem or defect": *My phone is* **broken**. *She has a* **broken** *arm*. In contrast, **broke** means "not having money": *After my long vacation, I was completely* **broke**.

Connecting Grammar and Vocabulary

Some past participles are used as adjectives much more frequently than others. Study this list of past participles that are frequently used as adjectives.

20 Most Frequent Past Participles Used as Adjectives			
1. unidentified	6. united	11. limited	16. lost
2. concerned	7. married	12. tired	17. advanced
3. involved	8. used	13. so-called	18. complicated
4. supposed	9. increased	14. armed	19. unknown
5. interested	10. surprised	15. broken	20. scared

Source: Reilly, N. (2013). *A Comparative Analysis of Present and Past Participial Adjectives and Their Collocations in the Corpus of Contemporary American English*. Thesis, University of Central Florida.

EXERCISE 8. Practicing Frequent Past Participle Adjectives in Sentences

Fill in the blanks with one of the common past participles from the box above.

1. Many people are _____ of spiders.

2. Three cars were _____ in an accident on Highway 77 today.

3. I'm in the beginning level, but the material is too _____ for me.

4. The paperwork for buying a new car was extremely _____.

5. Do you believe that _____ flying objects are real?

6. Most stores have a _____ and found department.

7. Our _____ bonus was only $50, much less than the $300 we had expected.

8. We had more rain than usual last month, but the _____ rainfall was very welcome because we had been in a drought.

9. In the _____ States, _____ couples have the right to file their taxes jointly or separately.

10. For a _____ time, three airlines are having a fare war.

EXERCISE 9. Speaking Activity: What Has Been Done?

Situation: You and your partner own a pizza shop. You have a list of things that need to be done. Some of these things have already been done, but the others haven't been done yet.

Step 1. There are twelve business activities listed on page 146. Put a check mark (✓) by any four of the activities. Do this on the lines from Your List column. These are the four items that you have done already.

Step 2. Next, work with a partner. Do NOT show your book to your partner. Take turns asking each other questions. Use passive voice in every question. Ask "Has/Have (item) been (past participle)?" Your partner will answer either with:

- Yes, [item] has/have <u>already</u> been [Past Participle] *OR*
- No, [item] hasn't/haven't been [Past Participle] <u>yet</u>.

Step 3: If your partner's answer is yes, then you can continue asking questions. If the answer is no, then it is your partner's turn to ask. Use Your Partner's List column to record the answers (yes/no) from your partner.

Step 4: The winner is the first student who can guess all four of his or her partner's checked (✓) answers.

<u>Remember</u>: Use passive voice in your questions and the words **already** or **yet** in your answers. Use complete sentences in your answers.

<u>Examples</u>:   A: Has gas been put in the delivery car?

B: No, gas hasn't been put in the delivery car yet. (The answer is no, so Student A writes no by put gas in delivery car in the column on the right in Student A's book. The no answer also means that it is now Student B's turn to ask a question.)

B: Has the rent been paid?

A: Yes, the rent has already been paid. (The answer is yes, so Student B writes yes by pay the rent in the column on the right in Student B's book. The yes answer also means that it is still Student B's turn to ask a question.)

Your List	Your Partner's List
_____ take out the garbage	_____ take out the garbage
_____ order a supply of pizza boxes	_____ order a supply of pizza boxes
_____ pay the rent	_____ pay the rent
_____ hire a delivery person	_____ hire a delivery person
_____ put gas in the delivery car	_____ put gas in the delivery car
_____ wash the entry door	_____ wash the entry door
_____ slice the pepperoni	_____ slice the pepperoni
_____ grate the cheese	_____ take out the garbage
_____ heat the oven	_____ grate the cheese
_____ copy the coupons	_____ heat the oven
_____ buy soap	_____ copy the coupons
_____ make the bank deposit	_____ buy soap

ONE-MINUTE LESSON
As your English proficiency increases, you need to focus heavily on increasing your vocabulary. In addition to new words such as **hire** and **grate**, you need to learn the words that usually accompany them: **hire a person, grate cheese.** Pay attention to words that usually occur with your new vocabulary.

Grammar Lesson

Passive Voice with *get*

| with **be** | A. The salesperson with the least sales last month **was fired** today. |
| with get | B. The salesperson with the least sales last month got fired today. |

Rule 1. The passive for the verb **get** consists of a form of the verb **get** followed by a **past participle**, as in B.

Rule 2. The **get** passive indicates a sudden change; the **be** passive indicates a result. Thus, We were lost describes our situation at a certain point, but We got lost indicates that we were traveling and suddenly did not know our location.

Rule 3. Formal writing generally avoids the use of **get**. Instead, use **become** as a synonym to express the same concept.

Rule 4. The use of **get** is considered informal language and is therefore much more common in spoken language than written language. Many past participles used with **get** indicate a **problematic situation: get lost, get killed, get stolen, get hurt.**

Connecting Grammar and Vocabulary

Thousands of verbs can be used in passive voice, but not as many are common in the *get* **passive** construction. Study this list of verbs frequently used in *get* **passive**.

12 Past Participles Frequently Used in *Get* Passive		
1. get rid (of)	5. get paid	9. get hit
2. get married	6. get involved	10. get elected
3. get started	7. get done	11. get fired
4. get caught	8. get dressed	12. get arrested

Source: Corpus of Contemporary American English, www.americancorpus.com.

EXERCISE 10. Mini-Conversations

Circle the correct words in these eight mini-conversations.

1. June: How long have you known Mike?

   Eve: Let's see. We got (marry, married) five years ago, but we (dated, were dated) for two years before that, so that means seven years.

2. June: How (did you meet, were you met) Mike?

   Eve: We (introduced, were introduced) by a mutual friend.

3. Agent: How (did, was) the accident happen?

   Client: From Evergreen Drive, I was (made, making) a left turn onto Atlas Road when all of a sudden my car (hit, got hit) on the driver's side by some guy who was (passed, passing) another car on Atlas.

4. Leslie: Where has Larry been lately?

   Monica: Oh, some friends took him surfing and he really got (hook, hooked), so now he's at the beach every weekend.

5. Taka: Hurry up or we're going to be late for the party.

   Leona: Ok, ok! I (am gotten, am getting, got) dressed now. Give me a minute.

6. Kevin: How long have you lived in your new house?

   Debbie: Just over two months, but I still (am not, did not, have not) gotten used to the place.

7. Mary: Are you aware that the Platte River flooded last night and many roads (are closed, closed)?

   Jose: No, I didn't know that.

8. Joey: Mom! What happened to my new wool sweater? It won't fit me!

   Mom: Oh, no! I guess it (was, got) shrunk in the dryer.

ONE-MINUTE LESSON
The adjective **aware** has two sentence structures. If we are talking about a noun, we use the preposition **of**: *We are* **aware of** *the problem*. If we are talking about a clause (a subject and a verb), we use **that** or **nothing**: *We are* **aware that** *there is a problem*. OR *We are* **aware** *there is a problem*.

EXERCISE 11. Sentence Study for Critical Reading

Read the numbered sentences. Then read the three answer choices and put a check mark (✓) in the yes or no box in front of each sentence to show if that answer is true based on the information in the original sentence. If there is not enough information to mark something as yes, then mark it as no. Remember that more than one true answer may be possible.

1. The world's largest collection of Star War's memorabilia, with more than 300,000 individual pieces, is owned by Steve Sansweet. The collection is housed in Rancho Obi-Wan, a museum that he operates.

   ☐ yes ☐ no   a. Rancho Obi-Wan is where Mr. Sansweet keeps his collection.

   ☐ yes ☐ no   b. Steve Sansweet has more Star War's collectibles than any other person.

   ☐ yes ☐ no   c. The Star Wars films are owned by Steve Sansweet.

2. The office manager's instructions for what to do with these files were confusing to both of the assistants.

   ☐ yes ☐ no   a. The files were confusing.

   ☐ yes ☐ no   b. There are two assistants.

   ☐ yes ☐ no   c. The assistants were confusing.

3. A zookeeper was attacked by a brown bear at the Hillsdale Zoo. An investigation by officials found that the cage door was unlocked.

   ☐ yes ☐ no   a. The zookeeper unlocked the bear's cage.

   ☐ yes ☐ no   b. A brown bear attacked someone who was working at the zoo.

   ☐ yes ☐ no   c. Officials unlocked the cage door.

4. Nearly 5,000 tourists were stranded in Acapulco when the airport was flooded with water and mud following several days of heavy rains that were brought about by two colliding tropical storms.

   ☐ yes ☐ no   a. Nearly 5,000 tourists were stuck at the airport in Acapulco.

   ☐ yes ☐ no   b. The tourists could not leave Acapulco on airplanes.

   ☐ yes ☐ no   c. A single tropical storm caused water to fill the airport.

5. FBI agents were told that D. B. Cooper was last seen jumping out of a plane with a bag that had been filled with $200,000.

   ☐ yes ☐ no   a. We don't know who saw Cooper jump from the plane.

   ☐ yes ☐ no   b. We know who talked to the FBI agents.

   ☐ yes ☐ no   c. Most of the money was used to purchase the suitcase.

EXERCISE 12. Review Test 1: Multiple Choice

Circle the letter of the correct answer. Some are conversations.

1. The Space Needle in Seattle was _____.

   a. built in 1962 by people   c. built in 1962

   b. in 1962 built by people   d. in 1962 built

2. Flight attendant: "All electronic devices must

   _____ off while we are taking off."

   a. get turn   c. be turned

   b. get turning   d. be turning

3. Your daughter looks about the same age as mine. When

   _____?

   a. was born she   c. did she get born

   b. was she born   d. she got born

4. "How was the restaurant last night? Was the food good?"

   "My steak _____ enough, so I had to send it back to the kitchen."

   a. was not cooking   c. was not cooked

   b. has not cooked   d. was not cook

5. "Are you ready to go home now?"

   "Yes, I am. These letters _____ tomorrow morning, but I have to

   put stamps on them first."

   a. have to be sent   c. must send

   b. are sending   d. have been sent

6. In some countries, food _____ with the right hand instead of with

   a fork or a spoon.

      a. eats   c. is eating

      b. has been eaten   d. is eaten

7. [Someone calls 911 at 8:00 AM] "Hello, police? Can you send someone ASAP?

   My car _____ into some time last night."

      a. was broken   c. was broke

      b. broke   d. is breaking

8. In 2009, Sonia Sotomayor _____ to be the first Latin-American

   woman to serve as a Supreme Court Justice of the United States of America.

      a. nominated   c. was nominated

      b. was nominating   d. has been nominated

Do Online Exercise 5.3. My score: _____ /10. _____ % correct.

EXERCISE 13. Review Test 2: Production and Evaluation

Part 1.

Fill in each blank with the correct form of the verb in parentheses. Both active and passive voices (with **be** or **get**) are used. A variety of tenses are used. Pay attention to key time words.

Missing Pacific Crest Hikers Found Alive

MOUNT HOOD – A 26-year-old woman ❶_____ (report) missing by her 29-year-old hiking companion late yesterday. Gary Ayers ❷_____ (tell) local officials that he ❸_____ (separate) from his 26-year-old companion, Katrina Tekin, during a sudden snow storm two days ago.

    Ayers ❹_____ (find) by a search team yesterday afternoon. He ❺_____ (be) reportedly wet and tired, but otherwise he was in good condition.

According to local authorities, Ayers ❻_____ (use) his cell phone to call rescuers for help. He ❼_____ (locate) by the search team using the GPS coordinates from his phone.

    Search teams ❽_____ (continue) to look for Tekin.

Part 2.

Read each sentence carefully. Look at the underlined part. If the underlined part is correct, circle the word *correct*. If it is wrong, circle the word *wrong*. Then write the correction above.

correct   wrong   1. My dog <u>was give</u> to me as a gift.

correct   wrong   2. She <u>was received</u> her vaccinations when she was three months old.

correct   wrong   3. We <u>were named</u> her Lady.

correct   wrong   4. She <u>is loved</u> to play chase.

correct   wrong   5. She <u>chases</u> squirrels in our neighborhood.

correct   wrong   6. How often <u>does she have to be groomed</u>?

correct   wrong   7. Lady's sweater <u>made</u> by my aunt.

correct   wrong   8. She is a good dog. She <u>never get punished</u>.

correct   wrong   9. The vet told me that she <u>should never be feed</u> chocolate.

correct   wrong   10. In the morning, Tina sits by the door because <u>she is expected me</u> to take her for a walk.

EXERCISE 14. Reading Practice: Locating Specific Details

Read the magazine article, and then answer the comprehension questions that follow. The grammar from this unit is underlined for you.

World Roller Coaster Races Reach New Heights

The race for building the tallest, fastest, steepest, and longest roller coaster with the most inversions <u>has been ongoing</u> for some time. Coaster fans <u>are motivated</u> to find the most thrilling ride that gives them the greatest amount of air time or speed. Air time <u>is caused</u> by a sudden drop in height or upside down loops that give the rider the sensation of zero gravity. Some people <u>have been known</u> to travel the world in order to ride the top roller coasters.

Currently, there are more than 3,000 roller coasters throughout the world that <u>are listed</u> in the Roller Coaster Database. Interestingly, nearly one-half of all roller coasters <u>have been built</u> in Asia, and North America has only half as many roller coasters as Asia. The continents with the fewest number of coasters are Africa and Australia.

The fastest roller coaster in the world <u>is named</u> Formula Rossa and it <u>was built</u> at Ferrari World in Abu Dhabi, United

Arab Emirates. Passengers on the Rossa <u>are rapidly accelerated</u> to a speed of 149 mph in just 4 seconds. Safety glasses <u>are required</u> on this ride in order to protect passengers' eyes. The coaster that ranks second for speed <u>is called</u> Kingda Ka. It <u>is located</u> at Six Flags in Jackson, New Jersey. Kingda Ka reaches speeds that <u>have been recorded</u> at 128 mph. The main differences between these two super-fast coasters is that Formula Rossa is nearly twice as long, but Kingda Ka has a 90° vertical spiral, a 270° vertical spiral and a 418-foot drop. Formula Rossa is a longer ride, but it <u>was not designed</u> with loops, spirals, or drops. In fact, Formula Rossa only reaches a height of 170 feet.

According to *Time Magazine*, one of the craziest roller coasters in the world <u>is called</u> Superman: Escape from Krypton. It <u>is located</u> at Six Flags Magic Mountain in Los Angeles, California and <u>was constructed</u> at a cost of $20 million. What makes this ride so thrilling is the fact that the passengers <u>are propelled</u> backward to a height of 400 feet at a speed of 100 mph. Once the coaster cars arrive at the top of the structure, the cars <u>are released</u> to free fall down the same tracks. This free fall allows passenger to feel 6.5 seconds of zero gravity.

Whether coaster fans are searching for a coaster with speed, loops, free fall, acceleration, or new designs in which they <u>are suspended</u> without a floor, there is likely one that <u>is being planned</u> somewhere at this very moment. Roller coaster fans love the excitement, so the demand for roller coasters continues to increase.

1. Approximately how many roller coasters are in North America (Canada, the U.S., Mexico, and Central America)? _____

2. What is the world's fastest roller coaster? Where is it? How fast can it travel?

   _____

3. What is the world's second fastest roller coaster? Where is it? How fast can it travel?

   _____

4. Which of the three described rides would you most like to experience? Why?

   _____

   _____

   _____

5. Which Asian country has the most coasters? How many does it have? _____

   _____

EXERCISE 15. Vocabulary Practice: Word Knowledge

Circle the answer choice on the right that is most closely related to the vocabulary on the left. Use a dictionary to check the meaning of words you do not know.

Vocabulary	Answer Choices	
1. constantly	always	never
2. an aisle	in a bank	in a store
3. soil	air	dirt
4. essential	absolute	necessary
5. carve	cut	fly
6. a task	a small house	a small job
7. scared	afraid	difficult
8. straightforward	complicated	simple
9. a loop	a circle	a line
10. cultivate	grow	happen
11. a flood	not enough water	too much water
12. be hooked	be angry about	be crazy about
13. a device	a small machine	a small report
14. a drought	not enough water	too much water
15. a number of	two or three	several
16. stranded	you cannot go anywhere	you have no more food
17. steep	a long river	a tall mountain
18. eventually	after a long time	very quickly
19. the status	the condition	the fare
20. accelerate	go faster	go slowly
21. consume	use	wish
22. rescue	destroy	save
23. collide	crash	fix
24. design	operate	plan
25. get rid of	eliminate	participate

EXERCISE 16. Vocabulary Practice: Collocations

Fill in each blank with the answer on the right that most naturally completes the phrase on the left. If necessary, use a dictionary to check the meaning of words you do not know.

Vocabulary	Answer Choices	
1. staple these _____	cans	papers
2. a hybrid _____	car	test
3. _____ your taxes	file	listen
4. is based _____ my idea	in	on
5. _____ you involved?	Did	Were
6. a supply of _____	classes	paper
7. _____ a reply	receive	take
8. a suitable _____	climate	storm
9. _____ terms of	in	on
10. no damage was _____	reported	suggested
11. an _____ flying object	unaffected	unidentified
12. belong _____	you	to you
13. a mutual _____	friend	job
14. _____ you aware?	Did	Were
15. a _____ term in office	second	young
16. a broke _____	person	window
17. throughout _____	the book	the idea
18. nominate a _____	clock	person
19. your _____ are justified	beverages	complaints
20. a loyal _____	business	customer
21. _____ rains	heavy	undone
22. a delivery _____	package	person
23. look _____ a word	on	up
24. come up with an _____	idea	opinion
25. _____ belongings	two	your

EXERCISE 17. Writing Practice: Explaining a Difficult Situation and a Suitable Solution

Part 1. Editing Student Writing

Read these sentences about a difficult subway ride in Japan. Circle the 15 errors. Then write the number of the sentence with the error next to the type of error. (Some sentences may have more than one error.)

_____ a. passive voice   _____ d. wrong verb tense

_____ b. wrong preposition   _____ e. singular-plural of nouns

_____ c. missing article   _____ f. an infinitive is needed

Navigating a Subway Station in a Foreign Language
1. I'll never forget first time I rode the subway in Tokyo.
2. My host family gave me map and marked the stops where I was supposed to get on and get off.
3. This task was seemed easy enough because all I needed remember was to get on at Yotsuya and then off at Ikebukuro.
4. The words were written in Romanized letters in the map and at the stations.
5. However, to my dismay, when I got off the subway at Ikebukuro and walked to the top of the stairs, I couldn't read the street names because they are written in Japanese hiragana, not Romanized letters.
6. I was doom, and I didn't know which street to walk on getting to the university.
7. I guess I must have looked confused because a gentleman was stopped and asked me if I was lost.
8. I was so relieved when he has spoken to me with English.
9. I told him I needed to find the Ikebukuro campus, and he pointed in the direction of the university and was told me to walk five block past the bank.
10. After this experience, I made sure that I never got separate from my Japanese dictionary so that I would be able to understand street sign better.

Part 2. Original Student Writing

Write a paragraph or a short essay in which you explain some kind of problem that happened to you or someone you know. Explain what happened. Explain why it happened. Explain what you did to solve the problem.

Use at least four verbs in passive voice. Underline these verbs so the teacher can see what you are trying to practice.

Unit 6

Adjective Clauses

Discover the Grammar

Read the conversation between two parents. Then answer the questions that follow.

Line	
1	**Mr. Rios**: Hello, I don't think I've seen you at baseball practice before.
2	**Mr. Wilson**: Oh, no, this is my first time. My wife is usually the one who
3	brings Jake to practice. Maybe you know her? Her name's Karen.
4	**Mr. Rios**: Karen . . . well, I don't know all the parents' names . . .
5	**Mr. Wilson**: She's the one with long red curly hair.
6	**Mr. Rios**: Isn't she the woman who works as a horse doctor?
7	**Mr. Wilson**: Yes, that's the one. I'm her husband Ken, by the way.
8	**Mr. Rios**: Hi, I'm Rick Rios.
9	**Mr. Wilson**: And which boy out there is yours?
10	**Mr. Rios**: Mine's the kid that's wearing the dirty baseball cap.
11	**Mr. Wilson**: Well, I think almost all of them have dirty caps!
12	**Mr. Rios**: True. He's over there next to the really tall kid.
13	**Mr. Wilson**: Is he the boy that threw the ball just now?

14	**Mr. Rios**: Yes, that's Alex. And your boy is … ?
15	**Mr. Wilson**: He's the player who's up at bat now. His name is Jake.
16	**Mr. Rios**: Oh, I know him. He'll be a great pitcher some day.

1. Study these two sentences with *who*.

Line	Sentences with **who** as Subject
6	Isn't she the woman **who works as a horse doctor?**
15	He's the player **who's up at bat now**.

   a. What kind of word follows *who*? _____

   b. What kind of word comes before *who*? _____

2. Study these two sentence with *that*.

Line	Sentences with **that** as Subject
10	Mine's the kid **that's wearing the dirty baseball cap.**
13	Is he the boy **that threw the ball just now?**

   a. What kind of word follows *that*? _____

   b. What kind of word comes before *that*? _____

3. The bold words in each sentence are **adjective clauses**. What is their function?

_____

_____

Grammar Lesson

KEY
9

Recognizing an Adjective Clause

An **adjective clause** is a group of words with a subject and a verb that functions as an adjective. An adjective clause is a dependent clause, and it needs to be connected to an independent clause.

independent clause	The book was interesting.
adjective clause	that you gave me
a sentence with an adjective clause	The book that you gave me was interesting.

While adjectives usually go before nouns, adjective clauses occur after a noun. Adjective clauses can begin with a pronoun such as **who, that, which,** or **whom** to connect the adjective clause to the main sentence (independent clause). We also use **whose, where,** and **when** sometimes.

Connectors	Examples with an Adjective Clause
who	The person who lives in the big brick house on Elm Street is my friend.
that	A store that sells doughnuts is a bakery.
which	Miami, which is the largest city in Florida, is not the capital.
whom	Mrs. Jones is the teacher whom the high school honored last year.
whose	Dr. Thomas is the professor whose work I value the most.
where	The city where I was born has a large network of hospitals.
when	People of a certain age can still remember the day when President Kennedy was shot.

<u>**Rule 1**</u>. Use **who** or **that** to talk about a person in the subject position.

<u>**Rule 2**</u>. Use **whom** or **that** to talk about a person in the object position. (**Who** may be used instead of **whom** in informal language.)

<u>**Rule 3**</u>. Use **that** or **which** to talk about a thing.

<u>**Rule 4**</u>. Use **whose** to talk about a possessive for a person or a thing.

<u>**Rule 5**</u>. Use **where** to talk about a place.

<u>**Rule 6.**</u> Use **when** to talk about a time.

 BE CAREFUL!

Common Learner Errors	Explanation
1. The student ~~which~~ who (or that) made 99 on the test is Megan.	Do not use *which* for people or *who* for things in adjective clauses.
2. ~~Vienna which is the capital of Austria is my home.~~ Vienna, which is the capital of Austria, is my home.	Only use commas if the adjective clause contains extra information that describes, not identifies, the noun.

EXERCISE 1. Identifying Adjective Clauses in Context

Underline the adjective clause in each sentence.

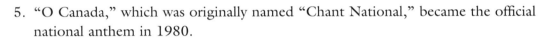

Interesting Facts about Canada

1. Canada is a country that has 3,800,000 square miles, but it has only 35,000,000 people.

2. Ottawa, which is the capital city, is not the largest city.

3. The city that has the largest population is Toronto.

4. The largest city where most of the people speak French is Montreal.

5. "O Canada," which was originally named "Chant National," became the official national anthem in 1980.

6. The border that is between Canada and Alaska is 1,538 miles long.

7. Lucy Maud Montgomery, who was a famous Canadian writer, is best known as the author of *Anne of Green Gables*.

8. Along the Bluefish River, there are caves where 20,000-year-old stone tools have been found.

9. Paul de Chomedey de Maisonneuve and Jeanne Mance, whose vision was to establish a missionary city, founded Montreal.

10. Banff, which is located in the Rocky Mountains, is Canada's oldest national park.

ONE-MINUTE LESSON

The word **found** can have two different meanings. The most common meaning of **found** is the irregular past tense of **find**: *They* **found** *the missing wallet.* However, the word **found** can also be a regular verb that means "to establish something": *Our company will* **found** *a new library for nearby residents.* It is related to the word **foundation**. The past tense and past participle form of **found** in the second meaning is **founded**: *New York was* **founded** *in 1624.*

EXERCISE 2. Identifying Adjective Clauses in Longer Context

Underline the ten adjective clauses in this short essay.

An Unusual Athlete

Mixed martial arts is a sport that mixes wrestling, tai kwon do, judo, and other martial arts elements. It is also known by another name, cage fighting, which refers to the "cage" that keeps the fighters in the ring. There are rules that fighters have to follow. For example, they cannot stick their fingers into their opponent's eyes, nose, or mouth. Shots to the back of the head and groin are prohibited, as are shots to the spine because these are all shots that could kill an opponent.

Most of the fighters who engage in this cage fighting are men. However, there are exceptions. One person who most certainly is not the stereotypical fighter is Sherilyn Lim, a Singaporean woman in her 20s whose hobbies used to include such non-violent activities as table tennis and playing the piano. She is an athlete whom others look to as a pioneer in the sport. She reportedly started cage fighting to lose weight; she thought she was fat. Darren De Silva, who has been Lim's trainer for several years, has publicly stated that he does not think she will ever get hurt. Lim's family and friends are accepting of her participating in mixed martial arts, and she has achieved her initial goal.

Grammar Lesson

Adjective Clauses with *that/who/which* in the Subject Position

The man <u>that</u> is standing by the door **works at the bank.**

This sentence is composed of two clauses: One clause provides the main information, and the other clause gives extra information.

The main clause is **The man works at the bank.** The subject here is **the man**, and the verb is **works**. The second clause is **that is standing by the door**. The subject is **that**, and the verb is **is standing**. The analysis looks like this.

The <u>**man**</u>	<u>that</u>	<u>is standing</u> by the door	<u>works</u> at the bank.
Subj 1	Subj 2	Verb 2	Verb 1

Here are the steps to create this kind of adjective clause correctly.

Step 1. Find the word that is the same in both sentences.	• The **book** is a bestseller. • The **book** talks about the death of President Kennedy.
Step 2. Change the word to the correct pronoun connector (**who, that, which, whom, whose**) and make sure that word begins the adjective clause.	• The **book** is a bestseller. • **that** talks about the death of President Kennedy
Step 3. Put the adjective clause just after the noun that it describes.	• The book **that talks about the death of President Kennedy** is a bestseller.
Sometimes you can change the order of the words, but the meaning may change.	• The book **that is a bestseller** talks about the death of President Kennedy.

<u>Rule 1.</u> To describe people, the subject of the adjective clause should be **who** or **that**. To describe things, the subject of the adjective clause should be **that** or **which**.

people	a. I know the boy who won the spelling contest. b. I know the boy that won the spelling contest.
things	a. The movie that won the award shows life in rural Japan. b. The movie which won the award shows life in rural Japan.

Rule 2. An adjective clause can modify a noun in several positions, such as a subject, a direct object, or an object of a preposition.

The **man** that lives in the brown house is my basketball coach.   subject
We saw the **man** that lives in the brown house.   direct object

We talked to the **man** that lives in the brown house.
        object of
        preposition

 BE CAREFUL!

Common Learner Errors	Explanation
1. The doctor ~~which~~ who (or that) treats my mother is from China.	Do not use the wrong word to begin an adjective clause. Do not use *which* for people or *who* for things.
2. What is the name of the ~~airline flies~~ airline that flies from Los Angeles to Ireland every day?	Do not omit the pronoun connector when it is the subject of the adjective clause.

EXERCISE 3. Creating a New Sentence with an Adjective Clause

From each pair of sentences, create a new sentence that has an adjective clause by putting the information from the second into the first. Underline the adjective clause.

1. The sentence has a mistake. The sentence is on the board.

   _____

   _____

2. A gym membership includes use of all the equipment, the tennis courts, and the pool. A gym membership costs only $100 a year.

   _____

   _____

3. A woman gave me an umbrella this morning. The woman was a complete stranger to me.

   _____

   _____

4. My cousin does all of her family's grocery shopping. She pays for more than half her groceries with coupons from newspapers and the Internet.

   _____

   _____

5. My brother doesn't have to leave his house very much. My brother is very shy.

   _____

   _____

6. The intersection is near the top of a very steep hill. It had two dozen accidents last year.

   _____

   _____

EXERCISE 4. Identifying Adjective Clauses and Independent Clauses in Context

Each sentence has two clauses: a main clause and an adjective clause. Put parentheses around the adjective clause. Put one line under the subject of each clause; label these S1 and S2. Then put two lines under the verb in each clause; label these V1 and V2. The first one has been done for you as an example.

1. Our city park has trails (that run along an

      S1 V1   S2 V2

old railroad route).

2. I bought an umbrella that fits in my purse.

3. I don't eat fast foods which have a high percentage of fat.

4. The person who gave you your refund is the manager of the store.

5. I can't stand people who listen to music without headphones on the train.

6. We'd like a slice of pizza that does not have any broccoli on it.

7. Most new car shoppers these days want a car that gets great gas mileage.

8. She developed an app that amplifies individual sounds in the environment.

Do Online Exercise 6.1. My score: _____ /10. _____ % correct.

EXERCISE 5. Creating Adjective Clauses to Connect Two Sentences

Read the two sentences, and then complete an adjective clause to create a new sentence. Sometimes the information from the second sentence goes in the first. Other times, information from the first goes in the second. The first one has been done for you as an example.

1. The man sells cheese at the farmer's market. The man is teaching a cheese-making class at the library.

    The man _who (or that) sells cheese at the farmer's market_ is teaching a cheese-making class at the library.

2. The guy mows our lawn. The guy is on vacation next month.

    The guy _____ is on vacation next month.

3. The quilt was made by my grandmother. It was given to me by my mother.

    The quilt _____ was given to me by my mother.

4. The cat destroyed my sofa. The cat was an orange tabby.

    The cat _____ was an orange tabby.

5. We wrote the poem. The poem will be read at Ben's wedding.

    We wrote the poem _____.

6. The people voted for the president. Some of the people are disappointed.

    Some of the people _____ are disappointed.

7. My mother chose the suit. The suit has silver buttons.

    My mother chose the suit _____.

8. Firefighters made the soup. The soup will be sold to help the homeless in our town.

    Firefighters made the soup _____.

Grammar Lesson

Adjective Clauses: *that/whom/which* in the Object Position

The man that we saw yesterday **works at the bank.**

This sentence is composed of two clauses. The main clause is **The man works at the bank**. The subject here is **the man** and the verb is **works**. The second clause is **that we saw yesterday**. The subject here is **we**, and the verb is **saw**. The word **that** here is a pronoun that replaces the word **man**. The word **that** is in the object position here. The analysis looks like this:

The <u>man</u>   that <u>we</u>   <u>saw</u> yesterday   **<u>works</u> at the bank.**

   Subj 1   **Subj 2**   **Verb 2**   **Verb 1**

Step 1. Find the word that is the same in both sentences.	• The **man** works at the bank. • We saw the **man** yesterday.
Step 2. Change the word to the correct pronoun connector (**that, whom, which**) and make sure that word begins the adjective clause.	• The **man** works at the bank. • that we saw yesterday
Step 3. Put the adjective clause just after the noun that it describes.	• The man **that** we saw yesterday works at the bank.

<u>Rule 1.</u> To describe people, the pronoun of the adjective clause in the object position can be **whom, who,** or **that.** In formal English, **whom** is used, but in everyday conversation and emails, **who** is preferred. To describe things, the subject of the adjective clause should be **that** or **which.**

people	1a. I know the boy whom you saw. 1b. I know the boy that you saw. 1c. I know the boy who you saw (informal).
things	2a. The movie that we saw yesterday showed life in 1800. 2b. The movie which we saw yesterday showed life in 1800.

Rule 2. In addition, when the pronoun connector is in the object position, the connector is optional and is in fact frequently omitted in writing and in speaking. Therefore, there is another option for Rule 1.

people	1d. I know the boy – – – **you saw.** (no connector)
things	2c. The movie – – – **we saw yesterday** showed life in 1800. (no connector)

Rule 3. An adjective clause can modify a noun in several positions, such as a subject, a direct object, or an object of a position.

The **man** that you know is my basketball coach.
The **man** who you know is my basketball coach.
The **man** whom you know is my basketball coach.
The **man** you know is my basketball coach.
subject

We saw the **man** that you know.
We saw the **man** who you know.
We saw the **man** whom you know.
We saw the **man** you know.
direct object

We talked to the **man** that you know.
We talked to the **man** who you know.
We talked to the **man** whom you know.
We talked to the **man** you know.
object of preposition

Rule 4. In academic language, it is best to avoid ending a clause with a preposition whenever that is possible. If you put the connector pronoun after a preposition, you must use only **whom** for a person and only **which** for a thing. Remember: **for whom, with whom, to whom, for which, with which,** and **to which**.

the most formal	We thanked the manager with **whom** we talked.
↑ ↓	We thanked the manager **whom** we talked with.
	We thanked the manager **that** we talked with. We thanked the manager **who** we talked with.
informal	We thanked the manager – – – we talked with.

BE CAREFUL!

Common Learner Errors	Explanation
1. The doctor ~~which~~ who (or that or whom) I met last week is from China.	Do not use the wrong word to begin an adjective clause. Do not use *which* for people or *who* for things in adjective clauses.
2. The citizens ~~who~~ whom this law impacts the most understand its importance.	In the direct object position, use **whom** for people in formal language.
3. As this report indicates, the reasons for ~~that~~ which people seek overseas employment vary tremendously.	In the object of preposition position, use **which** for things and **whom** for people.
4. Jenica Smith is the teacher ~~that we met her~~ that we met at the meeting yesterday.	Do not include a pronoun after the verb of an adjective clause. The pronoun is a redundant word.

EXERCISE 6. Creating Adjective Clauses to Connect Two Sentences

Read the two sentences, and then complete the new sentence. Include information from the second sentence in the first sentence. Write Ø if no pronoun connector is needed. The first one has been done for you as an example.

1. The fish was huge. I caught the fish.

   The fish _____that I caught was huge. (OR: which, Ø)_____.

2. My father doesn't like the music. My sister listens to the music.

   My father doesn't like the music _____

3. Did you see the photographs? I found the photographs in the attic.

   Did you see the photographs _____

4. The students cheated on the test. The principal expelled the students.

   The students _____

5. Is that the boy? The bees chased the boy.

   Is that the boy _____

6. The bill was passed by congress today. People have been talking about the bill.

   The bill _____

ONE-MINUTE LESSON
We use **the + adjective** to refer to a whole group of people. The word *homeless* is an adjective, but if you say **the** *homeless*, then *homeless* becomes a noun that refers to homeless people. Other examples include **the** *blind*, **the** *deaf*, **the** *old*, **the** *young*, **the** *rich*, **the** *poor*.

EXERCISE 7. Creating a New Sentence with an Adjective Clause

Read the two sentences, and then write a new sentence by including the second one within the first.

1. The young woman bought a car. The car has a sun roof.

    _____

    _____

2. The young woman bought a car. It had been owned by her neighbor.

    _____

    _____

3. Did you find the key? The key was in the drawer.

    _____

    _____

4. Did you find the key? You were looking for the key.

    _____

    _____

5. Malaria is a disease. Malaria kills many people.

    _____

    _____

6. Malaria is a disease. We know how to prevent malaria.

    _____

    _____

Do Online Exercise 6.2. My score: _____ /10. _____ % correct.

EXERCISE 8. Identifying Optional Pronoun Connectors in Adjective Clauses

Read the sentences. Underline the adjective clause. If the adjective clause pronoun is optional, put parentheses around it. The first one has been done for you an example.

1. The student <u>that joined our class yesterday</u> is from Jordan.

2. The people who were wearing black hoods were protestors.

3. Do you ever park in the lot that is across from the office?

4. What is the name of the noodle dish that you made?

5. I don't like the color of the car that he bought.

6. The airlines that cancelled flights gave customers refunds.

7. I hate to eat fish that has been overcooked.

8. The woman who was my assistant ten years ago is now president of the company.

9. The woman whom I hired as my assistant ten years ago is now the company president.

10. The coffee cup that has a crack in it is the one I like best.

11. The coffee cup that my grandmother gave me has a crack in it.

12. Sal thinks that we should not buy products which are made with micro-fiber.

13. The problems that you mention can all be solved.

14. The problems that have come up can be solved.

15. The man to whom the reporter spoke was not an eyewitness.

 Grammar Lesson

KEY 14

Adjective Clauses with *whose*

When the second sentence has a possessive form of a word also found in the first sentence, we use **whose** to connect the two sentences.

> **The author** whose works are the most interesting to me **is O. Henry**.

This sentence is composed of two clauses. The main clause is **The author is O. Henry**. The subject here is **the author** and the verb is **is**. The second clause is **whose works are the most interesting to me**. The subject here is **works**, and the verb is **are**. The word **whose** here is replaces the possessive word **O. Henry's**. The analysis looks like this:

> The <u>author</u>   whose <u>works</u> <u>are</u> the most interesting to me <u>is</u> **O. Henry**.
>
> **Subj 1**   **Subj 2** **Verb 2**   **Verb 1**

Here are the steps in creating an adjective clause using **whose**:

Step 1. Find the word that is the same in both sentences.	• The **painter** is Monet. • I really like the **painter's** work the most.
Step 2. Change the word to the correct pronoun connector (**who, that, which, whom, whose**).	• The **painter** is Monet. • I really like **whose** work the most.
Step 3. Move the connector word to the beginning of the adjective clause.	• The **painter** is Monet. • **whose** work I really like the most.
Step 4. Put the adjective clause just after the noun that it describes.	• The painter whose **work I really like the most** is Monet.

<u>Rule 1.</u> To create an adjective clause that replaces a possessive word such as *Henry's* or *his* and describes a person, use **whose**.

a possessive word referring to people	a. She was an architect **whose work stood out in the 1990s**. b. I don't think I know the girl **whose mother used to work here**.

<u>Rule 2.</u> To create an adjective clause that replaces a possessive word such as **the word's** or **the planet's** and describes a thing, use **whose**.

| a possessive word referring to things | a. What is the Spanish word **whose translation can be either** *kitchen* **or** *she cooks*? |
| | b. The planet **whose distance is farthest from the sun** is Pluto. |

 BE CAREFUL!

Common Learner Errors	Explanation
1. The two countries ~~which~~ whose capital cities are nearest each other are Slovakia and Austria.	Though it may sound strange at first, it is correct to use **whose** for things.
2. I prefer to visit a dentist ~~who's~~ whose office is peaceful and quiet.	Do not confuse **whose** and **who's**.

EXERCISE 9. Creating a New Sentence with an Adjective Clause with *whose*

Combine the two sentences using **whose**.

1. The students will be on TV. The students' invention won first prize.

   _____

   _____

2. The boy is sad. His mother is in the hospital.

   _____

   _____

3. We might get a discount from a friend. The friend's father owns the restaurant.

   _____

   _____

4. Pilots will make less money. The pilots' contracts begin in January.

   _____

   _____

5. I have a cat. The cat's favorite place to sleep is on my computer keyboard.

   _____

   _____

EXERCISE 10. Creating a New Sentence with an Adjective Clause with *whose*

Rewrite each sentence using an adjective clause with **whose**. You may have to use different verbs.

Example: People who have clean desks are usually well-organized.

People whose desks are clean are usually well organized.

1. People who have stressful jobs sometimes get sick.

   _____

2. Instructors who give interesting and well-prepared lectures usually get good student evaluations.

   _____

3. Students who have perfect attendance will receive an award at the end of the term.

   _____

4. A parent who has well-behaved children is a lucky person.

   _____

5. People with poor health generally aren't as active as healthy people.

   _____

6. Pets with violent owners sometimes show signs of mental illness.

   _____

7. Residents on my street who left their cars unlocked had items stolen.

   _____

8. Employees who have bosses who praise them are more productive.

   _____

ONE-MINUTE LESSON

The connector **whose** can refer to people: <u>Pilots</u> whose *contracts begin in January will make less money than current pilots.*

However, the connector **whose** can also refer to things: *I have a* <u>cat</u> **whose** *favorite place to sleep is on my computer keyboard.* OR *A dialect is* <u>a variety of language</u> **whose** *grammar, vocabulary, and pronunciation differ systematically from other variations of that same language.*

EXERCISE 11. Mini-Conversations

Choose the correct answers in these eight mini-conversations. Sometimes more than one answer is possible.

1. A: Excuse me, but can I use the phone that's in your office?

   B: Sure, or you can use the phone (that, which, who) is on the reception desk.

2. A: Where is the ladder (that, which, who) I used to paint the ceiling?

   B: I don't know. I'm not the one (that, which, who) used it last.

3. A: Is the class (that, which, who) you are taking now hard?

   B: Well, I like the professor (that, which, who) is teaching the course, but the course material is tough. In fact, the lesson (that, which, who) explains the Civil War is really beyond me.

4. A: Hey, what's the name of the TV show (that, which, who) comes on after the news?

   B: I don't know. I can ask my friend Lisa if you want. She is the kind of person (that, which, who) knows everything about TV and movies.

5. A: Do you want to see a movie later?

   B: Yes, let's see that new documentary (that, which, who) is at the Unison Theater.

   A: Do you mean the one (that, which, who) won the People's Choice Award? I can't remember the name of it.

6. A: Your father is a person (which, whose, whom) others admire a lot.

   B: Yes, but my mother's opinion is really the only one (that, who, whose) he cares about.

7. A: What do you remember about the day (which, when, who) your husband proposed to you?

   B: Oh, I remember everything about it. It's a day (that, where, when) I'll never forget.

8. A: This town is the place (when, where, whose) the revolution was won.

   B: Is there a monument or a historical site (that, where, who) is open to the public?

 **Grammar Lesson**

Restrictive and Non-Restrictive Adjective Clauses

There are two general types of adjective clauses: restrictive and non-restrictive.

- A **restrictive adjective clause** restricts or limits the noun.
- A **non-restrictive adjective clause** describes or adds information about the noun.

Type of Clause	Examples
Restrictive (no comma)	**High school students** who have a license **can drive.** Explanation: If you omit the adjective clause, you change the meaning of the sentence. You need this information. When you see *high school students*, you do not know who can drive.
Non-Restrictive (comma)	**Junior high students,** who are under the age of 18, **cannot vote.** Explanation: If you omit the adjective clause, the new sentence has the same meaning as the current one. All junior high students are under the age of 18, so the information in the adjective clause is extra and does not restrict the meaning of the subject.

<u>Rule 1</u>. Do not use a comma with a restrictive clause.

<u>Rule 2</u>. Use a comma with a non-restrictive clause.

EXERCISE 12. Writing with Non-Restrictive Adjective Clauses

Write three original sentences that have non-restrictive adjective clauses.

1. _____

   _____

2. _____

   _____

3. _____

   _____

Grammar Lesson

Reduced Adjective Clauses

Many adjective clauses can be reduced to an adjective phrase. The use of adjective phrases is very common, and sometimes they can be difficult to understand.

adjective clause: **The man** who is standing by the door **works at the bank**.

reduced adjective clause: The man standing by the door **works at the bank**.

In this sentence, **who** or **that** and **be** have been dropped. The meanings of the two sentences are the same. This is only one example of several ways to reduce an adjective clause.

<u>Rule 1.</u> You may drop the pronoun and the verb **be**. By doing this, you will end up with five possible options.

a prepositional phrase	The magazines **that are** on the table are mine. The magazines on the table are mine.
an adjective	The student **who was** absent the most last month was Jason. The student absent the most last month was Jason.
a present participle	The bird **that is** sitting on the top branch is a crow. The bird sitting on the top branch is a crow.
a past participle	The winner **that was** chosen in the contest received $1,000. The winner chosen in the contest received $1,000.
a noun (an appositive)*	George Washington, **who was** the first U.S. president, died in 1799. George Washington, the first U.S. president, died in 1799.

<u>Rule 2.</u> You may change a relative pronoun and a verb (other than **be**) by using just the *–ing* form of the verb. The tense of the original verb does not matter.

a present participle	People **who live** in glass houses should not throw stones. People living in glass houses should not throw stones.

*An appositive is a noun that explains or renames another noun and is usually set off by commas.

BE CAREFUL!

Common Learner Errors	Explanation
1. A book ~~that written~~ written before 1985 could not include a URL.	Don't forget to omit both the subject and the verb **be**, never just one of them.
2. We called ~~the people live~~ the people who live next to us.	Don't omit any words if the verb **be** is not present.
3. Every clerk ~~opened~~ opening more than 50 new accounts last month received a bonus in today's paycheck.	Be sure to use the **–ing** form of the verb.

 EXERCISE 13. Speaking Practice: Have You Ever Seen a Book That Didn't Have a Cover?

Step 1. Make a list of three questions that practice *have you ever* and adjective clauses.

   <u>Example:</u>   Have you ever been on a plane that experienced heavy turbulence?

Step 2. Work with a classmate (or interview a native speaker). Take turns asking each other your five questions. If your partner answers yes, talk more about that answer. Find out as much information as you can. For example, when did it happen? Where did it happen?

1. _____

_____

2. _____

_____

3. _____

_____

 ONE-MINUTE LESSON

It began to rain and the game was canceled**, which made the crowd furious**. A non-restrictive clause with **which** occurs frequently in spoken English at the end of a sentence. The purpose of this structure in spoken English is often to add the speaker's opinion about the information in the main clause. Other examples include:

They decided to send their son to private school, **which ended up costing a lot of money.**

As usual, my niece did not say thanks when I gave her her birthday present, **which made me mad.**

Joe has decided that he will marry Irene, **which I think is a huge mistake.**

EXERCISE 14. Practice Reducing Adjective Clauses

Underline the adjective clauses in these sentences. If these adjective clauses can be reduced, cross out the words not needed and rewrite the reduced phrase on the line. If they cannot be reduced, write *no change possible*.

A Famous Telescope

1. The Hubble is a telescope that orbits Earth.

   _____

   _____

2. We have learned many things from the images it has beamed back to Earth.

   _____

   _____

3. Lyman Spitzer, who first proposed a space observatory, spent 50 years working on the telescope.

   _____

   _____

4. Hubble, the name that was given to the telescope, was in honor of Edward Hubble, who proved, among other things, that the universe is expanding.

   _____

   _____

5. The first pictures that were taken by the Hubble were images that were of poor quality.

   _____

   _____

6. In 1993, the Space Shuttle Endeavor took a seven-person crew into orbit for a repair mission that lasted five days.

   _____

   _____

7. The year NASA released the first images from the Hubble was 1994.

   _____

   _____

8. In 2002, astronauts added the Advanced Camera for Surveys, which was the first new instrument to be added to the telescope since 1987.

   _____

   _____

EXERCISE 15. Editing: Is It Correct?

If the sentence is correct, write a check mark (✓) on the line. If it is not correct, write an X on the line and circle the mistake. Then make the change above the sentence. (*Hint*: There are ten sentences. Two are correct, but eight have mistakes.)

Cats in History

_____ 1. Thousands of years ago, humans domesticated cats to help control mice, which ate food grains.

_____ 2. In 1983 a grave was discovered in Cyprus who contained remains that belonged to a human, along with tools and other items.

_____ 3. About 40 centimeters away from it was a much smaller grave of a young cat, which body had been positioned to face the same way as the human skeleton.

_____ 4. It is not surprising that cat mummies have been found at many sites in Egypt human mummies have been located.

_____ 5. The cat in ancient Egypt was an animal was very respected.

_____ 6. In stark contrast, cats in Europe in the Middle Ages were associated with the devil, and some people who kept cats were tortured and even killed, and countless cats were executed.

_____ 7. Ironically, the Black Death, which killed 100 million people in the 14th century, was a plague where was spread mostly by rats and mice and the fleas they carried, and cats could have been helpful in lessening the spread of the disease.

_____ 8. In the eastern United States, too, there was a time when cats were executed because it was a period in that many women were accused of being witches, and it was thought that these witches had turned themselves into cats.

EXERCISE 16. Sentence Study for Critical Reading

Read the numbered sentences. Then read the answer choices and put a check mark (✔) in the yes or no boxes in front of each sentence to show if that sentence is true based on the information in the original sentence. If there is not enough information to mark something as yes, then mark it as no. Remember that more than one true answer may be possible.

1. I have a friend whose mother drives a car that runs on vegetable oil. She recycles oil used by local restaurants.

   ☐ yes ☐ no a. The restaurants use recycled oil.

   ☐ yes ☐ no b. My mother's friend drives a car that runs on vegetable oil.

   ☐ yes ☐ no c. My friend's mother works at a recycling company.

2. This television, which we bought less than six months ago, has a remote control that has over 15 buttons on it.

   ☐ yes ☐ no a. The television has more than 15 buttons on it.

   ☐ yes ☐ no b. The remote control has fewer buttons than the television.

   ☐ yes ☐ no c. The new remote control will have less than 15 buttons.

3. The bank where I have a checking account is locally owned. The manager, who has been there since the bank opened in 2003, greets me whenever I go there.

   ☐ yes ☐ no a. This bank is part of a national chain of banks.

   ☐ yes ☐ no b. The manager has been there more than two decades.

   ☐ yes ☐ no c. My checking account was opened with the help of the manager.

4. My brother, who lives in a rural area in the very northwestern part of the state of Washington, will spend two weeks in New York City next month as part of his new job. It will be interesting to see how Josh copes with life in a place that is so foreign to what he knows.

   ☐ yes ☐ no a. My brother lives in Washington.

   ☐ yes ☐ no b. I have only one brother.

   ☐ yes ☐ no c. Josh has lived in New York City for two weeks.

5. Czechoslovakia, which separated into Czech Republic and Slovakia in 1993, was created in 1918, meaning it was a country for only three quarters of a century.

   ☐ yes ☐ no a. Czechoslovakia became a nation in 1993.

   ☐ yes ☐ no b. Slovakia originated in 1918.

   ☐ yes ☐ no c. Czechoslovakia is the world's youngest nation.

EXERCISE 17. Review Test 1: Multiple Choice

Circle the letter of the correct answer. Some are conversations.

1. "How was the flight from Paris?"

   "I thought it was pretty good. I really liked my seat, but Kathy didn't like
   _____."
       a. the seat she got   c. she got the seat

       b. that she got the seat   d. the seat that was gotten

2. Do you remember the name of the artist _____ paintings you liked?
       a. who   c. whose

       b. whom   d. which

3. Can you remember the name of the first song _____?
       a. you learned it   c. that you learned it

       b. you learned   d. which you learned it

4. Not all of the CDs _____ are mine.
       a. on the shelf which   c. that they are on the shelf

       b. on the shelf that   d. that are on the shelf

5. "What did you think about Greg's speech?"

   "Actually, I didn't have a chance to hear _____."
       a. the speech was given by Greg   c. Greg gave the speech

       b. the speech Greg gave   d. the speech that Greg gave it

6. Students _____ for jobs in health, the food industry, hospitality and
   tourism, and airplane maintenance have good chances to find employment.
       a. train   c. that training

       b. which train   d. training

7. The person _____ was my college roommate.
       a. writing this song   c. whom she wrote this song

       b. who wrote this song   d. wrote this song

8. It can be very difficult to help people _____ don't want assistance.
       a. whose   c. which

       b. whom   d. that

EXERCISE 18. Review Test 2: Production and Evaluation

Part 1.

Read this short passage. Underline the 14 adjective clauses. Put parentheses ( ) around the 6 connector words that may be omitted.

A performance review is a meeting that can be stressful for both bosses and employees. Even employees who are confident about their work and who have good relationships with their bosses get nervous before their reviews. Are you someone who dreads them? Here is some information that can help you.

The people supervising your boss will expect him or her to be tough on you—to give you challenges and to find areas for improvement. Do not take it personally if your boss focuses on areas that are challenging for you. Respond gratefully to positive feedback, but respond gratefully to feedback that is negative. Tell your boss that you appreciate knowing ways that you can improve.

Be prepared. Before your meeting, think of things that you have accomplished at work. Make a list of extra work that you have taken on and of special projects that you have completed. Note all the deadlines that you met. Note all the sales you made. Note all the product or process improvements that you contributed to.

If you follow this advice, you will do well in your performance review.

Do Online Exercise 6.3. My score: _____ /10. _____ % correct.

Part 2.

Read each sentence carefully. Look at the underlined part in each sentence. If the underlined part is correct, circle the word *correct*. If it is wrong, circle the word *wrong*. Then write the correction above.

correct   wrong   1. Pet <u>owners want</u> to walk their dogs in the park must use a leash.

correct   wrong   2. What's <u>the name of the restaurant in Paris that you liked so much</u>?

correct   wrong   3. Do you like the man <u>whose</u> going out with your sister?

correct   wrong   4. <u>Who's</u> the current CEO of your company?

correct   wrong   5. The essay answer <u>that I wrote it</u> for question number 17 was incorrect.

correct   wrong   6. Can you remember the name of the <u>woman whom son</u> won the race?

correct   wrong   7. Before you can get a refund, you have to fill out <u>a form explains</u> why you want to return the product.

correct   wrong   8. A photograph <u>that taken</u> by a seven-year-old won the newspaper photography contest.

correct   wrong   9. The agent <u>who selling</u> the most homes last month got a big bonus.

correct   wrong   10. The woman <u>which</u> witnessed the accident gave a statement to the police.

correct   wrong   11. I got a phone call <u>asks me</u> to vote for Peterson for mayor.

correct   wrong   12. My son has a skateboard <u>runs on solar energy</u>.

EXERCISE 19. Reading Practice: Understanding a Fictional Event

Read this piece of fiction about a rescue, and then answer the comprehension questions that follow. The grammar from this unit has been underlined for you.

Nick Saves the Day

Nick McCarron is a man <u>who never thought he'd be a hero</u>, yet he's the person <u>to whom one young woman owes her life</u>. Normally, Nick jogs on one of the two tracks <u>which are located in City Park</u>. For some reason, however, he made a different decision on Saturday. This was a decision <u>that saved Jodie Sarton</u>.

Nick was jogging on a path along the river when his music stopped. He checked his iPod. He realized the device, <u>which hadn't been charged in a long time</u>, needed to be plugged in. He took out his earbuds. That was the moment <u>when he heard someone's voice</u>. The voice was frantically crying, "Help! Help!"

Nick looked around, but he couldn't tell where the voice was coming from. He listened closely and looked around. Finally, his eye caught something <u>that startled him into action</u>. About 50 yards downriver, there were some rocks <u>which formed a small rapids</u>. Clinging to the top of a large rock <u>that was out in the middle of the river</u>, Nick clearly saw a hand. He threw down his iPod, his phone, and his sunglasses, kicked off his shoes, and ran out into the water. A few feet from the bank, <u>where the river bottom dropped sharply</u>, he had to swim. When he got to the rapids, the current was strong. He had to use his hands to push against the rocks and to protect his head. It was very difficult for him to see or hear, but he finally reached the rock <u>where he had seen the hand</u>, which was still clutching the top of it. Just behind the rock, he found Jodie, terrified and crying, holding onto the rock for dear life. With her other hand, she held a life-jacket, <u>which was not doing her any good</u>.

Nick managed to support Jodie and help her get the life jacket on. Then he tried to lead her slowly back to shore. However, she had trouble moving, and Nick realized that this was a girl <u>who was close to going into shock</u>. He grabbed her around the waist from behind and began to half drag her, half float her, over the rocks, back to land. Jodie, <u>whose strength was gone</u>, did not resist much. When they got to shore, Nick ran to his phone to call 911. He then raced back to Jodie and positioned his body next to hers, <u>which was all he could do to keep her warm and steady</u>.

Paramedics arrived quickly, and Jodie was taken to a hospital, <u>where she was treated for shock and was kept one day for observation</u>. Nick, <u>who was quickly treated for scratches and bruises</u>, stayed at the hospital until Jodie's family arrived. When they got there, they ran to Jodie. After a couple minutes, they turned around to speak to the man <u>who had saved their daughter</u>. However, he was no longer there. He was on his way home to charge his iPhone.

1. Why did Nick stop jogging?

   _____

   _____

2. What did Nick do before running into the water?

   _____

   _____

3. What did Nick do when he reached Jodie?

   _____

   _____

4. What did Nick do after he got Jodie out of the water?

   _____

   _____

5. Where was Nick when Jodie's parents wanted to meet him?

   _____

   _____

EXERCISE 20. Vocabulary Practice: Word Knowledge

Circle the answer choice on the right that is most closely related to the vocabulary on the left. Use a dictionary to check the meaning of words you do not know.

Vocabulary	Answer Choices	
1. achieve	complete something	propose something
2. omit	not agree	not include
3. a necklace	a type of clothing	a type of jewelry
4. tough	difficult	easy
5. a bestseller	a delicious ingredient	a successful product
6. a ladder	you climb it	you grow it
7. a bakery	doughnuts	shrimp
8. a refund	pay money	receive money
9. seek	leave out	look for
10. rural	city	countryside
11. a grave	birth	death
12. a skeleton	bones	shoes
13. the ceiling	above you	below you
14. dread	look forward to	not want to do
15. a decade	10 years	100 years
16. a bruise	on your belt	on your skin
17. an opponent	a person	a place
18. stand out	be different	be friendly
19. an anthem	you cook it	you sing it
20. amplify	decrease	increase
21. a cap	you eat it	you wear it
22. a resident	an event	a person
23. steep	easy to purchase	hard to climb
24. shy	only	quiet
25. seek	look for	turn down

EXERCISE 21. Vocabulary Practice: Collocations

Fill in each blank with the answer on the right that most naturally completes the phrase on the left. If necessary, use a dictionary to check the meaning of words you do not know.

Vocabulary	Answer Choices	
1. an eyewitness _____ a crime	to	up
2. _____ my team	in	on
3. _____ employment	say	seek
4. a seven-person _____	crew	river
5. the top _____	bill	branch
6. curly _____	hair	meat
7. prevent a _____	beverage	disease
8. _____ TV	in	on
9. first _____	prize	trail
10. a network of _____	hospitals	menus
11. a brick _____	house	tree
12. _____ there	over	without
13. startle _____	someone	something
14. endangered _____	animals	storms
15. mow a _____	lawn	drain
16. _____ a red light	eat	run
17. a _____ stranger	complete	meaning
18. make 100 _____ his last test	in	on
19. _____ of tune	away	out
20. achieve a _____	goal	problem
21. _____ the way	at	by
22. _____ miles	circle	square
23. to _____ a new city	found	took
24. _____ the grocery shopping	do	make
25. on _____	company	vacation

EXERCISE 22. Writing Practice: Describing a Fictional Character

Part 1. Editing Student Writing

Read these sentences about a fictional character. Circle the 15 errors. Then write the number of the sentence with the error next to the type of error. (Some sentences have more than one error.)

_____ a. passive voice   _____ d. wrong adjective clause connector

_____ b. missing article   _____ e. singular-plural of nouns

_____ c. wrong preposition   _____ f. subject-verb agreement

Winnie the Pooh
1. The Winnie-the-Pooh stories, who are famous all over the world today, were written by A. A. Milne.
2. Winnie-the-Pooh was named after a toy bear who was owned by Milne's son, Christopher Robin.
3. The toy "Winnie" had named after a real bear that had been donated to the London Zoo.
4. The original bear had been purchased from a hunter by a Canadian army officer which was on his way for England to fight in the First World War.
5. He named the bear Winnie, which was short for Winnipeg, a cities that he liked.
6. Winnie, who was loved by many visitors to the zoo, became a favorite of young Christopher, so Christopher changed name of his teddy bear from Edward for Winnie.
7. The setting for the Winnie-the-Pooh stories was also based of a real place, Ashdown Forest, which is large area in Sussex, England, where the Milne family spent a lot of time.
8. E.H. Shepherd, who was drawn illustrations for the stories, incorporated many features of the Ashdown Forest landscape into his work.
9. 1926 was the year when the first collection of Winnie-the-Pooh stories were published at both the United States and England.
10. Stephen Slesinger, who was pioneer in the licensing industry, purchased the merchandizing, television, recording, and other trade rights to the "Winnie-the-Pooh" materials.
11. The red shirt that Winnie-the-Pooh always wear first appeared in 1932, and Walt Disney Productions bought the licensing rights to everything connected with Winnie-the-Pooh in 1961.
12. Since then, there has been many animations, TV show, and films that feature the characters from Milne's stories.

Part 2. Original Student Writing

Write a paragraph or a short essay in which you write about a fictional character (similar to Winnie the Pooh in Part 1). Your character can be from any culture. Describe the character. Explain why your selected character is popular. Use the Internet to search for interesting facts for your writing.

Use at least four adjective clauses. Underline the adjective clauses so the teacher can see what you are trying to practice.

Unit 7

Adverbs

Discover the Grammar

Read this safety demonstration given by a flight attendant on an international flight. Then answer the questions that follow.

Line	
1	"Ladies and gentlemen, welcome aboard Republic Airlines Flight 662 to
2	Sydney. At this point, we ask you to give your full attention as we explain some
3	extremely important safety information. We ask you to take your seats quickly
4	to ensure an on-time departure. Be sure to stow your carry-on luggage under
5	the seat in front of you or in an overhead compartment. Our captain has just
6	turned on the Fasten Seat Belt sign, so please fasten your seat belt tightly
7	around your waist and make sure your seat back and folding trays are in their
8	upright position.
9	If you're seated near an emergency exit, please read the special instructions
10	card in the seat pocket very carefully. If you do not wish to perform any of the
11	emergency functions described on the card, please ask a flight attendant to
12	reseat you immediately.

13	At this time, we request that all electronic devices be turned off or put in
14	airplane mode for the duration of the flight, as these items might cause serious
15	interference with the navigational and communication equipment on this plane.
16	We will notify you when it is safe to use these devices later.
17	We remind you that this is a non-smoking flight. Smoking is prohibited on
18	the entire aircraft, including the lavatories. Tampering with, disabling, or
19	destroying the lavatory smoke detectors is prohibited by law.
20	If you have any questions about our flight today, please don't hesitate to ask
21	one of the eight friendly flight attendants working today's flight. Thank you."

1. Write the six words ending in –ly:

    _____   _____   _____

    _____   _____   _____

2. Why is *extremely* used in Line 3 instead of *extreme*? Are both possible here?

    _____

3. Why is *serious* used in Line 14 instead of *seriously*? Are both possible here?

    _____

4. How is *friendly* (Line 21) different from the other five –ly words?

    _____

    _____

5. When do you have to use –ly?

    _____

    _____

Grammar Lesson

Adverbs

An **adverb** can consist of a single word, a phrase, or a clause. There are many different types of adverbs, depending on the question that the adverb answers: **Where? When? How? How often? To what degree? Why? How long?**

single-word	yesterday	extermely	so
phrase	on the first floor	with great difficulty	by studying hard
clause	because the plate was broken when it began to rain		

Type of Adverbs		
Type	**Question**	**Example**
place	Where?	The United Nations is **in New York**. You can buy used books **there**.
time	When?	**On July 28, 1914**, the war began. I was watching TV **when you called**. Our flight will depart **soon**.
manner	How?	The driver turned the corner **slowly**. They traveled **by bus**. He paid **with his mom's credit card**. She learned English **by watching TV**.
frequency	How often?	Roses are **usually** in full bloom in summer. Ostriches **never** fly.
degree	To what degree?	The history test was **very** difficult. This author's name is **widely** known.
purpose	Why?	We added more salt **to make the rice better**. **Because it was so cold,** I wore a heavy jacket.
duration	How long?	I've lived here **since 2010**, but Matt has been here **for almost 20 years**.

Rule 1. Adverbs modify (give information about) verbs, adjectives, or other adverbs.

adverb modifying a verb	The mayor spent the tax money **carefully**.
adverb modifying an adjective	China is an **extremely** large country
adverb modifying an adverb	The announcer spoke **too** quickly for me to understand her.

Rule 2. To form an **adverb of manner**, you add –ly to an adjective: *quick* → *quickly*. However, some adverbs of manner do not end in –ly (*fast, hard, well*), and there are a few adjectives that end in –ly (*friendly, likely, lovely, lonely, only, silly, ugly*).

Rule 3. Some words can be both adverbs and adjectives, depending on the word they modify: *fast, straight, hard, late, early, daily, only, enough, low, high.*

Rule 4: **Adverbs of manner** can be placed at the beginning, middle, or end of a sentence; however, they should not be put between the verb and the object.

Rule 5. **Adverbs of place and time** are generally placed at the end of a sentence or clause. Place comes before time unless the time is at the beginning of the sentence separated by a comma:

I worked at the library in 2005. → In 2005, I worked at the library.

Rule 6. **Adverbs of degree** are placed before the words that they modify. Some adverbs of degree are **very, really, too, so, almost, nearly, quite, fairly, just, hardly, scarcely, completely, extremely, widely.**

Rule 7. **Adverbs of frequency** are generally after the verb *be* but before all other verbs. If there is a helping verb, they go between the helping verb and the main verb. Some adverbs of frequency are **always, usually, often, sometimes, hardly ever, seldom, rarely,** and **never.**

Rule 8. The most frequent **adverbs of purpose** are **because + subject + verb** or an infinitive:

I went to the store because I needed some bread OR I went to the store to get some bread.

Rule 9. After **linking verbs** such as *look, seem, sound, taste, feel, become,* and *appear,* use an adjective, not an adverb:

She sings beautifully. Her voice sounds beautiful.

! BE CAREFUL!

Common Learner Errors	Explanation
1. He plays football very ~~good~~ well.	Do not use an adjective when you should use an adverb.
2. She ~~drank quickly the water~~ drank the water quickly OR quickly drank the water.	Adverbs of manner should not be placed between the verb and the object.
3. The rock hit the window so ~~hardly~~ hard that the glass shattered.	The adverb *hard* is the opposite of *softly*.
4. I ~~didn't hardly~~ hardly ate anything at dinner.	The adverb **hardly** is a negative word that means "at a very low amount." It is never used with *not* because English does not allow two negatives.

EXERCISE 1. Locating Adverbs in Context

Underline the adverb in each sentence. The number in parentheses indicates the number of adverbs in each sentence.

Skiing in the Alps

1. We are traveling around Austria now. (2)
2. We are here to visit our family. (2)
3. Tomorrow we will take the fast train to Innsbruck. (2)
4. Because the ski resort opens early, we will take the first train. (2)
5. The ticket agent said the train will depart at 6:00 AM exactly. (2)
6. The trains are seldom late. (1)
7. The Tyrolean Alps are incredibly beautiful but dangerously steep. (2)
8. My uncle has hardly seen us since we arrived. (2)
9. Because the weather has been good, we have been really busy skiing. (2)
10. We promised him we would go directly to his house as soon as the train arrives. (3)

Connecting Grammar and Vocabulary

Here are 40 frequently used adverbs of manner that end in **–ly**. They are listed in order of frequency as found in COCA, a database of actual English usage consisting of more than 450,000,000 words.

Except for *early*, all of these adverbs come from an adjective: *one → only, real → really.*

40 Frequent Adverbs of Manner Ending in –*ly*	
1. only	21. directly
2. really	22. immediately
3. early	23. completely
4. actually	24. generally
5. probably	25. slowly
6. finally	26. easily
7. especially	27. obviously
8. nearly	28. highly
9. simply	29. mostly
10. certainly	30. slightly
11. quickly	31. apparently
12. recently	32. relatively
13. exactly	33. fully
14. usually	34. basically
15. particularly	35. increasingly
16. clearly	36. carefully
17. suddenly	37. significantly
18. absolutely	38. largely
19. daily	39. currently
20. eventually	40. possibly

Source: Based on information in the Corpus of Contemporary American English, www.americancorpus.com.

EXERCISE 2. Mini-Conversations

Circle the correct words in these eight mini-conversations.

1. *Adam*: Whew! That was a difficult test we just took.

   Bob: I agree. Do you think you passed?

   Adam: I don't know, but I think I did pretty (good, well).

2. *Ed*: I need to see Dr. Frost, but it is so hard to find a convenient time.

   Don: I know what you mean. I (hard, hardly) have enough time to do anything.

3. *Chris*: How is your mom doing with her Spanish classes?

   Maria: I'm happy to say she has been learning Spanish rather (quick, quickly).

4. *Jorge*: Let's go to the amusement park and try the bungee jump.

   Luis: No way! That is a (total, totally) crazy idea.

5. *Bill*: Have you heard the story about the dog that (miracle, miraculously) swam home after falling off a boat 5 miles away?

   Tina: Are you (serious, seriously)?

   Bill: Yes, I am. I read it (recent, recently) on the BBC website.

6. *Mike*: You look (sleepy, sleepily), Jason. Are you all right?

   Jason: Sort of. (Late, Lately) I haven't been sleeping (good, well).

   Mike: Maybe you're drinking (so much, too much) coffee.

   Jason: Maybe. But that's the only way I can stay awake to study!

7. *Ryan*: Is that your running buddy I saw you with this morning?

   Kelly: No. She doesn't like the outdoors. She's (definite, definitely) not a runner.

8. *Steve*: Why don't you go outside? It's a (real, really) nice day.

   Reed: Would you play basketball with me?

   Steve: (Certain, Certainly)!

 Do Online Exercise 7.1. My score: ____ /10. ____ % correct.

EXERCISE 3. Using Adverbs in Context

Choose the correct word or phrase from the word bank to complete this story. Write the words on the lines.

word bank	after winning a silver medal also at the age of five during her junior years ever	four years earlier gracefully strongly to practice daily

Yuna Kim, A Skating Champion

World Champion figure skater Yuna Kim retired from skating

❶ _____ at the 2014 Sochi Winter Olympics.

❷ _____, she won the prestigious gold medal at the 2010

Vancouver Winter Olympics. Yuna is the first Korean figure skater to have

❸ _____ won an Olympic medal for figure skating.

Yuna began skating ❹ _____, and her instructors

❺ _____ encouraged her parents to continue her lessons.

❻ _____, she began winning national and international

competitions. Because it was difficult to find enough skating rinks in Korea, she

decided to move to Toronto in 2007 ❼ _____with her

coach at a private ice arena. Yuna ❽ _____ set many

world records for figure skating jumps that she powerfully and

❾ _____ executed.

Grammar Lesson

by and with

We use **by + noun** and **with + a/an + singular noun** to tell **how** something was done.

Preposition	Example	Notes
by	They arrived by bus. I sent the information by email.	We often use **by** with transportation or communication words. The noun after **by** often has no article or determiner.
with	The chef chopped up the peppers and onions with a knife. The meeting started with a short announcement about lunch.	The preposition **with** is used with an instrument or means. The noun after **with** usually has an article or determiner.
by + VERB + –ing	We got in better shape by running for 30 minutes every day.	We also use **by + verb + –ing** to indicate how something happened.
	By running for 30 minutes every day, we got in better shape.	A **by + gerund** phrase can come at the beginning or end of a sentence. When it begins a sentence, it is followed by a comma.

Rule 1. Use **by** for transportation and communication or **with** for an instrument or means to express **how.** The noun after **by** does not usually have an article, but the noun after **with** does.

Rule 2. The action word after **by** is a gerund, which is a verb form used as a noun. It always ends in **–ing.**

BE CAREFUL!

Common Learner Errors	Explanation
1. He saved ten dollars by ~~use~~ using a special coupon.	Use an **–ing** word (a gerund) after a preposition.
2. She won the game ~~for~~ by playing well in the last quarter.	Do not use *for* when you want to indicate how something happened.
3. He made his mother angry by ~~doesn't say~~ not saying anything.	Negate a gerund with **not**. Do not use *don't*, *doesn't*, or *didn't* with this grammar construction.
4. She won the game ~~to play~~ by playing well in the last quarter.	Do not confuse **to + VERB** and **by VERB + –ing**. Remember that *to +* VERB is a shorter form of **in order to + VERB** and tells why.

EXERCISE 4. Using *by* and *with* in Adverb Phrases in Context

Use **by** and **with** phrases of manner to express how something is done. Fill in the blanks with **by** or **with**.

1. I learned to make sushi _____ watching the Cooking Channel.

2. First, the rice was prepared _____ steaming it in a large pot.

3. Next, the chef sliced pieces of fresh, raw fish _____ a very sharp knife.

4. When the rice was cool, he stirred in some rice vinegar _____ a wooden spoon.

5. Then he formed the rice into oblong balls _____ using the palms of his hands.

6. After that, he smeared the rice _____ wasabi mustard.

7. He then finished the process _____ laying a slice of fish on top.

8. _____ saying, "*Itadakimasu*," the chef indicated that it was time to try his delicacy.

EXERCISE 5. Writing Original Sentences with *by* Phrases

Combine the two sentences into one sentence using a **by** phrase. The first one has been done for you as an example.

Janet's English Exam Results

1. Janet studied very hard. Janet passed the TOEFL exam.

   Janet passed the TOEFL exam by studying very hard.

2. Her friends congratulated her. They took her out for dinner.

   _____

3. She read various books and newspapers. She improved her vocabulary.

   _____

4. She practiced writing. She did additional homework assignments.

   _____

5. She didn't stay up late. She got plenty of rest.

   _____

6. She exercised three times per week. She reduced her stress level.

   _____

7. She made sure her body had good nutrients. She didn't eat junk food.

   _____

8. She did well on the test. She used all of these strategies.

   _____

Do Online Exercise 7.2. My score: _____ /10. _____% correct.

EXERCISE 6. Editing: Is It Correct?

If the sentence is correct, write a check mark (✓) on the line. If it is not correct, write an X on the line and circle the mistake. Then make the change above the sentence. (*Hint*: There are eight sentences. Two are correct, but six have mistakes.)

_____ 1. I am real hungry, but mom said I can't eat anything now.

_____ 2. We are going to Aunt Jane's new home for having dinner soon.

_____ 3. By don't eating now, I will have a better appetite later.

_____ 4. We will be able to find her house easily with our new GPS unit.

_____ 5. Aunt Jane moved in February to a condominium.

_____ 6. We need to turn left immediately after we see the sign.

_____ 7. By entering the front gate, we need a keycard.

_____ 8. We can also go through the gate for call Aunt Jane to ask her for the gate code.

ONE-MINUTE LESSON
We use the preposition **on** to talk about a test or examination. *What was your score* **on** *the test? How many questions will be* **on** *the final exam?* A common error is to use in with text or examination. The correct preposition is **on**.

EXERCISE 7. Speaking Practice: Interviewing a Classmate

Ask your partner about a favorite activity. Fill in the blanks for Questions 2–5 with the name of the activity your partner tells you in the first question. Answer the questions using adverbs, adverb phrases, or adverb clauses. When you are finished, your partner will ask you about your favorite activity. When you are both finished, report to the class about your partner's favorite activity.

Question	My Partner's Answers
What is your favorite activity?	
When (or How often) do you _____?	
Where do you _____?	
Why do you _____?	
How well do you _____?	
Which adverbs of manner best describe how you do this activity? (at least 3)	

EXERCISE 8. Sentence Study for Critical Reading

Read the numbered sentences. Then read the three answer choices and put a check (✔) in the yes or no box in front of each sentence to show if that answer is true based on the information in the original sentence. If there is not enough information to mark something as yes, then mark it as no. Remember that more than one true answer is possible.

1. In order to save money, Vincent began to take much shorter showers because he thought that using less water was one concrete step toward cutting his monthly expenses.

   ☐ yes ☐ no   a. Vincent wants to save the planet by saving water.

   ☐ yes ☐ no   b. By reducing the amount of water used, Vincent can save money.

   ☐ yes ☐ no   c. Vincent started to shower more frequently.

2. The local college orchestra will gain public recognition by performing with the Seattle Symphony during its annual Gershwin Festival.

   ☐ yes ☐ no   a. The location of the college performance is in Gershwin.

   ☐ yes ☐ no   b. The purpose of the Gershwin Festival is to gain support from the college.

   ☐ yes ☐ no   c. The purpose of the Seattle Symphony is to perform for local colleges.

3. The new window coverings for our home are called Sheer Shades because they lightly filter the sunlight when they are open and completely block the sun when they are closed.

   ☐ yes ☐ no   a. Our windows are covered with a fabric that allows us to choose between a little sunlight or no sunlight.

   ☐ yes ☐ no   b. Sheer Shades are light, not heavy.

   ☐ yes ☐ no   c. The reason that the window coverings filter the sunlight is because the blocks are complete.

4. For the last year, Gary and Miguel have been training daily to compete in the newly formed Ironman Triathalon competition. In June, they will join other athletes from around the world in the extremely strenuous swim, run, and bike competition.

   ☐ yes ☐ no   a. They are preparing by swimming, running, and biking.

   ☐ yes ☐ no   b. The Ironman Triathalon competition began in June of last year.

   ☐ yes ☐ no   c. Every day they do something to prepare for the race.

5. Occasionally, when I leave for work, I see my neighbor running with his dog early in the morning.

   [yes] [no]   a. I occasionally work in the morning.

   [yes] [no]   b. The dog runs away when I leave for work.

   [yes] [no]   c. Sometimes my neighbor runs in the morning.

6. After we moved to Ecuador, my son quickly learned to speak Spanish.

   [yes] [no]   a. My son learned Spanish quickly.

   [yes] [no]   b. My son speaks Spanish quickly.

   [yes] [no]   c. My son didn't speak Spanish before we moved to Ecuador.

7. Natasha is nervous about today's exam. She hardly studied for it.

   [yes] [no]   a. Natasha didn't study much.

   [yes] [no]   b. Natasha studied hard.

   [yes] [no]   c. Natasha studied only a little.

8. The chef doesn't have nearly enough flour to bake bread today.

   [yes] [no]   a. The chef can't bake bread today.

   [yes] [no]   b. The chef can bake bread today.

   [yes] [no]   c. The chef doesn't have any flour today.

ONE-MINUTE LESSON
The word **nearly** means "almost." It may combine with many different words, but a common example is before a number: **nearly** *5,000 died;* **nearly** *one hundred degrees;* **nearly** *three months.* The word **nearly** can also appear before a verb: *He* **nearly** *hit that cat! We* **nearly** *fell today due to our eyesight.* The word **nearly** may also be used in front of an adjective: *The time for the exam is* **nearly** *finished. My wallet is now* **nearly** *empty.*

Do Online Exercise 7.3. My score: _____ /10. _____ % correct.

EXERCISE 9. Review Test 1: Multiple Choice

Circle the letter of the correct answer.

1. After class, I waited _____ to my teacher.

    a. by talking   c. for talking

    b. to talk   d. with talk

2. Max and I love to visit _____.

    a. Paris during the summer   c. in Paris the summer

    b. during the summer Paris   d. the summer in Paris

3. Please speak _____. The baby is sleeping.

    a. slowly   c. quiet

    b. slow   d. quietly

4. Karla will save more money _____ every night.

    a. by not eating out   c. to not to eat out

    b. for not eating out   d. for don't eating out

5. _____, you should practice daily.

    a. To speak English fluently   c. Fluently, to speak English

    b. To speak fluently English   d. Fluently, English to speak

6. I find most of my recipes _____ online.

    a. to looking   c. to look

    b. by look   d. by looking

7. It's almost 9:00 AM. The instructor will be here _____.

    a. fast   c. soon

    b. quick   d. rapid

8. Nico takes a lot of photos _____ his smart-phone.

    a. by   c. for

    b. with   d. in

EXERCISE 10. Review Test 2: Production and Evaluation

Part 1.

For each exercise, use all the given phrases and words to create a sentence with correct word order. Be sure to add capital letters and punctuation as needed to write correct sentences.

1. announced / an entirely / that the students would learn / the teacher cheerfully / new language game today

   _____

   _____

2. very / the rules quickly / after her explanation / confused / the teacher explained / , so some students were

   _____

   _____

3. formed groups /, and then / the students eagerly /around the room to observe / the teacher walked / the students' progress

   _____

   _____

4. in the game / , but some / were participating actively / were noticeably quiet / most students

   _____

   _____

5. really / provided the students / the teacher patiently / whenever they / needed help / with hints

   _____

   _____

Part 2.

Read each sentence carefully. Look at the underlined part in each sentence. If the underlined part is correct, circle the word *correct*. If it is wrong, circle the word *wrong*. Then write the correction above.

correct   wrong   1. I didn't enjoy the movie because it was too unrealistic.

correct   wrong   2. During the concert, Bianca played the piano very good.

correct   wrong   3. The teacher has read carefully my paper.

correct   wrong   4. Our flight was late because of fog.

correct   wrong   5. Colleen didn't get enough sleep last night, so she performed poorly during today's volleyball match.

correct   wrong   6. A young man on the bus offered kindly his seat to an elderly woman.

correct   wrong   7. There is not hardly enough water in the pond for the ducks to swim.

correct   wrong   8. The roads in Omaha are real bad.

EXERCISE 11. Reading Practice: Noticing Details

Read this story, and then answer the comprehension questions that follow. The grammar from this unit is underlined for you. (Only the first word of some phrases has been underlined.)

My Skiing Accident

<u>After</u> riding the ski lift <u>to</u> the top of the mountain, Paul and I began <u>gracefully</u> skiing <u>down</u> the mountain <u>through</u> the <u>freshly</u> fallen snow. I felt weightless. Gravity was pulling me <u>down the hill</u>, yet the powdery snow was keeping me afloat. It was <u>almost</u> like a dream. Then <u>suddenly</u>, all I could see was white, and I realized my body was tumbling <u>wildly</u> down the slope. Cold snow filled my mouth and nose. Ugh! I had fallen and was <u>nearly</u> buried in snow. <u>Frantically</u>, I began to wave my arms and shouted, "Stop. Paul, stop." <u>Luckily</u>, he heard me. Paul removed his skis and began to climb <u>strenuously</u> <u>up</u> the slope <u>through</u> the deep snow <u>to help</u> me.

<u>By the time</u> he arrived <u>at</u> my side, my right leg was in severe pain. I told him that I thought it was broken. Paul <u>calmly</u> told me to relax <u>while</u> he called for help. He reached <u>into</u> his pocket, and his eyes widened. "I left my phone <u>in</u> our room!" he exclaimed.

"Let's <u>just</u> wait," I said. "<u>Perhaps</u> someone will see us <u>soon</u>."

Paul sat beside me. He decided that we should have a flag <u>in order to signal</u> another skier. So, he took one of my ski poles and the scarf from <u>around</u> his neck, and by pushing his scarf <u>through</u> the tip of my pole, we had a flag. <u>Now</u> the only thing to do was to sit <u>quietly</u> and wait for another skier.

<u>Roughly</u> one hour had passed <u>when</u> we heard the happy cries of skiers approaching. <u>Quickly</u>, Paul grabbed the flag and began waving it <u>high</u> <u>in</u> the air.

They spotted it and skied <u>toward</u> us. Paul asked if they could call the ski patrol. I felt relieved <u>when</u> the man called to report our location.

<u>Within</u> another 30 minutes, two ski patrollers wearing red parkas were kneeling beside me and examining my injured leg. They determined that I would need to be taken <u>down</u> the hill and <u>to</u> the clinic <u>with</u> a sled. <u>Before</u> they lifted me onto the sled, they protected my leg <u>by</u> strapping it to a splint. The pain was <u>very</u> bad and I screamed <u>loudly</u>. Paul walked back to his skis and finished skiing the run. He would meet me <u>at</u> the clinic <u>later</u>.

The doctor at the clinic x-rayed my leg and wrapped it in a cast. <u>When</u> we returned to our cottage, it was <u>already</u> past 5:00 PM. <u>As</u> Paul helped me enter the room, I saw his phone lying <u>on</u> the desk. He <u>deeply</u> apologized <u>for</u> forgetting it. I told him that I had <u>only</u> suffered an extra hour <u>because</u> of it. My leg would heal, but the day was lost. That didn't matter to Paul. He was <u>just</u> thankful that we weren't <u>still</u> sitting <u>on</u> the slope <u>in</u> the dark.

1. How did Paul go up the hill?

   _____

2. Why did Paul climb the ski slope?

   _____

3. To what degree was the narrator buried in snow?

   _____

4. How did Paul make a signal flag?

   _____

   _____

5. The narrator says that he "only suffered an extra hour because of it." What does *it* refer to?

   _____

   _____

EXERCISE 12. Vocabulary Practice: Word Knowledge

Circle the answer choice on the right that is most closely related to the vocabulary on the left. Use a dictionary to check the meaning of words you do not know.

Vocabulary	Answer Choices	
1. to tumble	enjoy	fall
2. a recipe	for cooking	for washing
3. to reduce	to decrease	to increase
4. to stow	to give up	to put away
5. eager to do something	avoid doing	want to do
6. upright	horizontal	vertical
7. to spot	see	take
8. cheerful	happy	jealous
9. fog	like an animal	like a cloud
10. a buddy	a friend	a house
11. a fabric	a cloth	a vehicle
12. strenuous	easy to do	hard to do
13. hints	small facts	suggestions
14. a cast	for a broken arm	for a bad worker
15. elderly	old people	young people
16. a scarf	a type of beverage	a type of clothing
17. a pond	a very large mountain	a very small lake
18. ensure	guarantee	not guarantee
19. the palm	part of your hand	part of your mind
20. prohibit	allow	not allow
21. shatter	break	seldom
22. sort of	50-50	100%
23. tumble	approach	fall
24. heal	forget	improve
25. fragrance	you eat it	you smell it

EXERCISE 13. Vocabulary Practice: Collocations

Fill in each blank with the answer on the right that most naturally completes the phrase on the left. If necessary, use a dictionary to check the meaning of words you do not know.

Vocabulary	Answer Choices	
1. widely _____	known	unknown
2. a _____ shattered	cloud	window
3. retire _____ a job	from	of
4. don't _____ to call me	hesitate	interrupt
5. _____ great difficulty	by	with
6. encourage someone _____	doing something	to do something
7. you look _____	sleepily	sleepy
8. fasten a _____	figure skater	seat belt
9. dangerously _____	cheap	steep
10. _____ a new record	make	set
11. _____ of the bad weather	although	because
12. too _____	delicious	dirty
13. be in severe _____	business	pain
14. be in full _____	bloom	cast
15. the _____ quarter of a game	last	most
16. get plenty _____ rest	of	in
17. _____ good	beautiful	pretty
18. a _____ step	concrete	fluent
19. _____ recognition for	find	gain
20. chop up the _____	answers	onions
21. to perform an _____	action	emergency
22. _____ a record	put	set
23. _____ in shape	get	take
24. steamed _____	candy	rice
25. an elderly _____	person	place

EXERCISE 14. Writing Practice: Providing Supporting Details

Part 1. Editing Student Writing

Read these sentences about spring. Circle the 15 errors. Then write the number of the sentence with the error next to the type of error. (Some sentences may have more than one error.)

_____ a. subject-verb agreement   _____ d. wrong preposition

_____ b. verb tense   _____ e. gerund

_____ c. adjective-adverb   _____ f. singular-plural of nouns

Why I Like Spring	
1. Of all four seasons, spring is my favorite seasons without a doubt.	
2. Every year I welcomed the spring sun after a bleak winter that always seems too longly.	
3. After spend most of the winter indoors, I can't wait to get outside to be on the sun again.	
4. Temperatures begin to rise, flowers started to bloom, and birds become more active in the sky.	
5. The ugly brown grass covering my lawn turn green.	
6. The lovely fragrance of spring flower gently drift across my front porch.	
7. Just after the start of spring, I think about being able to exercise every day by ride my bike on the dirt road by the river.	
8. My brother and I take photos from all the greenery to send to our extreme envious relatives whose weather is still cold.	
9. I have a new phone by an amazing camera, so I'm eagerly to try it out.	
10. I will like summer, fall, and winter, but certainly spring is my favorite season.	

Part 2. Original Student Writing

Write one or two paragraphs about why you like something. Use specific reasons and concrete examples. Provide details using adverbs of time, place, purpose, manner, and degree. Use as many adverbs as possible, but try to include at least one of each type. Underline these adverbs so the teacher can see what you are trying to practice.

Unit 8

Connectors

Discover the Grammar

Read the passage about a repair café. Then answer the questions that follow.

Line	
1	An organization in our town has started hosting a Repair Café every month.
2	Although the Repair Café is held in an old school, this organization is not con-
3	nected to education. Everyone in the community is welcome to attend, so the
4	Repair Café is very well attended.
5	What exactly happens at a Repair Café? On the third Saturday of the
6	month, people who are skilled at various kinds of repairs set up tables and tools
7	in the former school so they can help repair people's broken items. They are
8	available to repair electronics, clothing, small appliances, jewelry, and other
9	items. However, when possible, they help the people who bring in the items to
10	do the repairs themselves. All repairs are free. People who bring in items have
11	to sign a form saying they will not hold the volunteers responsible for breakage.
12	In addition, the form indicates that some items may not be repaired because the
13	volunteer considers the repair too difficult or because significant costs would be
14	involved.

15	People are allowed to bring more than one item for repair, but if the table
16	they need is busy, they are asked to place their names on a waiting list so that
17	everyone has a chance to get at least one item repaired. Since people spend
18	some time waiting around, people may get hungry. Water, coffee, and tea are
19	free, but there is a charge for baked goods and fruit.

1. Underline the three examples of *so*. Why do you think the first example has a comma, but the second and third one do not?

   _____

   _____

   _____

2. Circle the four examples of *and*. Why do you think the second and third examples have a comma, but the others do not?

   _____

   _____

   _____

3. Look at the word *although* in Line 2. What does *although* mean? Could you use the word *but* here instead? Why?

   _____

   _____

   _____

4. You learned earlier that the word **since** tells when an action started, as in *I've lived here since 2010*, which means "I started living here in 2010." Look at the one example of **since** in Line 17. What does **since** mean here?

   _____

   _____

   _____

Grammar Lesson

Coordinating Conjunctions: *and, but, so*

Coordinating conjunctions connect two (or more) equal items, such as two nouns, two verbs, or two clauses. The three most common of these connectors are and, but, and so. Their meanings are different, but their functions in a sentence are similar.

and, but		
Examples	**Meaning**	**Punctuation**
I have class on Monday and Wednesday.	also	no comma between two items in a series
I have class on Monday, Wednesday, and Friday.	also	comma between three or more items in a series
I have class on Monday, and I work on Tuesday.	also	comma between two independent classes
I have class on Monday and work on Tuesday.	also	no comma between a subject and two verbs (= one clause)
It was cold, but it was sunny.	contrast	comma between two independent classes
It was cold but sunny.	contrast	no comma between two items in a series
All of the students but me got an A on the test.	except	no comma when **but** is a preposition

so		
Examples	Meaning	Punctuation
I have class on Monday, so I can't go with you to the mall.	as a result, therefore	comma between two independent clauses (same as **and** and **but**)
He took a course in France for two months so he could improve his French. OR He took a course in France for two months so that he could improve his French.	in order that	no comma when **so** introduces a dependent clause (<u>Note</u>: The word **that** is optional here.)
So he could improve his French, he took a course in France for two months. OR So that he could improve his French, he took a course in France for two months.	in order that	comma after a dependent clause when it begins a sentence (<u>Note</u>: The word **that** is optional here.)
The weather in Kuwait in summer is so hot.	very	no comma when **so** is used as an adverb of degree

<u>**Rule 1**</u>. A comma is used to separate three or more items in a series. We do not use a comma when there are only two items in a series.

<u>**Rule 2**</u>. A comma is used to separate two independent clauses in the same sentence. This rule applies to seven connectors—**for, and, nor, but, or, yet, so**—that are often remembered by the acronym FANBOYS. However, the three most useful connectors for writing are **and**, **but**, and **so**.

<u>**Rule 3**</u>. We do not use a comma to separate a subject and a verb in one independent clause even if there are two subjects or two verbs.

<u>**Rule 4.**</u> The word **but** can also be a preposition and is followed by a noun or object pronoun.

<u>**Rule 5.**</u> We do not use a comma before **so** when it means "in order that."

BE CAREFUL!

Common Learner Errors	Explanation
1. The president visited ~~Honduras Nicaragua and El~~ Honduras, Nicaragua, and El Salvador.	Use a comma when there are three or more items in a series.
2. The South American countries of Brazil and Colombia have impressive mountainous ~~regions, and produce~~ regions and produce large quantities of coffee.	Do not use a comma to separate a subject and a verb in one independent clause even if there are two subjects or two verbs.

EXERCISE 1. Using Commas with *and, but, so*

Underline all the examples of **and, but,** and **so** in these sentences about eating only local food. Then add commas if necessary.

Trying to Eat Only Local Food

1. In Community-Supported Agriculture (CSA) groups, members pay for produce from local farms in advance so they have food even if the growing season is bad.

2. Most CSA memberships involve weekly pick-up of produce, volunteer hours, and social activities.

3. Each week any vegetables that are ready are distributed and some CSAs also distribute fruit.

4. Some CSAs allow members to take as much of each item as they need but usually there is a limit.

5. The food is often organically grown, which means it is free of pesticides and other chemicals.

6. Members volunteer to help a few hours in the fields or at weekly distributions so costs are kept as low as possible.

7. Often CSA farms sell eggs and meat from other local farms.

8. A few CSAs also sell raw milk but buyers have to go to the farm to get it due to government regulations.

EXERCISE 2. Using Commas with *and, but, so*

Fill in the blanks with **and, but,** or **so**. Then add a comma if necessary.

Possible Remedies for a Toothache

1. My tooth has been hurting _____ I called my dentist to make an appointment.

2. There were no appointments for the next day _____ I took the first available date, which meant my appointment was on Monday, June 16.

3. The pain was _____ bad that I couldn't think.

4. I looked online _____ I found articles that said clove, a spice, could stop the pain.

5. I tried clove powder from my kitchen cabinet _____ that didn't help.

6. I had some whole cloves _____ I tried chewing them.

7. Up to that point, I had tried everything _____ clove tea.

8. I boiled some cloves in water _____ swished it around in my mouth until the pain subsided.

ONE-MINUTE LESSON
Prepositions can be difficult to use correctly. For days and dates, we use **on**: on *Monday*. We use **at** for clock time: **at** *noon*. We use **in** for months, seasons, and years: **in** *July,* **in** *summer,* **in** *2015.*

Do Online Exercise 8.1. My score: _____ /10. _____ % correct.

EXERCISE 3. Using Commas with Subordinating Conjunctions

Fill in the blanks with **and, but,** and **so**. Then add a comma if necessary.

Cooking with Substitute Ingredients

1. Let's imagine that a recipe calls for a certain ingredient _____ you don't have it at that moment. What do you do?

2. Of course my first reaction is to go buy the ingredient _____ another solution is to use a suitable substitute product for that ingredient.

3. For example, crackers can be used in place of bread crumbs _____ they will change the texture of the dish a little.

4. When cooking, I often use butter if I have it _____ I use oil and salt if I don't.

5. _____ it will be a bit sweet, I add sugar to cocoa when I need a good substitute for baking chocolate.

6. If I have everything for cookies _____ eggs, I substitute tofu or mayonnaise or even smashed banana.

7. I use sour cream _____ yogurt when I am out of mayonnaise.

8. In baking, sometimes I use applesauce as a substitute for butter _____ cranberries as substitutes for raisins.

9. Honey tastes better than white sugar in most recipes _____ it's better for you.

10. I don't drink alcohol _____ I use chicken broth or a little fruit juice mixed with a little vinegar if the recipe calls for white wine.

Grammar Lesson

Subordinating Conjunctions: *after, although, because, before, if, since, so, when, while*

Subordinating conjunctions introduce a dependent clause. Their purpose is to connect their dependent clause to an independent clause. These connectors usually show a time, cause, or effect relationship. In addition, these conjunctions help the reader or listener understand that the information in the clause that it introduces is not as important as the information in the independent clause.

A comma is used when the dependent clause comes before the independent clause. If the independent clause comes first, no comma is used.

Examples	Punctuation
independent clause dependent clause I was eating dinner **when the rain began.**	**independent + dependent:** no comma is possible
dependent clause independent clause **When the rain began,** I was eating dinner.	**dependent + independent:** comma is required

Rule 1. A subordinating conjunction introduces a dependent clause.

Rule 2. When a dependent clause comes before an independent clause, a comma separates them. We do not use a comma when an independent clause precedes a dependent clause.

Rule 3. Other subordinating conjunctions include:

after	as soon as	even though	since	until
although	as though	if	so that	when
as	because	in order that	though	whenever
as if	before	now that	till	wherever
as long as	even if	provided that	unless	while

Rule 4. Many subordinating conjunctions can also be other parts of speech.

    Conjunction: I arrived after you left.
    Adverb: I arrived after.
    Preposition: I arrive after you.

BE CAREFUL!

Common Learner Errors	Explanation
1. As soon as the heavy rain ~~started we~~ started, we stopped playing baseball.	Use a comma when a dependent clause comes before an independent clause.
2. ~~As soon as the heavy rain started .~~ As soon as the heavy rain started, we left the park.	A dependent clause is never a complete sentence. It must have an independent clause in order to be complete. Otherwise, your sentence is a fragment.

Connecting Grammar and Vocabulary

11 Common Subordinating Conjunctions	
Examples	Meaning
The teacher told us the answers **after** the test was over.	time
Although people don't like taxes, they pay them.	concession
Hundreds of flights have been canceled **because** the weather is so bad.	cause-effect
Before the election took place, the president spoke to the nation.	time
Sarah would pay off her student loan **if** she had the money now.	condition
Since no one made an A, the teacher gave everyone five extra points.	cause-effect
He took a course in France **so** he could improve his French.	purpose
When Flight 729 took off, the weather was starting to deteriorate.	time
Someone stole my bag **while** I was talking to the clerk.	time

Source: Folse, Keith S. (2009). *Keys to Teaching Grammar to English Language Learners*. Ann Arbor: University of Michigan Press.

EXERCISE 4. Using the Correct Subordinating Conjunction

Underline the correct subordinating conjunction in each sentence.

My First Flash Mob

1. (While / After) I was riding the train to work, I was expecting a normal day.

2. I was very surprised (when / because) I got off the train and walked into the terminal.

3. There were a few hundred people standing (as if / although) they were frozen, but all at once they all started to sing the same song.

4. I would have taken a photograph (if / since) I hadn't been in a hurry.

5. (Since / Before) these people were all gathered in the center of the terminal, commuters had to go around them.

6. No one seemed very upset (although / if) the flash mob was in the way.

7. A lot of commuters stopped to observe the event for a few minutes (before / although) continuing on their way.

8. (Because / Since) of the crowd, the police showed up.

9. (When / Although) the police appeared, the people in the flash mob moved again.

10. (Since / After) there was no violence, there were no arrests.

Do Online Exercise 8.2. My score: _____ /10. _____ % correct.

EXERCISE 5. Mini-Conversations

Circle the correct words in these eight mini-conversations.

1. A: I want to get a really great new phone. I've been looking at them online.

   B: (However / While / In fact) a great phone is nice, it's also important to get a great service plan.

2. A: Do you think I should sign a (contract or / contract, or / contract or,) should I try to avoid one?

   B: It's hard to avoid contracts if you want good service and a lot of options.

3. A: You're probably right, (and / but / so) I think I'll choose a phone first.

   B: Actually, you should select the service, (so / therefore / and) after that, you'll probably be able to select a really good phone at a discount.

4. A: Maybe you and your wife should get a family plan (for / in order to / so) you can save money.

   B: Yeah, I should talk to her about it (so / to / for) find out what kinds of things she needs in a phone plan.

5. A: She probably needs the basics, such as phone, text, (in addition / moreover / and) data.

   B: Yes, she likes to store photos and lots of other things on her phone.

6. A: You probably also use your phone to check things online, don't you?

   B: (Although / Consequently / Whereas) I don't really connect to the Internet that often, sometimes I do use my phone to check my email.

7. A: (I am, too. / So do I. / Me either.) However, my parents don't text. They just email.

   B: Oh, you're lucky. My parents don't even email that much. They like to talk.

8. A: I know you have been looking at information online, (and / although / but) maybe it would be good to go into a place where they sell phones and talk to someone about plans.

   B: OK, but I'll talk to my wife first. Thanks.

 **Grammar Lesson**

Sentence Connectors: *however, therefore*

Two of the most common sentence connectors are however and therefore. Their meanings are different. **However** is similar to **but** or **although**. **Therefore** is similar to **so** or **as a result**. The grammatical function of these two words is the same. These words connect the ideas in one sentence with the ideas in a related sentence.

Examples	Meaning
The operation was quite difficult. However, the procedure was successful.	**but, although**
The operation was quite difficult. Therefore, it took a team of three doctors seven hours to finish the procedure.	**so, as a result**

Sentences with **however** and **therefore** may be punctuated in several different ways.

Examples	Location	Punctuation
The operation was quite difficult. However, the procedure was successful.	beginning of sentence	a comma after the connecting word
The operation was quite difficult; however, the procedure was successful.	between the two clauses semi-colon	a semi-colon before and a comma after the connecting word
The operation was quite difficult. The procedure, however, was successful.	inside the second sentence	When the connecting word is inserted in a sentence as an intensifier, it is surrounded by commas.
The operation was quite difficult. The procedure was successful, however.	at the end of the second sentence	a comma before the connecting word

<u>**Rule 1**</u>. A connecting word introduces a second independent clause.

<u>**Rule 2**</u>. When a connecting word starts a sentence, it is followed by a comma.

<u>**Rule 3**</u>. When a connecting word separates two independent clauses in the same sentence, a semi-colon comes before and a comma comes after it.

<u>**Rule 4.**</u>   Other connecting words like **however** and **therefore** include:

as a result	for instance	in comparison	likewise	otherwise
consequently	furthermore	in contrast	meanwhile	similarly
conversely	however	in fact	moreover	subsequently
finally	in addition	in sum	nevertheless	therefore
for example	in brief	instead	on the contrary	thus

 BE CAREFUL!

Common Learner Errors	**Explanation**
1. Our flight departed late. ~~Therefore,~~ However, we arrived a little ahead of schedule.	Be sure to use the connecting word with the desired meaning.
2. My teacher is very ~~nice, however~~ nice; however, he is a tough grader. OR My teacher is very ~~nice, however~~ nice. However, he is a tough grader.	Do not use a single comma before connecting words like **however** or **therefore**.
3. California is the most populous ~~state however Texas~~ state; however, Texas may overtake California in the near future.	Do not use connecting words like **however** or **therefore** without any punctuation.

EXERCISE 6. Using Correct Punctuation with Connectors in Context

Add punctuation with the connectors if necessary.

The Positive Image of Dragons

Many people in our culture tend to think of dragons as evil. Throughout most of the world however dragons are considered good. In some cultures, dragons are related to gods. They are associated with myths of creation and with good luck. In China, dragons have been considered godlike therefore they were historically associated  with the emperor. Likewise in Japan dragons are considered to be good agents and omens. They are associated with both Shintoism and Buddhism and can be found in religious art and architecture. For example carvings and paintings of dragons can be found in many Japanese temples. In addition the image of the dragon is still used for some Buddhist temple weather vanes. In comparison some Native American and South American dragons are also considered benevolent. They are believed to have given humankind wisdom. Furthermore they are thought to be instrumental in birth and death.

Do Online Exercise 8.3. My score: _____ /10. _____ % correct.

Grammar Lesson

Sentence Connectors: *to, in order to, for*

All three of these introduce the reason or purpose for some action. In sum, they answer the question *Why?* The grammatical difference involves what comes after the connecting word. To and in order to are followed by a verb; in fact, **to + VERB** is a shortened form of **in order to + VERB**. For is followed by a noun and not ever by a verb.

Examples	Notes
I went to the post office to purchase some stamps.	**to + VERB** (infinitive)
I went to the post office in order to purchase some stamps.	**in order to + VERB**
I went to the post office for some stamps.	**for + NOUN**

Sentences may begin with **to** and **in order to**, but their phrases will be followed by a comma.

Examples	Location	Punctuation
The company hired 50 new employees to increase production at the San Diego factory.	after independent clause	no comma
To increase production at the San Diego factory, the company hired 50 new employees.	beginning of sentence	comma comes after the connecting phrase

<u>Rule 1</u>. To and **in order to** are followed by a verb (**to + VERB = infinitive**).

<u>Rule 2</u>. **For** is followed by a noun.

<u>Rule 3</u>. When **to** or **in order to** begins a sentence, a comma separates the introductory phrase from the independent clause.

 **BE CAREFUL!**

Common Learner Errors	Explanation
1. ~~For increase~~ To increase production at the San Diego factory, the company hired fifty new employees.	Do not use *for* with a verb.
2. ~~To apply for a job at the Weston branch of First Naitonal Bank.~~ To apply for a job at the Weston branch of First National Bank, you need at least four letters of recommendation from people in the local banking business.	A phrase with **to**, **in order to**, or **for** is never a complete sentence by itself. It must have an independent clause in order to be complete. Otherwise, your sentence is a fragment.

EXERCISE 7. Practicing Three Ways to Answer *Why* Questions

Questions with *why* often have three possible answers. Make questions with *why* and give three possible answers. Follow the example.

Example: The customer called the waiter to ask for more water.

Why did the customer call the waiter?

To ask for more water. / In order to ask for more water.

For more water.

1. I got a bus pass for my commute to work.

_____

_____

_____

2. Dan bought a bread machine so that he could make bread faster.

_____

_____

_____

3. Sophie went to the store because she needed milk.

_____

_____

_____

4. We went to the library for the lecture.

_____

_____

_____

5. My neighbors got an invisible fence that keeps their dog in the yard.

_____

_____

_____

6. I brought my binoculars for a better view of the moon and stars at night.

_____

_____

_____

EXERCISE 8. Using *to* or *for* in Extended Conversation

Write **to** or **for** on the line in order to answer the question why.

Shopping at the Mall

Noah: I'm going to the department store ❶ _____ a new tie. Do you want to go there ❷ _____ help me choose one?

Meg: Sure. I want to go ❸ _____ look for shoes. I need some ❹ _____ the gym. We can't wear our street sneakers inside.

Noah: Should we just go to the mall? You can check a few places ❺ _____ get the best price. And there are lots of places ❻ _____ lunch.

Meg: Well, OK, but if we go to the mall, I'd like to go to the bed and bath store ❼ _____ check the bridal registry. I need something ❽ _____ a wedding.

Noah: No problem. I need to pick up a couple things ❾ _____ my camping trip. I was thinking the drugstore would be a good place ❿ _____ go to look for those candles that keep mosquitoes away.

Meg: Yes, we should go to the drugstore ⓫ _____ see if they sell them. I'll definitely be hungry after that, so maybe we can go to the food court ⓬ _____ lunch.

Noah: Oh, I don't want to go to the food court ⓭ _____ have lunch. Let's go somewhere nicer. Hey, let's go to The Grill ⓮ _____ use those coupons we found in the newspaper.

Meg: OK, sure. But I think we have to order more than $25.00 of food ⓯ _____ use those coupons. Why don't you save them ⓰ _____ use them for dinner sometime?

Noah: Well, OK. My trip is coming up soon, so we'll have to go out for dinner this week ⓱ _____ use the coupons before they expire. They're good ⓲ _____ anything except alcohol.

Meg: Are you ready? I need to stop at a gas station ⓳ _____ put air in my tire. I think it's low. It will just take me a minute ⓴ _____ check.

Grammar Lesson

Sentence Connectors: *so, too, neither, either*

Four connectors—so, too, neither, and either—are used to agree with the information in the previous sentence.

So and **too** have the same meaning in agreement statements. In this case, they are used when the second statement agrees with the first statement, and both are affirmative. However, **so** and **too** have different grammatical structures.

Statement 1	Statement 2	Combined Sentence
China is in Asia.	Japan is in Asia.	China is in Asia, and Japan is, **too**.
		China is in Asia, and so is Japan.
Argentineans eat a lot of beef.	Uruguayans eat a lot of beef.	Argentineans eat a lot of beef, and Uruguayans do, **too**.
		Argentineans eat a lot of beef, and so do Uruguayans.

Either and **neither** have the same meaning in negative agreement statements. They are used when the second negative statement agrees with the first negative statement. However, **either** and **neither** have different grammatical structures.

Statement 1	Statement 2	Combined Sentence
Switzerland is not a flat country.	Austria is not a flat country.	Switzerland is not a flat country, and Austria is not, **either**.
		Switzerland is not a flat country, and neither is Austria.
Bolivia does not have a seacoast.	Paraguay does not have a seacoast.	Bolivia does not have a seacoast, and Paraguay does not, **either**.
		Bolivia does not have a seacoast, and neither does Paraguay.

Choosing the Second Verb

The second verb depends entirely on the first verb.

1st Verb	2nd Verb	Example
be	**be**	Canada and Brazil **are** big, and so **is** China.
modal	modal	Penguins **can't** fly, and turkeys **can't**, either.
auxiliary verb	auxiliary verb	Joe **is** eating popcorn, and we **are**, too.
		Flight 62 **has** arrived, and so **has** Flight 63.
		The Internet **did** not exist before 1980, and cell phones **did** not, either.
verb	**do, does, did**	Joe **likes** popcorn, and we **do**, too.
		Indonesia **has** active volcanoes, and Chile **does**, too.
		Flight 62 **arrived** early, and so **did** Flight 63.

<u>Rule 1</u>. Use **so/too** with affirmative statements.

<u>Rule 2</u>. Use **either/neither** with negative statements.

<u>Rule 3</u>. If the verb in the first sentence is **be**, use a form of **be** in the second.

<u>Rule 4</u>. If the verb in the first sentence is a **modal**, use a **modal** in the second.

<u>Rule 5</u>. If the verb in the first sentence is an **auxiliary verb**, use an **auxiliary verb** in the second.

<u>Rule 6</u>. If the verb in the first sentence is a **VERB**, use **do, does,** or **did** in the second.

BE CAREFUL!

Common Learner Errors	Explanation
1. Kevin is a good football player, and his cousin ~~does, too~~ is, too.	Chose the verb in the second clause based on the verb in the first clause.
2. Many Swiss speak more than one language, and many Moroccans ~~speak more than one language, too~~ do, too.	Don't repeat the whole second clause.
3. Mark plays baskeball on the weekend, and Liam ~~plays, too~~ does, too.	Don't repeat a verb in the second clause. Use *do, does,* or *did.*
4. Florida has beautiful beaches, and California ~~has, too~~ does, too.	Don't use **have** or **has** in the second clause as a main verb.
5. Egypt is in North Africa, and ~~so Morocco is~~ so is Morocco.	Invert the subject and verb with **so** and **neither.**
6. Japanese does not have a word for *the,* and Russian ~~doesn't, neither~~ doesn't, either.	Don't use two negatives (double negative) in the same clause.

EXERCISE 9. Using Connectors in Affirmative Sentences

Connect these sentences in two ways. Follow the examples.

Example: Keith learned to play tennis when he was a kid. Ken learned to play tennis when he was a kid.

Keith learned to play tennis when he was a kid, __and Ken did, too__.

Keith learned to play tennis when he was a kid, __and so did Ken__.

1. Tamar has a canoe. Arnold has a canoe.

_____

_____

2. Sarah's car is getting old. Michael's car is getting old.

_____

_____

3. Stephen has visited all the continents of the world. Sam has visited all the continents of the world.

_____

_____

4. John went to the concert last weekend. Karen went to the concert last week.

_____

_____

5. Jodi is taking a vacation in May. Pete and Don are taking a vacation in May.

_____

_____

6. We cook a big meal for Thanksgiving. Our neighbors cook a big meal for Thanksgiving.

_____

_____

7. My colleagues can't agree with our boss. I can't agree with our boss.

_____

_____

8. My classmates want to have a party on the last day of class. Our teacher wants to have a party on the last day of class.

_____

_____

EXERCISE 10. Using Connectors in Negative Sentences

Connect these sentences in two ways. Follow the examples.

Example: Carla doesn't do any sports. Ted doesn't do any sports.

Carla doesn't do any sports, _<u>and Ted doesn't either</u>_ .

Carla doesn't do any sports, _<u>and neither does Ted</u>_ .

1. James doesn't like crowds. Deb doesn't like crowds.

   _____

   _____

2. James isn't good at small talk. Deb isn't good at small talk.

   _____

   _____

3. Deb and James don't dance. Most of their friends don't dance.

   _____

   _____

4. Deb doesn't have a very outgoing personality. James doesn't have a very outgoing personality.

   _____

   _____

5. James won't go to Joe's party on Friday. Deb won't go to Joe's party on Friday.

   _____

   _____

6. Deb and James won't go out Saturday night. We won't go out Saturday night.

   _____

   _____

7. Deb won't be bored this weekend. James won't be bored this weekend.

   _____

   _____

8. Deb hasn't gone to a party in two years. James hasn't gone to a party in two years.

   _____

   _____

EXERCISE 11. Using Connectors in Context

Read the sentences, and then complete them with **so, too, neither, either,** and other missing words.

Twins

1. Tom has curly hair, and _____ his twin sister, Nell.

2. Nell's hair is brown, but Tom's _____. It's red.

3. Tom's eyes are blue, and Nell's _____.

4. Tom is tall, but Nell's _____.

5. Tom isn't overweight, and Nell _____.

6. Nell doesn't wear bright colors, and _____ Tom.

7. Nell shops at discount stores, but Tom _____.

8. Nell really doesn't like shopping, and Tom _____.

9. Tom usually shops online, and _____ Nell.

10. He always compares prices from different sellers, and Nell

     _____.

11. Tom is careful with his budget, but his sister _____.

12. Nell has always been a good student, and _____ Tom.

Do Online Exercise 8.4. My score: ____ /10. ____ % correct.

EXERCISE 12. Editing: Is It Correct?

If the sentence is correct, write a check mark (✓) on the line. If it is not correct, write an X on the line and circle the mistake. Then make the change above the sentence. (Hint: There are twelve sentences. Four are correct, but eight have mistakes.)

Making Money at a Craft Fair

_____ 1. My friend wanted to try to make money at a craft sale, and I wanted, too.

_____ 2. She had never sold items at a craft sale before, and so had I.

_____ 3. I called the sale organizers for find out how to get tables.

_____ 4. My friend had knitted a lot of scarves, and so I had.

_____ 5. My friend decided to sell the scarves, or I chose to keep my scarves to give as gifts.

_____ 6. I decided to sell some birdhouses I had painted. In addition, I decided to sell some hand-painted flower pots, vases, and napkin holders.

_____ 7. On the day of the sale, I couldn't decide whether to take my car but my husband's truck.

_____ 8. I finally decided to take the truck so that I could load and unload my things easily.

_____ 9. I went early in order to set up before customers started arriving.

_____ 10. So did my friend go early.

_____ 11. I didn't sell much at the sale, and neither didn't my friend.

_____ 12. Although we didn't sell much, we didn't mind because we met a lot of great people.

EXERCISE 13. Speaking Activity: Talking about Actions

This chart gives information about four people and eight actions or situations. The words yes or no in the chart refer to that person and that action. For example, yes under Duc's name by "likes coffee" means that Duc likes coffee. The no under Chie's name in the same line means that Chie doesn't like coffee.

Step 1. Look at the chart. Write eight statements about the people and the information on page 246. Make some of the statements true and some false. Practice *and . . . too, and so . . . , and . . . either, and neither . . . ,* and *but.* Circle T for true or F for false to indicate whether your sentence is really true or false.

Step 2. Work with a partner. Student A will read all of his or her sentences. Student B will look at this chart and say True or False for each statement. Keep track of the number of correct answers.

Step 3. After Student A has read all of his or her sentences, then it is Student B's turn to read his or her statements, and Student A must say True or False for each statement.

Action/Situation	Chie (female)	Sam (male)	Duc (male)	Adila (female)
likes coffee	no	yes	yes	no
has gone to Turkey before	no	yes	no	yes
speaks Chinese fluently	yes	no	yes	no
bought a phone last year	no	yes	no	yes
has a bike	yes	no	no	yes
is a shy person	yes	yes	no	no
can play the guitar	yes	no	no	yes
might get married soon	yes	no	yes	yes

T F   1. _____

T F   2. _____

T F   3. _____

T F   4. _____

T F   5. _____

T F   6. _____

T F   7. _____

T F   8. _____

EXERCISE 14. Sentence Study for Critical Reading

Read the numbered sentences. Then read the three answer choices and put a check mark (✔) in the yes or no box in front of each sentence to show if that answer is true based on the information in the original sentence. If there is not enough information to mark something as yes, then mark it as no. Remember that more than one true answer is possible.

1. When you eat a lot of garlic, you may not be fun to kiss, but your health may benefit.

   ☐ yes ☐ no a. Kissing keeps you healthy.

   ☐ yes ☐ no b. You may be healthy if you don't kiss after eating garlic.

   ☐ yes ☐ no c. People might not enjoy kissing you after you eat a lot of garlic.

2. Garlic can kill mosquitoes, fight infection, and kill mold; moreover, it has many additional uses.

   ☐ yes ☐ no a. Too much garlic can give you an infection that can kill you.

   ☐ yes ☐ no b. Garlic can protect your health, but it does not have many other uses.

   ☐ yes ☐ no c. Garlic has many uses because it can kill mold.

3. Some fishermen say that bass are attracted to garlic, and trout are, too.

   ☐ yes ☐ no a. Some fishermen like to eat fish with garlic.

   ☐ yes ☐ no b. Bass are attracted to garlic and to trout.

   ☐ yes ☐ no c. It is said that garlic can be useful for fishing.

4. Some women use garlic on their skin to help keep it clear; however, the garlic is usually used with other ingredients.

    ☐ yes ☐ no a. Some women use garlic because they cannot use other ingredients on their skin.

    ☐ yes ☐ no b. Some women use a combination of garlic and other ingredients on their skin.

    ☐ yes ☐ no c. Some women eat food without garlic to keep their skin clear.

5. Many babies do not like the taste of garlic, and some adults don't either.

    ☐ yes ☐ no a. Some baby food includes garlic.

    ☐ yes ☐ no b. You should only give garlic to sick babies.

    ☐ yes ☐ no c. There are both babies and adults who don't like garlic.

6. Diego's cookbooks do not have any dessert recipes that use garlic, and neither do his favorite online cooking sites.

    ☐ yes ☐ no a. His favorite online cooking sites are better than his cookbooks for garlic recipes.

    ☐ yes ☐ no b. He has some favorite online sites for recipes.

    ☐ yes ☐ no c. He makes unusual desserts in the summer.

7. Even though the recipe called for sliced garlic, Gina crushed a clove and then chopped it finely in order to release more flavor.

    ☐ yes ☐ no a. Gina wanted to get a stronger garlic taste in what she was cooking.

    ☐ yes ☐ no b. Gina crushed a clove of garlic, so she had to use it in her dish.

    ☐ yes ☐ no c. Gina was using a recipe.

8. Scapes are a tender, curly, stem-like, green part of the garlic plant that appear before the bulb forms. Because they are difficult to find at supermarkets, many people are eager to buy them when they are finally available at farmer's markets.

    ☐ yes ☐ no a. Scapes are a part of the garlic plant that can be eaten.

    ☐ yes ☐ no b. Scapes are a kind of garlic plant.

    ☐ yes ☐ no c. Many people look for scapes at farmer's markets.

EXERCISE 15. Review Test 1: Multiple Choice

Circle the letter of the correct answer. Some are conversations.

1. "What did you two do yesterday?"

   "I went to the library, and _____ Maria."

   a. went, too   c. did, too

   b. so went   d. so did

2. Travis wasn't in class yesterday, but Steve _____.

   a. did   c. was

   b. didn't   d. wasn't

3. We ate pie for dessert, and they _____.

   a. did, too   c. did either

   b. ate, too   d. neither did

4. He is attending that school specifically _____ get computer training.

   a. for   c. in order

   b. to   d. so

5. _____, and so do my sisters.

   a. I never exercise   c. I am a good artist

   b. I have joined a gym d. I live in a small town

6. "Have you finished your paper?"

   "Yes, I have, and so _____ Fahad."

   a. did   c. has

   b. have   d. had

7. There was no bus to the airport, _____ we had to take a taxi.

   a. therefore   c. for

   b. in order to   d. so

8. "Can you help me move some furniture next weekend?"

   "Sure. I am free in the morning, and I think Diego _____."

   a. so, too   c. is, too

   b. can, too   d. so can

EXERCISE 16. Review Test 2: Production and Evaluation

Part 1.

Read this short passage. Circle the correct words in parentheses.

The Tough Job of a Catering Waiter

A catering waiter's job is similar to any other waiter's job, (but / so) there are some significant differences. For one thing, catering involves large groups of people who order meals for (banquets, receptions, / banquets receptions) and other big celebrations. Usually the menu is set by the customers, (for / so) the waiter doesn't have to keep track of a lot of different orders. However, sometimes there are a couple of different choices for each course of a meal. (In addition / In addition,) sometimes people are free to order a range of drinks. (Therefore, / As though) a catering waiter might have to remember a few things. Moreover, catering waiters have to be very fast (in order to / for) serve everyone at about the same time and in order to get warm food out before it gets cold. It is also important for a waiter to be fast (so that / since) his team gets a good tip. Usually a company or other organization pays for catered meals. (While / When) this is not the case, usually the catering is for a private celebration. (Consequently, / Conversely,) the event planners may feel more generous than usual when tipping. However, the event planners do not have any control over the actual food preparation, and (neither / so) do catering waiters, so the waiter's tips depend largely on the chef and kitchen staff.

Part 2.

Read each sentence carefully. Look at the underlined part in each sentence. If the underlined part is correct, circle the word *correct*. If it is wrong, circle the word *wrong*. Write the correct form above.

correct   wrong   1. I was tired after the party, and my wife <u>did too</u>.

correct   wrong   2. Yesterday was rainy, <u>and</u> today isn't.

correct   wrong   3. The train is faster than the bus. <u>Although</u>, the train is noisier.

correct   wrong   4. I don't want to move, and my wife <u>doesn't, either</u>.

correct   wrong   5. My office isn't messy, and my house <u>isn't, too</u>.

correct   wrong   6. My sister took off work for six months <u>for</u> take care of her new child.

correct   wrong   7. I shop online <u>in order to</u> convenience.

correct   wrong   8. The oil spill resulted in the deaths of thousands of sea animals and birds; <u>whereas</u>, it is not correct to say that it was only a small shipping accident.

EXERCISE 17. Reading Practice: Understanding an Extended Definition

Read this passage about a new business concept, and then answer the comprehension questions that follow. The grammar from this unit is underlined for you.

What Is Advergaming?

Advergaming, a term that comes from the words *advertising* <u>and</u> *gaming,* refers to games that help sell products which are often found on company websites. Sometimes they are offered <u>in order to</u> encourage people to spend more time on the site. The game will draw people in <u>and</u> keep them playing. They may tell friends <u>and</u> family members about the game, which may increase traffic to the company site. <u>Moreover,</u> the entire time they are playing, people will see ads, slogans, the brand name, <u>and</u> so on.

<u>In addition,</u> companies sometimes offer games to give information about a product, issue, or event. <u>While</u> these advergames are intended to educate, they are not all about serious issues. The U.S. military may use advergames to motivate people to join the army, <u>but</u> a company may use advergames simply to give people information about a new product. <u>Although</u> this is commonly accomplished within the game itself, sometimes the advertising happens before people can play. <u>After</u> the launch button to start the game is pressed, an instructional video clip <u>or</u> ad may come up. People have no choice <u>but</u> to sit through this <u>while</u> they wait to play the game.

<u>Although</u> advergaming is relatively new in some ways, in other ways it is similar to TV and movie advertising. <u>For example,</u> product placement is one very common advertising strategy in games. <u>However,</u> because of the game environment, a player can interact with the product in ways that would not be possible in a movie ad. Players might try on target brand clothes, <u>or</u> they might engage in an arcade-style car race, driving a target brand car. Some companies

have gone beyond this. One company, for instance, invited players to design their own cars <u>and</u> race them. <u>Consequently</u>, valuable information about color, style, <u>and</u> design preferences was obtained.

Players can <u>also</u> see a target company's ads in a virtual world. <u>Even if</u> there is no interaction with the brand, it can be advertised within the game on billboards, computer <u>or</u> TV screens, <u>or</u> print media. <u>Furthermore</u>, ads surrounding the game screen are possible.

<u>In fact</u>, there are games in which players interact with outside links <u>and</u> websites that advertise things. There is even the possibility of games within games, <u>so</u> a person could go to a game kiosk <u>and</u> play a game in a virtual world—with another layer of advertising embedded in the second game!

<u>Since</u> so many children play games online, of course marketers have geared advergames to children, <u>and</u> this raises concerns. <u>For example</u>, junk foods containing high levels of fat, sugar, <u>and</u> salt can be featured in games. <u>However</u>, maybe of greater concern to critics is the idea of stealthily associating material things with achievement—that is, linking the product to reward. Despite any criticism, it looks like advergaming might be around for a long time.

Some people are hopeful about other potential uses of advergames. Advergames could be used to further environmental initiatives <u>or</u> human development projects. Advergames could send strong messages against crime, racial prejudice, <u>or</u> gender bias. True, children would be especially vulnerable to whatever messages games relayed; <u>however</u>, there is potential for truly positive messages to be promoted. Imagine, <u>for example</u>, a game in which peace is advertised or, <u>even more ironically</u>, a game promoting less consumerism.

1. What is the origin of the word advergaming?

_____

_____

2. What does *game within a game* mean? Can you give an example?

_____

_____

3. What is the concern about advergames and children? Do you think this concern in warranted?

_____

_____

4. Of the potential uses of advergaming, which one holds more promise in your opinion and why? What are the main ideas in this passage? List 3 to 5.

_____

_____

_____

_____

_____

_____

_____

EXERCISE 18. Vocabulary Practice: Word Knowledge

Circle the answer choice on the right that is most closely related to the vocabulary on the left. Use a dictionary to check the meaning of words you do not know.

Vocabulary	Answer Choices	
1. commute	at only one place	between two places
2. subside	increase	lessen
3. flat	no hills	no water
4. distribute	announce to everyone	give to everyone
5. all at once	especially	immediately
6. upset	angry, bothered	quiet, introverted
7. concentrate	put ideas together	think really hard
8. instrumental	very important	extremely diffuclt
9. deteriorate	from bad to good	from good to bad
10. provided that	if	since
11. a pesticide	a poison	a relaxant
12. hygiene	clean	clear
13. in contrast	and	but
14. due to	because of	in spite of
15. purchase	accept	buy
16. a colleague	a person	a place
17. to show up	appear somehere	locate an answer
18. a solution	an answer	a question
19. in brief	a few words	a lot of words
20. quite	very	not loud
21. raw	uncooked	uninjured
22. a clerk	a concept	a person
23. a mob	many people	much money
24. instrumental	famous	important
25. invisible	can't fly	can't see

EXERCISE 19. Vocabulary Practice: Collocations

Fill in each blank with the answer on the right that most naturally completes the phrase on the left. If necessary, use a dictionary to check the meaning of words you do not know.

Vocabulary	Answer Choices	
1. on the _____	summer	weekend
2. _____ for more growth	early	potential
3. to _____ on	depend	follow
4. be skilled _____ something	at	by
5. _____ of people	hundred	hundreds
6. an _____ substitute	appropriate	individual
7. _____ sum	at	in
8. block _____ the sunlight	off	out
9. an outgoing _____	person	place
10. hold you responsible _____ something	for	in
11. to agree _____ someone about	for	with
12. she is _____ to him	attracted	believed
13. the _____ expired	coupon	storm
14. to _____ a business	run	say
15. to _____ an appointment	let	make
16. this recipe _____ for an egg	acts	calls
17. to pay _____ your loan	by	off
18. I think it is _____ my time.	friendly	worth
19. to turn _____ an invitation	after	down
20. the test was _____ by noon	over	under
21. a _____ list	waited	waiting
22. _____ goods	baked	fried
23. to store _____	information	people
24. be _____ with	associated	related
25. an outgoing _____	person	thing

EXERCISE 20. Writing Practice: Discussing an Experience with a New Product

Part 1. Editing Student Writing

Read these sentences about a cooking vacation. Circle the 15 errors. Then write the number of the sentence with the error next to the type of error. (Some sentences may have more than one error.)

_____ a. comma error with a connector   _____ d. verb tense

_____ b. subject-verb agreement   _____ e. adverb-adjective

_____ c. preposition   _____ f. singular-plural of nouns

Cooking Vacation
1. My friends Deborah and Mary Beth take a "cooking vacation" last summer.
2. They wanted to go back to Italy but they wanted to do something they had not done before.
3. The cooking vacation concept has started in Italy at 1998, and today these cooking tours are offered throughout Europe and Central and South America.
4. Most culinary vacations lasts about a week, and include tours of local attraction as well as farms and wineries.
5. Of course the highlights are the cooking lessons (in English), and the chance to taste regional foods and wines.
6. Deborah and Mary Beth's tour was in Umbria (Italy), and they stayed on the grounds of a farm and could pick the freshly produce for their recipes.
7. They learned to make all kinds of traditional Italian food with hand, including Bolognese sauce, ravioli (from scratch), herb-roasted chicken, wood-fired pizza, eggplant parmesan, tiramisu, biscotti, and gelato.
8. Deborah took a separate course to learn how to make cheese, and so does Beth.
9. Their tour guide also took them for an olive oil factory, the famous Deruta ceramics factory, and the three city of Assisi, Orvieto, and Pienza.
10. Deborah and Mary Beth have been good cooks before they had their culinary vacation but now they say that their cooking is more authentic.

Part 2. Original Student Writing

Write one or two paragraphs about your experience with a new product. Use a variety of connectors from this unit. Underline each connector you use so that the teacher can see what you are trying to practice.

Unit 9

Review of Verb Tenses

Discover the Grammar

Read the passage about a recent trip. Then answer the questions that follow.

Line	
1	Most people have heard of the Panama Canal, but what do they know
2	about it? I know a great deal because I sailed through the canal last year.
3	The history of the canal is very interesting. France began construction work
4	on the canal in 1881. However, French attempts ended in 1894 because the
5	project cost $287,000,000 and approximately 22,000 lives. These deaths were
6	due to construction accidents and to diseases, especially malaria and yellow
7	fever. While the U.S. worked on the canal between 1904 and 1914, an addi-
8	tional 5,000 people died. The canal officially opened on August 15, 1914.
9	Last year I sailed on a ship with 800 passengers through this canal. It took
10	us approximately eight hours to complete the 48-mile journey. The canal uses
11	an intricate system of locks that raise and lower huge ships so that they can pass
12	from one end of the canal to the other. Each lock is as tall as a six-story build-

13	ing. However, the most surprising thing to me was how close other ships were
14	to our ship. In fact, when our ship was passing by another ship, I couldn't
15	believe that we were only about 30 feet apart.
16	The Panama Canal is extremely busy. In 1914, about 1,000 ships used the
17	canal, but more recently, the annual traffic has grown to 13,000 ships per year.
18	One day I am going to do this trip again because it was such an adventure.

1. Underline the two examples of **present perfect tense**. Is it possible to use **simple past tense** instead of **present perfect** in either of these examples? Explain each answer.

    _____

    _____

2. Circle the example of **past progressive tense**. Why is that tense used here?

    _____

    _____

3. Compare **uses** (Line 10) and **used** (Line 16). Why is **simple present** possible in one case but not in the other?

    _____

    _____

4. One verb tense that is not used anywhere in this passage is **present progressive**. Why is this tense not used here?

    _____

    _____

 **Grammar Lesson**

Simple Present Tense

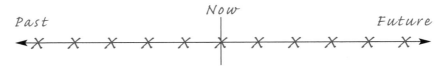

usage	Use the simple present tense for facts, habits, routines, or customs.	
common time words	*every _____ (every day), always, frequently, usually, often, sometimes, occasionally, rarely, never*	
affirmative	I/you/we/they + VERB I wash my hands *frequently*.	he/she/-it + VERB + –s It looks cloudy today.
negative	I/you/we/they + do not + VERB They **don't produce** cars there.	he/she/it + does not + VERB He **does not rely** on anyone for money.
question	Do + I/you/ we/they + VERB Do you **initiate** all the contracts?	Does + he/she/it + VERB Does the contract **specify** the cost?

<u>Rule 1</u>. In the simple present tense, a verb has only two forms: VERB or VERB + –s.

<u>Rule 2</u>. SPELLING: For verbs that end in **consonant** + –y, change the –y to –i and then add –es: *study* → studies. However, if the verb ends in **vowel** + –y, only add –s: play → plays. For verbs that end in –*o*, –*sh*, –*ch*, –*s*, –*z*, and –*x*, add –es: do → does.

<u>Rule 3</u>. To make a negative statement, add **do not** OR **does not** before the base (simple) form of the verb. It is also possible to use contractions in informal English: **do not** = **don't**; **does not** = **doesn't**. Contractions are not used in formal academic English.

<u>Rule 4</u>. To make a question with a verb (not **be**), add **do** OR **does** before the subject. Be sure to use only the **base** (simple) form of the verb.

BE CAREFUL!

Common Learner Errors	Explanation
1. Kathy ~~prepare~~ **prepares** oatmeal for breakfast every day.	Remember to use **VERB + –s** when the subject is **he, she,** or **it.**
2. (A) The boxes that are on the bottom shelf ~~needs~~ **need** new lids. (B) The box with those magazines ~~need~~ **needs** a new lid.	In sentences with prepositional phrases or adjective clauses, be sure to locate the subject that belongs with the verb.
3. That color ~~doesn't looks~~ **doesn't look** good on me.	When using **does,** use the simple verb form (no –s). You need only one –s for **he/she/it.**
4. Does your wife ~~speaks~~ **speak** English?	If the question begins with **does,** the verb doesn't have –s. Use only the simple form of the main verb.

EXERCISE 1. Simple Present Tense in Context

Underline the correct verb.

A Martial Arts Legend

In my town, we ❶ (have, has) a martial arts legend from China. His name is grandmaster Pui Chan, and he ❷ (are, is) 74 years old. Although most people his age ❸ (isn't, aren't) so active, Grandmaster Chan ❹ (practice, practices) yoga and tai chi a few  hours per day. He still ❺ (give, gives) kung fu demonstrations and ❻ (travel, travels) all over the world promoting martial arts. His age ❼ (don't, doesn't) seem to matter really. Most of the people who watch his demonstrations ❽ (don't, doesn't) know how he has so much energy.

 **Grammar Lesson**

Simple Past Tense

KEY
3

usage	Use the simple past tense for actions or events that are finished.	
common time words	*yesterday, last* _____ (*last month*), _____ *ago* (*2 days ago*)	
affirmative	regular verbs: **subject + VERB + –ed** I washed my hands before dinner. wash → washed	irregular verbs: **subject + IRREGULAR VERB** We found a great restaurant. find → found
negative	**subject + did not + VERB** Our teacher did not take our homework.	
question	**Did + subject + VERB** Did you identify the problem with your car?	

Rule 1. In the simple past tense, a **regular** verb has one form: VERB + –ed. **An irregular form varies:** go → went, take → took, begin → began. (See Appendix C.)

Rule 2. For **one-syllable** verbs that end in **consonant + vowel + consonant** (**CVC**), **double the final consonant:** stop → stopped and plan → planned. However, do not double final letters for verbs that end in –w (snowed), –x (taxed), or –y (played)

Rule 3. For **two-syllable** verbs that end in CVC and have stress on the **second** syllable, **double the final consonant:** *ocCUR* → occurred and *perMIT* → permitted. However, if the stress is on the **first** syllable, just add –ed: *HAPpen* → happened and *LISten* → listened.

Rule 4. To make a negative statement, add **did not** before the base (simple) form of the verb. In informal speaking or writing, it is possible to use a contraction: did not → didn't. Contractions are not used in formal academic English.

Rule 5. To make a question with a past tense verb (not **be**), add **did** before the subject. Be sure to use only the **base** (simple) form of the verb.

BE CAREFUL!

Common Learner Errors	Explanation
1. My uncle Juan Carlos ~~lives~~ lived in Chicago 20 years ago.	Remember to use simple past tense. Don't use **VERB** or **VERB + −s** for a simple past affirmative action.
3. The meeting ~~didn't started~~ didn't start on time.	If you have the auxiliary verb **did, did not,** or **didn't,** then don't use −**ed** with the verb.
4. Did you ~~installed~~ install a new lock on your door?	Do not use −**ed** or the irregular past form of the verb in yes-no questions. Use only the base (simple) form of the verb. **Did** is past, and you only need a past tense form once.

EXERCISE 2. Using Affirmative and Negative with Simple Past Tense

Create affirmative or negative past tense statements (as indicated) for the following regular and irregular verbs. Use a variety of subjects. In other words, don't use *I* or *you* for all items. When you have finished, share your answers with a partner. Discuss any items that you think are not correct. The first one has been done for you as an example.

1. learn (affirmative) *Lucy learned that she got accepted into her first choice of college this morning.*

2. resign (affirmative) _____

3. drink (affirmative) _____

4. stop (negative) _____

5. understood (negative) _____

6. tell (negative) _____

7. need (affirmative) _____

8. love (affirmative) _____

EXERCISE 3. Conversations Using Regular and Irregular Past Tense

Circle the form of the verb in each set of parentheses.

The Post Office

Jimmy: I ❶ (go, went) to your house yesterday, but you weren't home. I didn't call you first, though. I ❷ (am, was) really bad about remembering to call first.

Kendall: Oh. I ❸ (had, have) to go to the post office.

Jimmy: I really ❹ (want, wanted) to find you that I caught you! I needed to mail something.

Kendall: I ❺ (was, were) really lucky, because the post office always ❻ (closes, closed) early on Saturdays. I almost didn't make it there on time.

Jimmy: What ❼ (did, do) you ❽ (did, do) for the rest of your afternoon?

Kendall: Well, I ❾ (have, had) to go shopping at the market. I ❿ (need, needed) to get a few items for our dinner party next week.

Jimmy: That's right! I don't ⓫ (get, got) many party invitations, so thank you for inviting me.

Kendall: No problem. That ⓬ (is, was) something that I love to do—have parties! Another reason why I ⓭ (have, had) to go to the post office was to mail the rest of the invitations.

Jimmy: ⓮ (Do you think, Do you thought) that the post office will deliver them in time?

Kendall: Oh, I really ⓯ (hope, hoped) so.

ONE-MINUTE LESSON
In the dialogue, Jimmy said, "I didn't call you first, though." The word **though** is very frequently used at the end of a sentence and has a similar meaning to the connector **but**. This usage is extremely common in spoken language.

EXERCISE 4. Editing: Is It Correct?

If the sentence is correct, write a check mark (✓) on the line. If it is not correct, write an X on the line and circle the mistake. Then make the change above the sentence. (*Hint*: There are eight sentences. Two are correct, but six have mistakes.)

How Coffee Came to the United States

_____ 1. It is a legend that the first coffee trees was in Ethiopia.

_____ 2. Colonialists in America drinked mostly tea until the Tea Act in 1773.

_____ 3. Coffee replaced tea as the country's favorite hot beverage.

_____ 4. Reforms in pricing rules after the Coffee Crash in 1881 help coffee to become more affordable.

_____ 5. Coffee drinking in the United States is the highest in the mid-1940s.

_____ 6. At that time, the average person consumed almost 20 pounds of coffee.

_____ 7. In the 1950s, advertising campaigns make the phrase *coffee break* popular.

_____ 8. The first store of the most popular coffee chain in the United States, Starbucks, open in 1971.

Do Online Exercise 9.1. My score: _____ /10. _____ % correct.

Grammar Lesson

Present Progressive Tense

usage	1. Use the present progressive tense for actions happening now.
	2. It is also possible to use present progressive tense for future plans, especially when a future time word is used.
common time words	*now, right now, today, tonight, this _____ (this month), currently, these days, at this moment/minute*
affirmative	**I am, you/we/they are, he/she/it is + VERB + –ing** It **is raining** really hard right now.
negative	**I am, you/we/they are, he/she/it is + not + VERB + –ing** It snowed a lot yesterday, but at least today it **is not snowing**.
question	**Am I, Are you/we/they, Is he/she/it + VERB + –ing** **Am I sitting** in your chair? I'm sorry.

<u>Rule 1</u>. In present progressive tense, a verb has three forms: am VERB + –ing; is VERB + –ing; and are VERB + –ing.

<u>Rule 2</u>. Do not use this tense with non-action verbs. Four kinds of verbs that typically do not occur in present progressive tense are: senses (**hear, see, smell, feel, sound**), emotions (**like, love, need, prefer, want**), mental states (**believe, forget, remember, seem**), and possession (**belong, have, own, possess**).

> <u>Exception 1</u>: You can say **I'm having a good time** or **We're having a test** because **have** is an action in these two examples. You cannot say ~~I'm having a new car~~ or ~~She's having a pencil~~ because in these examples, **have** shows possession and not action.

> <u>Exception 2</u>: You can also use **think** in the progressive if you are indicating it is a progressive action. You can say, **I am thinking about moving to a new apartment.** However, you would not express your opinion by saying ~~I am thinking that your car looks nice~~.

<u>Rule 3</u>. Use the word **not** to make a negative sentence with the verb **be** in present progressive tense: **am not, is not, are not**.

<u>Rule 4</u>. To ask a question using present progressive tense, invert the subject and the **be** verb.

BE CAREFUL!

Common Learner Errors	Explanation
1. The earth ~~is taking~~ takes one year to go around the sun.	Don't use present progressive for actions that happen every day or all the time.
2. ~~eatting~~ eating, ~~colorring~~ coloring, ~~takeing~~ taking, ~~openning~~ opening, ~~cuting~~ cutting, ~~listenning~~ listening	Be careful with the spelling of –ing verbs.
3. Why ~~are walking Petra and Melissa~~ are Petra and Melissa walking home?	Put the subject between **am, is,** or **are** and the **–ing** verb.

EXERCISE 5. Present Progressive Sentence Completion

Fill in the blanks with the correct form of the present progressive—*affirmative* or *negative*. Choose from among the verbs in the word list. Use all of the words. Add the correct form of **be (affirmative** or **negative)** to agree with the **subject.**

pack	fly	check	fight
travel	go	stay	make

Getting Ready for Summer Vacation

1. My family is excited! We _____ on summer vacation!

2. We _____ this year. We're taking the family car instead.

3. My dad _____ the oil in the car right now.

4. My sister _____ all of her books in her backpack.

5. My little brothers _____ over who will sit by the window first.

6. Our cat _____ with my cousin while we are on vacation.

7. My oldest brother _____ with us because he has to work at a law firm this summer.

8. My mom _____ some sandwiches for us to eat on the road.

EXERCISE 6. Speaking Practice: Charades

Work in pairs. Create a list of activities that you can act out without speaking. You can act alone or you and your partner can act together. The rest of the class has to guess what you are doing by asking yes/no questions (ex: *Are you cooking?*). You are only allowed to answer *yes* or *no* to continue guiding the class to guess the correct answer. If you answered yes to this question, continue acting using specific gestures until this class guesses correctly. The second guess might be *Are you baking a cake?* If that is what you have written down, say, *That's correct* and the turn passes to the next team.

A Few Ideas for Charades	
throwing a ball	climbing stairs
driving a bus	cooking soup
mowing the yard	vacuuming a floor

Grammar Lesson

KEY
4

Be Going To for Future Time

We commonly use be + going to + VERB to talk about the future.

    Affirmative: I **am**, you/we/they **are**, he/she/it **is** + **going to** (**VERB**)

    Question: **Am** I, **Are** you/we/they, **Is** he/she/it + **going to** (**VERB**)

Be + going to + VERB for the future and will + VERB for the future have similar meanings, and sometimes they seem interchangeable. However, the reasons we use one more than the other depend on the situation at the time of speaking or the information that the speaker knows:

1. **Future plans** (arranged prior to when you talk about them)

2. **Predictions** (based on current evidence)

	Examples
Affirmative	**A:** "I'm going to see my cousins in two more days." **Plan:** They talked about it on the phone weeks ago, and the plane tickets are already bought. **B:** "If he doesn't hurry, he is going to miss his flight." **Prediction:** The evidence is the clock time.
Negative	**C:** "You're not going to spend a lot of money, are you, June?" **Plan:** June is going shopping. Del is asking about her intentions. **D:** "According to the weather forecast, it is not going be below freezing tonight." **Prediction with evidence**—Weather forecasters use scientific instruments.
Yes-no question	**E:** "Are you going to buy a new car next year?" **Plan:** Asking about your future plans **F:** "**Pat,** is that tree going to fall?" **Prediction:** Asking Pat to make a prediction based on Pat seeing the tree.
***Wh–* question**	**G:** "When are your cousins going to be here?" **Plan:** Asking about plans made before the question was asked. **H:** "How many people are going to attend the Super Bowl?" **Prediction:** Asking the listener to make a prediction. The evidence is the size of the stadium and last year's attendance.

<u>Rule 1</u>. Use be + going to + VERB to talk about future plans that have been **arranged in advance:**

> A: "I am going to make a presentation tomorrow."
> B: "What time?"
> A: "At 1:30."

<u>Rule 2</u>. Use be + going to + VERB to talk about predictions based on **current evidence:**

> A: "Oh, the sky is really dark."
> B: "Yes, it's going to rain soon."

<u>Rule 3</u>. In spoken language, going to before VERB often sounds like **gonna.** This is acceptable in informal spoken language, but we never use **gonna** in academic writing.

BE CAREFUL!

Common Learner Errors	Explanation
1. If you don't go to bed now, you're ~~going be~~ going to be tired in the morning.	Don't forget the word **to**. It is part of the infinitive VERB that follows.
2. Your application for a new credit card is going to ~~taking~~ take four to six weeks.	The verb after **be going to** is the base (simple) form. Don't use **–s** or **–ed** or **–ing** with the verb after **to**.
3. Written language example: Many economists think these new policies are ~~gonna~~ going to help the average person.	We often pronounce **going to** as *gonna*, but we never write *gonna*. It is not a written word.
4. Spoken language example: I really think it's ~~gonna to~~ gonna rain OR going to rain soon.	If you want to say *gonna*, don't say *gonna to*. The pronunciation of *gonna* means "going to," so the error *gonna to* really means "going to to."

EXERCISE 7. Information Questions in Context

Fill in the blanks with the correct form of the future tense with **be going to**.

Plans after Graduation

1. *Sara*: Hey, Andi! We (graduate) _____ this month. Can you

    believe it?

2. *Megan*: It's definitely exciting. What (you, do) _____ after

    graduation?

3. *Sara*: I'm not sure. I (probably, move) _____ back to my parents'

    house.

4. *Megan*: Really? You (not, take) _____ that job offer in the city.

5. *Sara*: Well, the salary (not, be) _____ high enough to cover my

    rent.

EXERCISE 8. Editing: Is It Correct?

If the sentence is correct, write a check mark (✓) on the line. If it is not correct, write an X on the line and circle the mistake. Then make the change above the sentence. (*Hint*: Every sentence has an error.)

Planting an Urban Garden

_____ 1. As populations increase, there are going to be limited space in cities.

_____ 2. Many people is still going to want fresh vegetables.

_____ 3. Because of limited space, gardeners going to get more creative.

_____ 4. Apartment buildings goes to have gardening resources available to their tenants.

_____ 5. We are going to different types of planting materials available.

_____ 6. Even large items like an an apple tree is going to be more compact.

_____ 7. People with larger gardens going to need to reduce their plant size, too.

_____ 8. It's going to exciting to see the new kinds of tools and innovations for urban gardening in the next few years.

Do Online Exercise 9.2. My score: _____ /10. _____ % correct.

 **Grammar Lesson**

KEY
4

Will for Future Time

Will + VERB has the same grammar forms as other modals that you have learned.

Affirmative Form: I/you/he/she/it/we/they **will + VERB.**

Negative Form: I/you/he/she/it/we/they **won't (will not) + VERB**

The form is easy to learn, but the uses and meanings take time to acquire.

1. future plans that are made **at or near the moment of speaking**

2. predictions that are less certain **(evidence is not required)**

3. promises **(with I)**

4. offers to help / requests for help

5. formal announcements

	Examples
Affirmative	I/you/he/she/it/we/they will call you later. I'll call you later. (casual way of ending a conversation) I'll call you tomorrow. (promise, because of *I*) She'll call you tomorrow. (prediction) Sign on door: The bank will be closed tomorrow (formal announcement)
Negative	I will not call you tomorrow. (formal or possibly angry) I won't call you tomorrow. (plan made at moment of speaking)
Yes-no question	Will you call me tomorrow? (request)
***Wh–* question**	When will you call me? (wanting a prediction) Where will you be tomorrow? (wanting a prediction)
Short answers	Speaker 1: What are you going to wear to the party Friday night? Speaker 2: I'm going to wear black pants. Speaker 1: OK. I will, too. (plan made at moment of speaking)
	(a woman is at a store with a baby in her arms and she is trying to open a door) Speaker 3: Can someone get the door for me? Speaker 4: Yes, I'll help. (offer to help)

Rule 1. You cannot use **will** for future intentions that you have already planned. We ask, **What are you going to do tomorrow?** not usually ~~What will you do tomorrow?~~

Rule 2. You can use will for a last-minute change in plans. For example, if your friend has planned to play golf tomorrow, we can ask, **What will you do if it rains tomorrow?** In other words, if Plan A is to play golf, then we are asking about Plan B.

Rule 3. The contraction for will not is **won't,** and in conversation we usually use **won't** instead of will not.

EXERCISE 9. *will* vs. *be going to*

Circle the correct form of the verb. Sometimes both may be possible.

Zander's New Baby

1. Zander and his wife (are going to have, will have) their first baby.

2. The baby (will be, is going to be) born on July 24th.

3. Zander's mom said, "I (will help, am going to help) you when the baby arrives."

4. Zander's wife told her mother-in-law, "Don't worry. We (are going to call, will call) you if the baby comes early!"

5. Zander promised his wife that he (will go, is going to go) to the pre-natal classes with her.

6. Zander's wife thinks that everyone (will like, is going to like) the baby's name when they hear it.

7. Her mother (will make, is going to make) a baby hat and blanket for her new grandchild.

8. Zander is sure that his wife (is going to have, will have) a safe and easy delivery.

Grammar Lesson

Present Perfect Tense

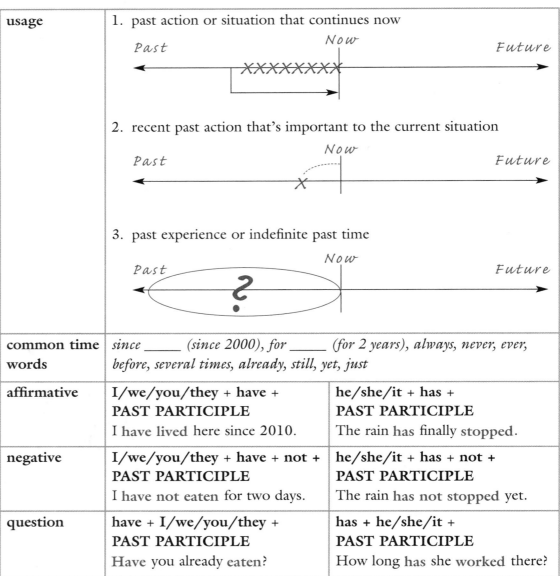

usage	1. past action or situation that continues now
	2. recent past action that's important to the current situation
	3. past experience or indefinite past time
common time words	*since _____ (since 2000), for _____ (for 2 years), always, never, ever, before, several times, already, still, yet, just*
affirmative	I/we/you/they + **have** + PAST PARTICIPLE I have lived here since 2010.	he/she/it + **has** + PAST PARTICIPLE The rain has finally stopped.
negative	I/we/you/they + **have** + **not** + PAST PARTICIPLE I have not eaten for two days.	he/she/it + **has** + **not** + PAST PARTICIPLE The rain has not stopped yet.
question	**have** + I/we/you/they + PAST PARTICIPLE Have you already eaten?	**has** + he/she/it + PAST PARTICIPLE How long has she worked there?

<u>Rule 1</u>. Use have for **I/you/we/they.** Use has for **he/she/it.**

<u>Rule 2</u>. The **PAST PARTICIPLE** is the second part of the present perfect tense. You can find a list of past participle forms in Appendix C.

<u>Rule 3</u>. The negative of present perfect is have not (haven't) or has not (hasn't).

Rule 4. To make a question with present perfect tense, move have or has before the subject: **Have you ever eaten sushi? OR** How long has **Maria lived in China?**

Rule 5. Present perfect tense has several distinct usages. Three common usages include:
  (A) an action that began in the past but continues now. (We **have lived** here for 10 years; I **have worked** here since 2002.)
  (B) a past (often recent) action that is important to now. (She **has** just **eaten** lunch.)
  (C) a past action that occurred at an indefinite time in the past. (I **have traveled** to Dubai.)

Rule 5. Ever and yet are used with questions (about indefinite time) and negative answers (about an action that has not happened so far).

 BE CAREFUL!

Common Learner Errors	Explanation
1. I ~~play~~ have played the piano since I was 10 years old.	Don't use simple present tense for an action that began in the past and still continues.
2. In 2010, I ~~have lived~~ lived in Bogota, Colombia.	Don't use present perfect tense for a specific past time (*in 2010*).

EXERCISE 10. Understanding Present Perfect Tense

Read each example of the present perfect. Determine which time is being expressed. Place a check mark in the appropriate column.

Examples with Present Perfect	Continues to Now	Recent Past	Indefinite Past
1. Have you ever bought roses before?			
2. Tammy taught at the college for 15 years.			
3. My wife has just told me we're having another baby!			
4. Pilar has worked on her master's thesis for 9 months now.			
5. Rob and Kelly have lived in their neighborhood for 2 years.			
6. Have they eaten at the Thai restaurant downtown yet?			

 **Grammar Lesson**

Present Perfect Progressive Tense

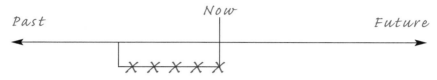

usage	The present perfect progressive tense is used to express an action that began in the past and is continuing now with emphasis on the fact that it is still happening.	
common time words	*since _____ (since 2000), for _____ (for 2 years), all _____ (all year)*	
affirmative	**I/we/you/they + have + been + VERB + –ing** I have been living here since 2010.	**he/she/it + has + been + VERB + –ing** The meat has been cooking all night.
negative	**I/we/you/they + have + not + been + VERB + –ing** I have not been sleeping well recently.	**he/she/it + has + not + been + VERB + –ing** That door has not been squeaking for a long time.
question	**have + I/we/you/they + been + VERB + –ing** Have you been waiting for a long time?	**has + he/she/it + been + VERB + –ing** How long has she been working there?

Rule 1. Use have/has + been + VERB + –ing to form the present perfect progressive.

Rule 2. Negatives are formed by adding not or n't after have/has.

Rule 3. Questions are formed by moving have/has in front of the subject: Has **she** been studying **all day?**

EXERCISE 11. Practicing Present Perfect Progressive Tense

Rewrite each sentence by changing the verb to present perfect progressive tense. In some cases, you can use the time words from the original sentences, but in many cases, you will need to change the time words.

1. Sean talked to his mother.

   _____

2. I felt sick last week.

   _____

3. My husband's volleyball team has won all their games so far.

   _____

4. We have worked at the local organic market.

   _____

5. We waited for the doctor for over an hour.

   _____

6. Jill tried to find a new job.

   _____

Do Online Exercise 9.3. My score: _____ /10. _____ % correct.

 **Grammar Lesson**

 KEY 3

Past Progressive Tense

usage	1. To emphasize what we were doing at a certain time in the past.
	2. To tell what action was happening in the past when another action interrupted it. In other words, the first had begun and was continuing when the second action occurred.
	3. To describe two or more actions that were happening at the same time.
common time words	*while, when*	
affirmative	I/he/she/it + was + VERB + –ing I was watching TV when my cell rang.	you/we/they + were + VERB + –ing You were preparing for your trip all day yesterday.
negative	I/he/she/it + was + not + VERB + –ing I was not watching TV when you called me.	you/we/they + were + not + VERB + –ing You were not preparing for your trip all day yesterday.
question	Was + I/he/she/it + VERB + –ing Was it raining at your house when you woke up this morning?	Were + you/we/they + VERB + –ing Were you sleeping when I called you last night?

Rule 1. Use was for **I/he/she/it.** Use were for **you/we/they.**

Rule 2. To make a negative, add *not*: was not (wasn't) or were not (weren't).

Rule 3. To make a question with past progressive tense, move was or were before the subject.

Rule 4. If one past action interrupts another past action, the longer action is usually in past progressive tense and the shorter action that interrupted it is in simple past tense.

Rule 5. We usually use while with 2 actions happening at the same time and when for the action that interrupts the other.

BE CAREFUL!

Common Learner Errors	Explanation
1. When I got my first job, I ~~was live~~ was living in Los Angeles.	Progressive tenses always need an **–ing** on the verb. Don't use two verbs in simple past if one was already in progress when the other one interrupted it.
2. From 2010 to 2011, I ~~was owning~~ owned two cars.	**Own** is not an action. Do not use **–ing** with a verb that does not show action.

EXERCISE 12. Past Progressive Tense to Talk about People's Actions

Tara is marrying her fiancé (Greg) this Saturday at a historic building in their town. Carolyn is Tara's mother, who is helping her with the wedding. Use the past progressive and/or simple past tenses with **while/when** to describe what they were doing earlier this morning. It is now lunch time. Use the information from this chart. The first one has been done for you as an example.

	Tara	Greg	Carolyn
6:00 AM	waking up	sleeping	
6:30 AM		sleeping	calling Tara
7:00 AM	texting bridesmaids	waking up	
7:30 AM		getting coffee	driving to Tara's
8:00 AM	getting her hair done		picking up the cake
8:30 AM		finding his tuxedo	getting her nails done
9:00 AM	getting her wedding dress on		arrived at the building
9:30 AM	texted Greg	eating breakfast	
9:35 AM		arrived at building	helping Tara's dad with his tuxedo
10:00 AM	walked down the aisle	smiled at Tara	

1. At 6:00, <u>Tara was waking up when Greg was still sleeping.</u>

2. At 6:30, _____

3. At 7:00, _____

4. At 7:30, _____

5. At 8:00, _____

6. At 8:30, _____

7. At 9:00, _____

8. At 9:30, _____

9. At 9:45, _____

10. At 10:00, _____

ONE-MINUTE LESSON

The word **just** has several meanings. When it refers to an action that happened a short time ago, we have the option in current English to use either present perfect or simple past tense. Some grammar books insist on present perfect tense only, but modern usage has changed, and now simple past tense is the same. Therefore, you can say *I have* **just** *cooked dinner* or *I* **just** *cooked dinner* with no difference in meaning.

EXERCISE 13. Contrasting Verb Tenses in Context

Read each sentence. Think about the time of the action, and then write the verb in the correct verb tense on the line. Use the tenses practiced in this unit.

1. **tell**

   a. We _____ you about the play yesterday.

   b. They _____ us about the play tomorrow.

   c. I _____ him about the play since last Friday.

2. **arrange**

   a. A travel agent _____ vacations every day.

   b. Next week I _____ our spring break plans.

   c. He _____ for us to stay at the best hotel when we went to Paris last summer.

   d. Sheila _____ flowers since she was a young girl.

3. **sit**

   a. My husband always _____ in the middle of the movie theatre.

   b. Jerry _____ next to his sister on the bus.

   c. Erin _____ in the café waiting for Steph right now.

   d. We wanted to be in the mezzanine seats for the opera, but a group _____ there already.

4. **walk**

   a. I _____ for one mile each day on my lunch break.

   b. Tony _____ Cheryl home last night because the weather was nice and they wanted the exercise.

   c. Sharon _____ through the grocery store when a shelf collapsed on her cart.

   d. I _____ that hiking path many times in the past.

   e. My grandma _____ with my son in our neighborhood right now.

EXERCISE 14. Mini-Conversations

Circle the correct words in these five mini-conversations.

1. A: How many countries in South America (are, were, have been, are going to be) landlocked?

   B: Two. Bolivia and Paraguay (do not have, did not have, have not had, are not going to have) direct access to a sea or ocean.

2. A: When you (are living, live, have lived, lived) in France last year, how many times (are you going, were you going, do you go, did you go, have you gone) to Paris?

   B: During that time, I (go, am going, was going, have gone, went) to Paris only twice, so I (am, was, have been, am going to be, was going to be) there a total of five times so far.

3. A: Wow, you (are, were, have been, are going to be, were being) all wet!

   B: Yes, I (don't take, didn't take, am not taking, was not taking, have not taken) my umbrella when I (leave, am leaving, left, have left, have been leaving) my house this morning because it (didn't rain, hasn't rained, hasn't been raining, wasn't raining) then, but on the way here, the sky suddenly (is opening, has opened, opened) up, so of course I (get, got, have gotten, are going to get, were getting) wet. I really need a towel now so I can dry off.

4. A: What's your plan for tomorrow?

   B: I (think, have thought, am going to think) we (stay, will stay, have stayed, have been staying) home.

5. A: Those onions that you (fry, are frying) smell great. What (do you cook, are you cooking, have you cooked)?

   B: It (is, was, has been, was being) a chicken dish. It's a little spicy, so I (am not knowing, don't know, haven't known, am not going to know, won't know) if you can eat it because you generally (aren't liking, don't like, have not liked) hot foods.

EXERCISE 16. Sentence Study for Critical Reading

Read the numbered sentences. Then read the three answer choices and put a check mark (✓) in the yes or no box in front of each sentence to indicate if that answer is true based on the information in the original sentence. If there is not enough information to mark something as yes, then mark it as no. Remember that more than one true answer may be possible.

1. Steve was eating a veggie pizza this afternoon when he burned his tongue very badly.

   ☐ yes ☐ no   a. Steve was eating hot sauce before he had veggie pizza.

   ☐ yes ☐ no   b. Steve burned his tongue because the pizza was hot.

   ☐ yes ☐ no   c. The pizza was hot at the time that Steve ate it.

2. I have three cats. I've had two of them for six years, and the third one is new.

   ☐ yes ☐ no   a. The cats are the same age.

   ☐ yes ☐ no   b. One cat is still a kitten.

   ☐ yes ☐ no   c. Seven years ago, I did not have any of these cats.

3. Cheryl and Penny have wanted to go to Paris since they were little girls. Cheryl won a trip to Paris and will take Penny next March.

   ☐ yes ☐ no   a. Cheryl and Penny went to Paris last March.

   ☐ yes ☐ no   b. Cheryl and Penny are in Paris now.

   ☐ yes ☐ no   c. Cheryl and Penny are going to Paris.

4. Lucy and Ron are expecting their fourth child soon. They need to get a minivan.

   ☐ yes ☐ no   a. Lucy and Ron have three kids now.

   ☐ yes ☐ no   b. Lucy and Ron's children have all moved out of the house.

   ☐ yes ☐ no   c. Ron thinks he should get a motorcycle.

5. Susan bought a house three years ago for $150,000. Last week, a similar house in her neighborhood sold for $250,000.

   ☐ yes ☐ no   a. Three years ago, houses in Susan's neighborhood were worth more.

   ☐ yes ☐ no   b. Susan spent $200,000 more than she should own her house.

   ☐ yes ☐ no   c. The price of a house like Susan's in her neighborhood now is $150,000.

6. When Katya gets a job, she will have to buy a new car.

    ☐ yes ☐ no   a. Katya has a job now.

    ☐ yes ☐ no   b. Katya needs a new car right now.

    ☐ yes ☐ no   c. We do not know if Katya has a car right now or not.

7. Jorge works for his wife, but he plans on starting his own business next year.

    ☐ yes ☐ no   a. Jorge's wife is his employee.

    ☐ yes ☐ no   b. Jorge started his own business last year.

    ☐ yes ☐ no   c. Jorge might stop working for his wife next year.

8. My dad bought a filter for his kitchen faucet because the water is not clear.

    ☐ yes ☐ no   a. My dad will need a water filter for his kitchen faucet.

    ☐ yes ☐ no   b. My dad bought a kitchen faucet.

    ☐ yes ☐ no   c. My dad didn't want to drink from his kitchen faucet as it was.

EXERCISE 16. Review Test 1: Multiple Choice

Circle the letter of the correct answer. Some are conversations.

1. "_____ the new romantic comedy that came out last Friday yet?"

   "No, but I want to."

a. Do you see	c. You are seeing
b. Are you seeing	d. Have you seen

2. "_____ some of Mom's blueberry pie?"

   "Yes! It was so delicious!"

a. Have you try	c. Do you try
b. Did you try	d. Did you tried

3. "What time _____ out of school on weekdays?"

   "At 3:45 p.m."

a. does your son get	c. is getting your son
b. does get your son	d. your son is getting

4. "Children! _____ this mess in the family room?"

   "Not me!"

a. Who does make	c. Who made
b. Who making	d. Who maked

5. "I called you three times last night to go see a movie with us, but you didn't answer."

   "Oh, sorry. I _____ for my big exam when you called."

a. studied	c. have studied
b. was studying	d. am studied

6. "Oh, no! I forgot to buy food for the turtles!"

   "Don't worry. Tina _____ some food for them earlier today."

      a. has already bought   c. already buy

      b. have already bought   d. did already buy

7. "Did you mow the yard?

   "No, but I _____ it later this afternoon."

      a. will do   c. will doing

      b. have done   d. do

8. "How long _____ sitting here on the counter?"

   "I don't know."

      a. has this milk be   c. have this milk being

      b. been this milk   d. has this milk been

EXERCISE 17. Review Test 2: Production and Evaluation

Part 1.
Read this short passage. Fill in the blanks with the correct tense of the word in parentheses.

Rob and Oksana, U.S. Paralympians

My friends Rob and Oksana (be) ❶ _____ athletes. They (represent)

❷ _____ the United States in rowing. They (begin) ❸ _____ training

together a year ago. What (make) ❹ _____ them unique is that they (not,

have) ❺ _____ legs. Rob (lose) ❻ _____ his legs while serving

with the Marines in Afghanistan, and Oksana (not, have) ❼ _____ legs

when she was born near Chernobyl in the Ukraine.

Oksana (start) ❽ _____ at the age of 13. She (win) ❾ _____

many races since she began rowing. Many of her medals (be) ❿ _____ gold

medals. Oksana (set) ⓫ _____ a world record at a young age, too.

Rob (not, start) ⓬ _____ rowing until after he (served) ⓭ _____

in the military. In addition to rowing competitions, he (participate)

⓮ _____ in triathalons—without legs!

Rob and Oksana (compete) ⓯ _____ against other disabled rowers

in the past and (set) ⓰ _____ world records. They (become) ⓱ _____

the U.S. representatives in the Trunk & Arms Rowing Paralympics. They (go)

⓲ _____ to the Paraplympics last summer, which (be) ⓳ _____ held

every four years. They (train) ⓴ _____ very hard for the future Paralympics

as well, and they (hope) ㉑ _____ to bring home even more gold medals

for their country. I (watch) ㉒ _____ them on television whenever they

have an event.

Part 2.

Read each entence carefully. Look at the underlined part in the sentence. If the underlined part is correct, circle the word *correct*. If it is wrong, circle the word *wrong*. Then write the correct form above.

correct   wrong   1. We <u>are going to watch</u> the play last week.

correct   wrong   2. Aaron <u>has eaten</u> at that Colombian restaurant many times.

correct   wrong   3. I <u>am wanting</u> to get a haircut this week.

correct   wrong   4. Ava <u>water</u> her herb garden every day.

correct   wrong   5. Dana <u>is going to be</u> in New York City next Tuesday.

correct   wrong   6. Barack Obama <u>has been</u> born on Auust 4, 1961.

correct   wrong   7. Tuna casserole <u>was made</u> from macaroni, tuna fish, and
                              vegetables.

correct   wrong   8. The giraffe is the tallest living creature that <u>lives</u> on land.

EXERCISE 18. Reading Practice: Thinking Critically about an Accomplishment

Read the passage about teenager who is getting his driver's license, and then answer the comprehension questions that follow. In this reading passage, at least one example of each verb tense that has been reviewed in this unit is underlined for you.

Jordan Gets His Driver's License

Jordan is 16 years old. He lives in Oklahoma City with his parents and older sister, Gabriela. Jordan has been driving with his learner's permit for six months. The learner's permit means that he cannot drive by himself, so he usually drives with his father, Ben. Gabriela is 18 and has her driver's license, but she does not like driving with Jordan.

When Jordan took his written test to get his learner's permit, he got a very high score. Since he passed the learner's permit test, he has shown that he knows driving rules, road signs, and general driving safety. He thought that since he scored very high, he would be a great driver. Unfortunately, Jordan was wrong.

One problem is that Jordan does not have confidence when he is driving. He knows that he should not be aggressive when driving, but he often waits too long to make simple driving decisions. This makes the people driving behind him very angry, and sometimes they will honk at him.

He also pulls out in front of other cars and drives slowly, causing them to slam on their brakes quickly. This is not safe. He also drives slowly in the left lane, which is the passing lane for cars that are traveling at a faster speed. These two things will cause an accident if Jordan continues to do them. His parents have told him to drive faster and have more confidence, and they think that he is driving a little better now.

Yesterday Jordan's mom <u>took</u> him to the driver's license office to take his driving test. She <u>sat</u> in the waiting room while Jordan and the driver's test administrator <u>took</u> her car out on the road. When she <u>looked</u> at Jordan's face when he <u>returned</u>, he <u>was smiling</u>. He passed! Because Jordan has his driver's license, he <u>will drive</u> to his part-time job and <u>pick up</u> groceries at the store for his mom. Jordan <u>is going to save</u> money for his own car.

1. Place a check mark (✓) to indicate if each description is true for Jordan, Gabriela, both of them, or neither of them.

Description	Jordan	Gabriela	Both	Neither
a. is 18 years old				
b. has been in an accident				
c. failed the learner's permit exam				
d. is saving money for a new car				
e. helped his/her sibling practice driving				
f. has a driver's license				

2. List at least 3 dangerous things that Jordan does while he is driving.

a. _____

_____

b. _____

_____

c. _____

_____

EXERCISE 19. Vocabulary Practice: Word Knowledge

Circle the answer choice on the right that is most closely related to the vocabulary on the left. Use a dictionary to check the meaning of words you do not know.

Vocabulary	Answer Choices	
1. quote	your goods	your words
2. fog	hard to see	hard to write
3. afford	able to pay	able to walk
4. ancient	very afraid	very old
5. pregnant	a janitor	a mother
6. a bypass	a type of house	a type of road
7. assisted	attended	helped
8. motivated	avoid doing	want to do
9. client	buyer	pilot
10. a patient	a sick person	a smart person
11. found out	discarded	learned
12. predict	the future	the past
13. struggle	with a gift	with a problem
14. off and on	from time to time	very easy to do
15. amount	statement	total
16. moist	a little expensive	a little wet
17. a pamphlet	food	information
18. a penguin	a type of bird	a type of vehicle
19. resign	begin a job	leave a job
20. vary	be different	be the same
21. malaria	a disease	a machine
22. a gem	an app	a jewel
23. a pyramid	like a circle	like a triangle
24. a checkout line	at the airport	at the supermarket
25. a boarding pass	at the airport	at the supermarket
26. to be fit	exercising	intervening
27. a shake	you drink it	you organize it
28. a compliment	"Don't do that!"	"Great job!"
29. a journalist	a nurse	a writer
30. a cruise	by plane	by ship
31. lately	not early	recently
32. went off	an airplane	an alarm
33. liquid	cream	ice cream

EXERCISE 20. Vocabulary Practice: Collocations

Fill in each blank with the answer on the right that most naturally completes the phrase on the left. If necessary, use a dictionary to check the meaning of words you do not know.

Phrase	Answer Choices	
1. install a _____	key	lock
2. intense _____	feelings	pickles
3. verify _____	your age	your new socks
4. in the 9th _____	floor	grade
5. rake _____	animals	leaves
6. _____ asleep	fall	take
7. the _____ is boiling	meat	soup
8. earn _____	money	taxes
9. rely _____ someone	in	on
10. take up our _____	papers	times
11. a boarding _____	pass	turn
12. come over to _____	the roof	my house
13. _____ my laundry	do	make
14. _____ a problem	identify	scramble
15. a _____ carton	coffee	milk
16. in 2 more _____	day	days
17. on the _____ shelf	average	bottom
18. an application _____ a job	for	to
19. I wonder _____ it will rain	by	if
20. variety of _____	search	subjects
21. _____ up	heavy	hurry
22. once _____ month	a	the
23. an _____ hour	almost	entire
24. _____ way	no	yes
25. a _____ battery	dead	silent
26. associate X _____ Y	for	with
27. I've lived here _____ 10 years	for	since
28. where we _____ our anniversary	brought	spent
29. the _____ forecast	supermarket	weather
30. a patient in a _____	bank	hospital
31. canned _____	sports	tuna
32. we feel _____	absent	upset
33. concerned _____ the weather	about	for

EXERCISE 22. Writing Practice: Describing a Person's Accomplishments

Part 1. Editing Student Writing

Read these sentences about a famous person. Circle the 15 errors. Then write the number of the sentence with the error next to the type of error. (Some sentences have more than one error.)

___ a. verb tense   ___ d. articles

___ b. subject-verb agreement   ___ e. prepositions

___ c. passive voice   ___ f. singular-plural of nouns

Nelson Mandela
1. Nelson Mandela was the South Africa's first black president.
2. To rest of the world, Nelson Mandela remembered for his determination to help his people become free.
3. His full name were Nelson Rolihlahla Mandela.
4. He was born on July 18, 1918, and dies on December 5, 2013.
5. For most of his lifetime, people of different race were separated in all aspects of public life through a system that called apartheid.
6. Because of his resistance to apartheid on South Africa, he spent more than 27 year in jail.
7. He released on 1990 after a huge international campaign against his imprisonment.
8. In 1993, he was awarded the Nobel Peace Prize for his efforts to make South Africa better country for all of its citizen.
9. In 2004, he has campaigned for South Africa to host the 2010 World Cup matches.
10. The whole world mourned the loss of this international symbol of hope for the better life.

Part 2. Original Student Writing

Write one or two paragraphs about someone who lived more than one hundred years ago. Be sure to include supporting details. Pay attention to the verb tenses you use. Underline each verb tense to show your teacher what you are trying to practice.

Unit 10

Review of Units 1–9

This unit contains two types of review practices for the grammar covered in *Clear Grammar 3*.

Part 1: Comprehensive Review (five tests of 25 multiple choice questions on all nine units)

Part 2: Individual Units (nine review practices, one for each of the nine units)

The multiple choice questions in the five tests in Part 1 can be used as an objective assessment of the material covered in this book. You may do this unit after completing all previous nine units, or you may take these tests after certain intervals such as every two units. Following this schedule, you would do Test 1 after Units 1 and 2, Test 2 after Units 3 and 4, etc. If you follow this schedule, your scores should be lower on Test 1 and much higher by Test 5 since you would be progressing through the material in the book and on the tests. Remember that the tests in Part 1 are comprehensive and each covers all nine units.

The completion questions in the nine tests in Part 2 cover each of the nine units one by one. Thus, there is a test for Unit 1, a test for Unit 2, etc. You may use these tests as a diagnostic pre-test to see if you need to complete a given unit. Of course the tests in Part 2 can also be used as additional assessments after you have completed the units.

Part 1: Comprehensive Review

Test 1.

Write the letter of the correct answer on the line.

1. Would you mind _____ us?

    a. to ask Jo helping   c. asking Jo helping

    b. to ask Jo to help   d. asking Jo to help

2. The number _____ wrote on the envelope is not my telephone number.

    a. that   b. that you   c. where   d. where you

3. I learned the vocabulary words _____ them five times every day.

    a. by writing   b. to write   c. for writing   d. written

4. The current Canadian flag _____ in 1965.

    a. was adopted   b. adopted   c. was adopting   d. had been adopting

5. How many people who are alive today _____ in World War I?

    a. have served   b. serving   c. was going to serve   d. served

6. Your brother reminds me _____ my best friend from elementary school.

    a. by   b. from   c. in   d. of

7. The watch that I wanted to buy was too expensive. _____ I couldn't buy it.

    a. Therefore   b. Therefore,   c. Although   d. Although,

8. In the story of Cinderella, the main character _____ with her step-family.

    a. has lived   b. living   c. was living   d. was lived

9. The teacher called _____.

    a. the sleeping student on   c. the slept student on

    b. on the sleeping student   d. on the slept student

10. The arrested man was found guilty _____ stealing the money.

    a. about   b. from   c. in   d. of

11. The items that _____ in the store window were on sale.

    a. placed   b. have placed   c. were placed   d. were placing

12. _____, I have not been sleeping very _____.

   a. Lately/good   b. Lately/well   c. Late/good   d. Late/well

13. The candidate _____ did not win the election.

   a. for whom we voted   c. whom we voted

   b. whose we voted for   d. for which we voted

14. Most of the workers come to the factory _____ a bus.

   a. by   b. with   c. for   d. on

15. When I finish writing this report, then I can concentrate _____ my project.

   a. about   b. for   c. on   d. with

16. A fire started because someone tried to _____ a cigarette in the trash can.

   a. put off   b. put out   c. took off   d. took out

17. They reacted to the news by _____ anything.

   a. do not say   b. no saying   c. not say   d. not saying

18. When I arrived at the airport, I found that the police _____ everyone's passports, tickets, and any other documentation for security reasons.

   a. checked   b. were checking   c. have checked   d. going to check

19. We do not use a comma _____ an independent clause precedes a dependent clause.

   a. which   b. , which   c. when   d. , when

20. Ottawa, _____ is the capital of Canada, is not the biggest city.

   a. which   b. that   c. where   d. whose

21. TV commercials being played now constantly urge _____.

   a. we to vote   b. we vote   c. us to vote   d. us voting

22. The bus waited _____ as long as possible, but eventually it left.

   a. for   b. in   c. on   d. up

23. English and German _____ from left to right.

   a. write   b. are written   c. is written   d. are writing

24. _____ relaxes some people, but we don't enjoy it very much.

    a. Going shopping   c. To go shopping

    b. Going to shop   d. To go to shop

25. The university entrance exam _____ last week was very difficult.

    a. that given   b. which given   c. that gave   d. given

Test 2.

Write the letter of the correct answer on the line.

1. If you keep _____ to the dentist, you will really regret it later in life!

    a. to avoid going   b. to avoid to go   c. avoiding going   d. avoiding to go

2. The children were tired _____ playing outside all day.

    a. by   b. from   c. in   d. to

3. Some students who have not completed their homework are known for _____ incredible stories to explain why they were not able to finish their work on time.

    a. putting on   b. put on   c. making up   d. make up

4. When Flight 330 took _____ the weather was just starting to get bad.

    a. off, so   b. off, and   c. off,   d. off

5. Benjamin Franklin traveled extensively, but who knows how many countries he _____?

    a. visited   b. was visiting   c. has visited   d. has been vistiing

6. People _____ in the downtown area of the city lost electricity last night.

    a. where live   b. whom live   c. lived   d. living

7. When lightning _____, there is a strong possibility of serious damage, injury, and even death.

    a. struck   b. has struck   c. strikes   d. is striking

8. Many teachers believe that your vocabulary knowledge _____ with your reading ability.

    a. connected   b. has connected   c. is connecting   d. is connected

9. Are you ready _____ your big interview tomorrow?

    a. about   b. for   c. in   d. on

10. When Jill visited Mexico City in 1985, there _____ a huge earthquake that _____ certain areas of the city for the next decade or so.

    a. was / has affected   c. has been / affected

    b. was / affected   d. has been / has affected

11. Restaurant customers often show their dissatisfaction by _____ a tip.

    a. not leave   b. not leaving   c. no leave   d. no leaving

12. Prices for dictionaries _____ from around $5 to about $25.

    a. range   b. are ranged   c. were ranged   d. can be ranging

13. Where is the main office _____ passports?

    a. issue   b. that issue   c. issues   d. that issues

14. The President spoke to the nation by radio _____ the election took place.

    a. , for   b. for   c. , before   d. before

15. Whenever I _____ to relax, I prefer to sit outside and read a good book that will take my mind away.

    a. wanted   b. have wanted   c. want   d. am wanting

16. I agree _____ you on nine of the ten topics.

    a. about   b. for   c. in   d. with

17. Coins _____ in the city of Denver bear the letter D.

    a. that minted   b. that are minted c. minting   d. have been minting

18. Is anyone _____ to a movie tonight?

    a. interesting in going   c. interesting in go

    b. interested in going   d. interested in go

19. I prefer to pay by _____ whenever it is possible.

    a. a credit card   b. credit card   c. a telephone   d. the telephone

20. The employee _____ name was announced at the meeting has won a trip to London.

    a. who   b. whose   c. who's   d. which

21. Parents get angry when their children don't put their things _____.

    a. away   b. in   c. on   d. to

22. The decision she made to leave the company _____ everyone off guard.

    a. caught   b. was catching   c. are catching   d. has been caught

23. I'm really looking forward _____ that actor's new movie.

    a. to seeing   b. to see   c. seeing   d. see

24. Today's special plate _____ fresh pasta with a little cheese.

    a. is contained   b. contains   c. that is contained   d. that contains

25. Here are the tomatoes you asked me _____ for you.

    a. buy   b. to buy   c. buying   d. have bought

Test 3.
Write the letter of the correct answer on the line.

1. A dictionary allows us to _____ the meaning of new words.

    a. call back   b. fill in   c. look up   d. turn on

2. Argentina is a country _____ people consume a great deal of meat.

    a. that   b. whose   c. for which   d. where

3. We made certain that we thanked the hosts _____ a great meal.

    a. for   b. in   c. on   d. to

4. The English alphabet _____ of 26 letters but many more sounds.

    a. that is consisted   c. is consisted

    b. that consists   d. consists

5. Good students always _____ before a major exam.

    a. go over their notes   c. pass away their notes

    b. go their notes over   d. pass their notes away

6. We have never traveled to Europe, so our trip next week _____ our first time there.

    a. has been   b. will be   c. have been   d. was

7. The movie was very interesting, _____ I enjoyed seeing all of my friends there.

    a. and   b. because   c. while   d. in order

8. She won the contest _____ an outstanding essay.

    a. by submit   b. by submitting   c. for submit   d. for submitting

9. Can anyone think _____ a different way to solve this problem?

    a. about   b. by   c. for   d. of

10. Some people enjoy _____ long distances.

    a. to drive   b. drive   c. from driving   d. driving

11. The box _____ contained more than 50 paperback books.

    a. that the company delivered   c. that delivered the company

    b. the company was delivered   d. was delivering the company

12. _____ their goals, the directors hired a manager who could help them with their objectives.

    a. To achieve   b. Achieving   c. Achieve   d. For achieve

13. _____ lose weight quickly, some people avoid all types of bread, rice, and pasta.

    a. For   b. If   c. Consequently,   d. In order to

14. Spanish is a language _____ many people assume is easy to learn.

    a. where   b. that   c. for   d. for which

15. The parents of the student submitted a request _____ more information.

    a. about   b. for   c. on   d. to

16. How long _____ at this company so far?

    a. have you worked   c. are you working

    b. did you work   d. will you work

17. I mailed a letter to Argentina, and it _____ ten days to reach Buenos Aires.

    a. took   b. was taking   c. has taken   d. takes

18. Parents expect their children _____ safe in school.

    a. being   b. be   c. to be   d. are being

19. _____ more money, I use coupons when I buy my groceries.

    a. For save   b. For saving   c. To save   d. To saving

20. A common reason _____ people want to work for an airline is that they want to see the world.

    a. because   b. that   c. when   d. whose

21. At first, no one in our group _____ the cat because it was hissing so fiercely.

    a. was approached   c. has approached

    b. approached   d. were approaching

22. If a bright shirt _____ with white clothing, the white clothing can sometimes turn colors.

    a. washes   c. which washes

    b. is washed   d. which is washing

23. We had to contact the airline _____ out where our luggage was.

    a. to finding   b. for find   c. for finding   d. to find

24. Most people have a positive opinion _____ the Vice President.

    a. at   b. for   c. of   d. to

25. Dr. Miller is the professor _____ we admire the most.

    a. which   b. whom   c. for which   d. for whom

Test 4.

Write the letter of the correct answer on the line.

1. We are sad to hear that Mrs. Jackson has _____.

    a. passed away   b. passed her away c. called on   d. called her on

2. Will your boss allow children _____ their parents' office during work hours?

    a. visit   b. visiting   c. to visit   d. are visiting

3. Three famous actors _____ in the new film about a hijacked airplane.

    a. star   c. who are starring

    b. starring   d. who are starred

4. They added two additional flights to Chicago _____ the heavy passenger demand.

    a. to handle   b. handling   c. for handling   d. have handled

5. I was so _____ when I was watching that movie.

    a. boring   b. bored   c. who are boring d. bore

6. The assignment is to make a list of ten _____ facts about Shakespeare's work.

    a. interested   b. interesting   c. interest   d. that interest

7. I want you _____ my uncle later.

    a. to remind me to call   c. to remind me calling

    b. reminding me to call   d. reminding me calling

8. A tornado is a powerful and destructive windstorm that _____ when warm and cool air masses collide.

    a. have occurred b. are occurring   c. occurs   d. occur

9. I misspelled the word by leaving one letter _____.

    a. away   b. by   c. out   d. over

10. _____ the problem better, the committee is having an extra meeting.

    a. For understand   c. To understand

    b. For understanding   d. To understanding

11. The newspaper _____ you want to buy will cost you two dollars.

    a. when   b. where   c. that   d. whose

12. The judge let the lawyer _____ the testimony a second time.

    a. to object to hearing   c. object to hear

    b. to object to hear   d. object to hearing

13. When all the votes have _____, we will know who the new president is.

    a. counted   b. been counting   c. are counting   d. been counted

14. Some people have switched to an electronic planner, but many others _____ to use a paper notebook as a planner.

    a. continue   c. have continued

    b. are continued   d. were continuing

15. My brother and I _____ go fishing when we were kids.

    a. were used to   b. used to   c. were ready for d. ready for

16. _____ you take a course in France, surely that will improve your French tremendously.

    a. Because   b. In order for   c. Consequently, d. If

17. _____ in a large restaurant can be a tedious and demanding job.

    a. Cooking   b. To cook   c. For cooking   D. Cook

18. _____ the best work possible, Jill is proofing her paper one more time.

    a. Producing   b. For produce   c. For producing d. To produce

19. In a _____ worded document, the workers hinted at a possible strike.

    a. careful very   b. very careful   c. very carefully   d. carefully very

20. People are genuinely _____ by the new tax rules.

    a. annoying   b. annoyed   c. who annoy   d. who annoyed

21. Time is up! Please pass _____ your exams.

    a. in   b. on   c. over   d. out

22. Abraham Lincoln, _____ was the sixteenth U.S. president, faced a difficult task with the Civil War.

    a. which   b. whose   c. whom   d. who

23. The famous French painter Monet was born in 1840 and _____ in 1926.

    a. who died   b. was died   c. died   d. who was died

24. A _____ number of elementary school students need help with their English language training.

    a. grow   b. grown   c. growing   d. is growing

25. _____ an airplane takes a great deal of practice as well as skill.

    a. Landing   b. To land   c. Land   d. When a pilot lands

Test 5.

Write the letter of the correct answer on the line.

1. The bride decided to call _____ the wedding because she had second thoughts.

    a. away   b. back   c. off   d. out

2. We believe that children who are taught in a class with no more than 18 students _____ better.

    a. learn   b. who learn   c. are learned   d. that are learned

3. Cats _____ orange, black, and white are called calico cats.

    a. are   b. that are   c. that   d. which

4. When I tried to walk to my car, the rain _____ sideways, so I went back in my house.

    a. blew   b. was blown   c. was blowing   d. has been blowing

5. When passengers _____ their flight, a flight attendant can help them find their correct seats.

    a. who are boarded   c. are boarded

    b. who board   d. board

6. I need _____ my father pay my rent this month because I'm broke.

    a. that   b. having   c. to have   d. have

7. The Sahara Desert _____ about one-third of Africa.

    a. that covers   b. covers   c. is covered   d. that is covered

8. I arrived at the office around 7 AM as usual, and then I _____ the windows to let some of the cool morning air into the room.

    a. was opening   c. am going to open

    b. opened   d. have opened

9. When people first visit that part of the world, they oftentimes _____ by all the modern technology available.

    a. amazed   b. are amazed   c. amazing   d. are amazing

10. It is not uncommon for _____ children to have nightmares.

    a. frightening   c. frightened

    b. who are frightening   d. whom are frightened

11. Why are you so interested _____ with kindergarten children?

    a. in working   b. for working   c. to work   d. by work

12. Our team was _____ defeated in our most _____ match.

    a. easy / recent   c. easily / recent

    b. easily / recently   d. easy / recently

13. The proverb "A penny saved is a penny _____" means that every cent that you save is one that you deserve because you have earned it.

    a. have earned   b. earned   c. that earned   d. earning

14. When I want to remember a new vocabulary word, I always _____.

    a. leave out it   b. leave it out   c. write down it   d. write it down

15. We'd really like _____ with us.

    a. that Miguel goes   c. inviting Miguel to go

    b. that Miguel to go   d. to invite Miguel to go

16. Rainy days are very _____ times for me.

    a. depressing   b. depressed   c. depress   d. to depress

17. A light _____ is the distance that light can travel in one year, is a huge number.

    a. year that   b. year, that   c. year which   d. year, which

18. The children quickly turned the _____

    a. boring show off   c. boring off show

    b. bored show off   d. bored off show

19. My neighbor's little children were fighting a few minutes ago, but now they have _____ up.

    a. made it   b. been made it   c. made   d. have been made

20. The president's decision _____ shocked everyone.

    a. resigned   b. resigning   c. to resign   d. has resigned

21. The rock _____ as pumice is the only rock that can float in water.

    a. which knew   b. which known   c. is known   d. known

22. I _____ to see how popcorn grows, and maybe one day I will get my wish.

    a. have always wanted   c. always want

    b. will always want   d. am always wanting

23. The news about the fire was very _____.

    a. disappoint   b. disappointed   c. disappointing   d. disappointment

24. I have been studying so much lately. I'm really _____.

    a. tired of study   c. tiring of study

    b. tired of studying   d. tiring of studying

25. To me, rice _____ with salt and a little butter is a simple and very delicious dish.

    a. that is cooked   b. that cooks   c. cooking   d. is cooked

Part 2: Individual Units

UNIT 1. Phrasal Verbs

Underline the correct word in parentheses.

1. The game has been cancelled. Both coaches decided to call (off it, it off).

2. I was out of the office for a week with the flu, and it took me a really long time to (catch with up, catch up with) all my work.

3. He is going to the store now because we have (come up with, looked up to, run out of) coffee.

4. Many people like living in an apartment, but I prefer a house so I don't have to put (up with noisy neighbors, with noisy neighbors up) so close to me.

5. Take this application and (fill out it, fill it out, put on it, put it on).

6. We are (counting, going, putting, taking) on you.

7. When you finish using my laptop, can you please put (back it, it back) on my desk?

8. Students who have not read the assigned chapters usually hope that the professor does not (call on them, call them on, tear up them, tear them up).

9. He tore (away, down, off, on, up) the letter because he didn't want to see it again.

10. When you visited your sister's kids, did you have to look (after them, them after) when your sister was at work?

11. The boy turned (in, off, on, out, up) the TV because he couldn't hear it well.

12. I think my apartment has fleas. How can I get rid (at, of, off, out) them?

13. It's usual in Japan to take your shoes (away, down, in, off, out, over) when you enter a house.

14. Let's (open up, put on, turn on) the TV to watch the news.

15. She made a mistake, so she (crossed, figured, found, picked) her answer out and rewrote it.

16. Driver, please stop here. We're going to that hotel across the street, so we can get (by, out, over, with) here.

17. When I clean my sofa cushions, I sometimes (come across lost coins, come lost coins across, look over lost coins, look lost coins over).

18. As an excuse for being late again, I (crossed out, made up, tried on) a story about (running into an old friend, running an old friend into) at the bank.

19. I took my notes with me to the interview so I could look (over them, them over) again.

20. Joe and Sue had an argument a few hours ago, but I think they have already made (up, it up, up it).

UNIT 2. Infinitives and Gerunds

Write the correct form of the word in parentheses. You must use the base form at times.

1. It is raining hard right now, so both coaches have decided (put) _____ off the start of the game until the weather clears up.

2. According to this report, hot air (balloon) _____ may (become) _____ an incredibly popular sport.

3. The thief denied (take) _____ the wallet, but a police photo convinced the jury (lock) _____ up the man for at least seven years.

4. We need (persuade) _____ our boss (permit) _____ everyone (take) _____ an additional day off.

5. The schedule has a problem in it, so I hope no one will (object) _____ to (change) _____ some of the meeting dates.

6. We expect all job seekers (have) _____ enough managerial experience (be) _____ able to run an office of fifteen employees.

7. (find) _____ an item that you lost a long time ago is always a surprise.

8. I was so excited about (pick) _____ up my uncle at the airport that I almost forgot (fill) _____ up the gas tank before I went to get him.

9. If you don't want (miss) _____ your flight, you should (leave) _____ for the airport by 7 AM.

10. Some children enjoy (pick) _____ out their own dinner dishes, but most of them need (have) _____ an adult who can (help) _____ them (make) _____ better choices.

11. In Dr. Sanderson's class, it is very difficult (succeed) _____ in (make) _____ an A on both the midterm and final exams.

12. You can (watch) _____ what you want by (select) _____ the channel and then (adjust) _____ the volume.

13. The teacher decided (have) _____ her students (make) _____ short speeches.

14. While I appreciate (be) _____ able (exercise) _____ in the morning, I would really like to work out more at home.

15. Would you mind (ask) _____ your brother (let) _____ us (use) _____ his car?

16. Our teacher came to class with a test for us, but the problem was that she forgot (tell) _____ us about the exam, so no one thought about (prepare) _____ for the test.

17. Do you think that pet owners should (allow) _____ their pets (lie) _____ on the furniture?

18. Because pumpkins grow on vines, they need (have) _____ a very large area (spread) _____ out.

19. Are you eager (start) _____ classes at Ford University?

20. Has your business ever considered (get) _____ a loan (increase) _____ its true sales potential?

UNIT 3. Participial Adjectives

Underline the correct word in parentheses.

1. I think that movie was one of the most (boring, bored) I've ever had to watch.

2. One of the (underlying, underlaid) reasons for the closure of that company is their recent decision to charge more for shipping, which is always a sore point for customers.

3. Are you (interesting, interested) in playing tennis tomorrow afternoon?

4. Is your boss a very (demanding, demanded) person?

5. Some well-(preserving, preserved) mummies are on display in the Cairo museum.

6. A robbery is a (terrifying, terrified) event for all those present.

7. The (injuring, injured) bus passengers were taken to the hospital at once.

8. A green (blinking, blinked) light means that there is a potential problem.

9. "A (watching, watched) pot never boils" is a proverb that means you cannot watch some things actually happen.

10. Making the final payment on a loan is a very (satisfying, satisfied) accomplishment.

11. No one was (surprising, surprised) at the boss's decision to retire.

12. The professor handed out our (grading, graded) papers yesterday.

13. What was your (deciding, decided) factor in choosing who you would vote for?

14. Even several hours after my tennis match, I still couldn't believe the (shocking, shocked) results.

15. People were (perturbing, perturbed) when they found out the concert had been canceled.

16. Dinner tonight consists of (frying, fried) rice with (steaming, steamed) vegetables.

17. Tuna salad with a generous helping of spicy mustard, lemon juice, and a little black pepper is an (energizing, energized) dish.

18. One of the most (amazing, amazed) animals is the owl.

19. The results of the football match were (disappointing, disappointed) for Asian fans, but the South Americans are still doing well in the tournament.

20. After swimming all afternoon, the children were clearly (exhausting, exhausted) and fell asleep just after dinner.

UNIT 4. Adjectives/Verbs/Nouns + Preposition

Underline the correct word in parentheses.

1. Your face is swollen. What happened (for, from, of, to, with) you?

2. Name something that most people are afraid (at, by, in, of, to).

3. The main reason (about, for, of, to, with) coming here today was to apply for a new job.

4. Some people are opposed to (change, changing) the name of the company.

5. There may be a new tax (about, in, of, on, with) tourist items such as hotel rooms and rental cars.

6. How is Korean different (by, from, in, on, with) Chinese?

7. Most of us are (aware from, familiar with, interested on) the travel route already.

8. I am always ready to help you, so you know you can count (about, by, of, on, with) me for sure.

9. Most of the children were successful (about, of, in, on, to) finishing their project on time.

10. Teenagers are not accustomed (for wake, for waking, to wake, to waking) up very early.

11. Water is composed (about, from, of, on, to) hydrogen and oxygen.

12. I like science, but I am really (accustomed by, excited with, good at) math.

13. My parents approve (by, for, in, of, with) my decision to work in New York.

14. How is this information relevant (about, from, of, to, with) your report?

15. Our departure time depends (about, for, on, to, with) several factors.

16. How similar is Portuguese (at, from, in, to, with) Spanish or French?

17. One advantage (at, by, in, of, on) your plan is that each person does less work.

18. Some of the students complained (about, for, of, to with) the new teacher's tests.

19. Are you worried at all (about, from, in, of, to) the weather forecast?

20. The United States consists (at, in, of, on, with) fifty states.

UNIT 5. Passive Voice

Underline the correct word in parentheses.

1. The proverb "practice (makes, is made) perfect" means that people (need, are needed) to practice something many times before it can (become, be become) perfect.

2. Flying from Miami to Singapore (requires, is required) at least two and quite possibly four different flights.

3. Many of the sweaters that (sold, are sold) in this store (produced, were produced) in Thailand.

4. An online credit card payment will (guarantee, be guaranteed) receipt of the product within a week.

5. Over time, planes can (damage, be damaged) due to a high number of take-offs and landings.

6. All applications for replacement passports due to theft or loss must (complete, be completed) online.

7. If the number of passengers (exceeds, is exceeded) the number of dinners on the plane, then the flight attendants (will have, will be had) to solve the problem on the spot.

8. To (reduce, be reduced) the amount of refined sugar in this recipe, you can (substitute, be substituted) applesauce or honey instead of using plain white sugar.

9. How much money (do you think, are you thought) you might (need, be needed) for retirement?

10. Flight 661 has already (taken, been taken) off, so you can now (track, be tracked) the flight online.

Write the correct form of the verb in parentheses.

11. Harvard University, which (call) _____ New College, (establish) _____ in 1636.

12. Sara Hale, who (work) _____ so hard to establish the American holiday of Thanksgiving, (write) _____ the famous children's poem "Mary Had a Little Lamb."

13. There is a proverb that (say) _____ "Lightning (no strike) _____ twice," which means that a bad thing (no happen) _____ twice.

14. Surprisingly, the first fax machine (invent) _____ in 1843.

15. Water (boil) _____ at 212 degrees Fahrenheit or 100 degrees Celsius.

16. The original White House (burn) _____ in the War of 1812.

17. Arabic (write) _____ from left to right.

18. The guillotine (use) _____ in France from 1792 to 1977, which means it (last) _____ 185 years.

19. In the summertime, the sun (set) _____ between 8:30 p.m. and 9:15 PM.

20. If you want to sign into your account, you must (enter) _____ the password correctly.

UNIT 6. Adjective Clauses

Underline the correct word in parentheses.

1. The book (whose, where, that) is on the table belongs to Joseph.

2. Although Miami (which is, who is, is) the largest city in Florida, it is not the capital city.

3. The police questioned the two passers-by (witnessed, that were witnessing, who witnessed) the accident.

4. George Washington, (that, whom, who) was born in 1732, was a very important historical figure.

5. This is the park (when, that, where) we used to play many years ago.

6. "Wheat Field with Crows" (is, which is, who is) believed to be Van Gogh's last painting.

7. Martha worked at Plymouth Bank, (that, which, where) had more than 100 full-time employees.

8. The grade (that received, which receiving, I received) was not expected.

9. Mr. Jones is the client for (who, which, whom) we have been preparing an extensive report.

10. The weather was very bad, (that, this, which) caused the buses and trains to be late.

11. People (who living, are living, who live) in glass houses should not throw stones.

12. My friend Terry is the realtor (sold, that was sold, who sold) the apartment building on Green Street to the coach of the football team.

13. "May I help you?" is a question (that, that is, is) frequently heard in businesses.

14. Applications (that submitted, when submitted, submitted) after the deadline will not be considered.

15. There are five people in my class who (has, have, are had) a new computer.

16. The winning team was the one (that had, who had, had) the most consistent players.

17. The Canadian, Greek, Peruvian, and Saudi flags (have, which have, having) only two colors.

18. Sweden, which is the fifth largest country in Europe, (ranks, which ranks, ranking) only eighteenth in terms of population.

19. The answer (that you wrote, whose was written by you, was writing) is only partially correct.

20. This map is the kind of map (we, which, where) needed on our last trip to Chile.

UNIT 7. Adverbs

Underline the correct word in parentheses.

1. She plays basketball very (good, well).

2. He made his father angry by (no say, no saying, doesn't say, not saying) anything all day.

3. Max and I love to visit (Paris during the summer, during the summer Paris).

4. She explained the lesson again (for help, for helping, to helping, to help) the weaker students.

5. They improved their English (by, for, with) finding many chances as possible to speak with natives.

6. The driver will be here (good, quick, soon, rapid).

7. I would like to get a new cell phone (for being, to be, for be, to being) able to talk to my family better.

8. This painting is (so, too) beautiful to keep in one person's house.

9. I failed the exam because it was (difficult extremely, extremely difficult).

10. Jack London is an author whose name (widely known is, is widely known).

11. I learned to make sushi (by watch, by watching, with watch, with watching) the Cooking Channel.

12. Unfortunately, we do not have (nearly money enough, nearly enough money, enough money nearly) to buy that beautiful house now.

13. The rock hit the window so (hard, hardly) that the glass went everywhere.

14. (Cutting after, After cutting, Cut after, After cut) the onions, put them in the frying pan.

15. You may pay by (credit card, a credit card) if you wish.

16. Jackie takes more pictures (by, for, in, with) her phone than anyone else I know.

17. I've been so busy these past few days that I (hard, hardly) had enough time to watch any of my favorite news programs on TV.

18. I got in better shape (by running, by run, by to run, by to running) 30 minutes every morning.

19. (To speak French fluently, To speak fluently French, Speaking fluent French, Speaking French fluent), you should practice every day.

20. They (didn't hardly, hardly, hardly did not) ate anything at lunch.

UNIT 8. Connectors

Underline the correct word and punctuation in parentheses.

1. Ten is not an odd number, and (so / either / neither / too) is twenty.

2. The operation was very difficult (, however, / ; however, / , therefore, / ; therefore,) it was successful.

3. It was raining heavily when the game was supposed to start. (Consequent / So / Consequently, / So,) the players as well as the fans had to wait an additional hour.

4. The flight leaves at noon (so /, so /so,) you should be at the airport by ten at the latest.

5. Customers need to have their original (receipts, to / receipts for / receipts and) a full refund.

6. (For / Although / But) I was in the kitchen, I was still able to hear the TV from the living room.

7. (So / Although / Therefore / While) every guest would have enough to eat, we ordered two sandwiches for each person.

8. My best friend plans to get a job in Mexico, (however / and / so) I do, too.

9. Brazil is a large country in South America, and (so is Argentina / Argentina is so).

10. When the phone (rang / rang, / , rang) we were eating dinner.

11. I would buy a new house for my (parents if / parents, if / parents so if) I won the lottery.

12. Most of the customers use a credit card (to / for / , to / , for) all of their major purchases.

13. Some cooks prefer to use limes instead of lemons (for / so / to) add a special flavor to their dishes.

14. The weather was (so cold, / so cold / too cold / to cold,) that I had to wear a sweater and a jacket.

15. When a connecting word starts a (sentence, therefore / sentence, / sentence so) that opening clause is followed by a comma.

16. A ticket from Miami to Boston is more than $500 (; however, / , however, / , however) a one-way ticket is almost $400.

17. Switzerland is a mountainous country, (and so is Austria / and Austria is so / but Austria is).

18. Mario loves popcorn, and his sister (loves too / does too / loves, too / does, too).

19. Clothing costs more this year (, because / because, / because) there is a new tax now.

20. Flight 882 never arrives early, and (so does / either arrives / neither does) Flight 881.

UNIT 9. Review of Verb Tenses

Underline the correct word in parentheses.

1. If you don't close the door, mosquitoes (come, have come, came, are going to come) in the house.

2. When I (check, checked, have checked) into my flight, I noticed that my suitcase was very close to the weight limit.

3. Some people are so addicted to video games that they (play, played, have played, have been playing, were played) them for more than ten hours every day.

4. In 1958, Sweden (host, hosts, was hosting, has hosted, hosted, was hosted) the World Cup, which was the only time that Sweden did so.

5. Joe said something, but no one (was understanding, understood, has understood) his words.

6. In 1989, the Berlin Wall (took, was taking, was taken, has taken, has been taken) down.

7. After the onions have been chopped up, the next step (is, was, has been) to sauté them in olive oil.

8. This medicine has a new ingredient that (allow, allows, allowed, have allowed) patients to sleep better.

9. I am pretty sure that the Chinese dish we ordered (has, had, was having) sesame oil in it because I could taste it.

10. Helsinki (is, was, has been, is being) the capital of Finland since 1812.

11. Because aspirin prevents blood from clotting, doctors sometimes (prescribe, are prescribing, have prescribed, are prescribed) it as a way to help prevent a heart attack.

12. We know that you have many banking options, so we (thank, thanked, have thanked, are thanked) you for your continued business with our institution.

13. Millions of years ago, dinosaurs (roam, were roamed, roamed, have roamed) all over the Earth.

14. In general, most adult hearts (have beat, beat, were beating, are beating) between 60 and 100 times per minute, with athletes experiencing a lower number.

15. According to the forecast for the next six hours, the weather (deteriorates, deteriorate, has deteriorated, was deteriorating, will deteriorate) even more.

16. If you need to talk with my supervisor, she (meets, met, has met, is meeting) with another client but can be with you in about fifteen minutes if you can wait a bit.

17. Space travel for humans may seem difficult, but humans (visit, are visiting, have visited, were visiting) the Moon and will one day set foot on a planet.

18. In English, prepositions come before nouns, but in Japanese, prepositions (follow, are following, were followed) nouns.

19. A valve is an instrument that (control, controls, controlled, has controlled, was controlling) the flow of a liquid by opening and closing passageways.

20. When the ambulance arrived at the scene of the accident between a truck and a car, the medics found that the driver of the car (was not breathing, did not breathe, has not been breathing, will not breathe).

Appendix A: Parts of Speech

Category	Definition	Examples
noun	a name of a person, place, thing, or abstract idea	*Maria, a store, a book*
verb	shows action or state of being	*eat, take, is*
pronoun	takes the place of a noun	*he, him, myself, mine, anything*
adjective	describes a noun or pronoun	*good, delicious, green*
preposition	shows relationships	*in, with, for*
conjunction	connects	*and, because, if*
adverb	describes verbs, adjectives, or other adverbs	*quickly, very, extremely*
interjection	expresses strong emotion	*Wow! Oh! No!*

Appendix B: Verb Tenses

Tense	Example
simple present	*I* drive *to my office every day.*
simple past	*I* lived *in an apartment in 2009.*
simple future	*I* will help *you with that job.*
present progressive	*I* am reading *these verbs right now.*
past progressive	*I* was watching *TV during the storm last night.*
future progressive	*I* will be flying *to Japan at midnight tonight.*
present perfect	*I* have been *here since 9 AM today.*
past perfect	*I* had been *in France twice before.*
future perfect	*I* will have finished *this work by midnight.*
present perfect progressive	*I* have been living *in Sacramento for two years.*
past perfect progressive	*I* had been reading *all night.*
future perfect progressive	*I* will have been working *here for thirty years.*

Appendix C: Irregular Past and Past Participles of Verbs

The vast majority of verbs in English are regular verbs, which means that their past tense and their past participles end in –ed.

Present	Past	Past Participle
add	added	added
like	liked	liked
map	mapped	mapped

Other verbs, however, are irregular, which means that their past tense and past participles are formed in some other way, including internal vowel changes (*sing–sang–sung*), *–en* or *–ne* (*choose-chose-chosen* or *go-went-gone*), and no change at all (*cut-cut-cut*). (Note that the present participle has not been included here because it always ends in *–ing*.)

Though some sources claim to have more than 350 irregular verbs, these lists often include rare words such as *forego* (*forego-forwent-forgone*), *hew* (*hew-hewed-hewn/hewed*), and *unspin* (*unspin-unspun-unspun*). The following chart lists 155 of the most frequently used irregular verbs. A list of 155 items may seem daunting to ELLs, but these verbs should be introduced in much smaller groups. For example, beginning students are often given a list of 25 of the most common verbs, and this list is increased as ELLs attain intermediate proficiency. See Teaching Technique 15 in ***Keys to Teaching Grammar to English Language Learners*** (Folse, 2009) for specific ideas for teaching these verb forms.

Present	Past	Past Participle
arise	arose	arisen
awake	awoke	awoken
be	was / were	been
bear	bore	born / borne
beat	beat	beaten / beat
become	became	become
begin	began	begun
bend	bent	bent
bet	bet	bet
bid	bid	bid
bind	bound	bound
bite	bit	bitten
bleed	bled	bled
blow	blew	blown
break	broke	broken
bring	brought	brought
broadcast	broadcast	broadcast
build	built	built
burst	burst	burst
buy	bought	bought
cast	cast	cast
catch	caught	caught
choose	chose	chosen
come	came	come
cost	cost	cost
creep	crept	crept
cut	cut	cut
deal	dealt	dealt
dig	dug	dug
dive	dove	dived
do	did	done
draw	drew	drawn
dream	dreamed / dreamt	dreamed / dreamt
drink	drank	drunk
drive	drove	driven
eat	ate	eaten
fall	fell	fallen
feed	fed	fed
feel	felt	felt
fight	fought	fought
find	found	found
fit	fit	fit
flee	fled	fled

fly	flew	flown
forbid	forbade	forbidden
forecast	forecast	forecast
foresee	foresaw	foreseen
forget	forgot	forgotten
forgive	forgave	forgiven
forsake	forsook	forsaken
freeze	froze	frozen
get	got	gotten
give	gave	given
go	went	gone
grind	ground	ground
grow	grew	grown
hang	hung	hung
have	had	had
hear	heard	heard
hide	hid	hidden
hit	hit	hit
hold	held	held
hurt	hurt	hurt
input	input	input
keep	kept	kept
kneel	knelt	knelt
know	knew	known
lay	laid	laid
lead	led	led
leave	left	left
lend	lent	lent
let	let	let
lie	lay	lain
light	lit / lighted	lit / lighted
lose	lost	lost
make	made	made
mean	meant	meant
meet	met	met
mislead	misled	misled
mistake	mistook	mistaken
misunderstand	misunderstood	misunderstood
overcome	overcame	overcome
overdo	overdid	overdone
override	overrode	overridden
oversee	oversaw	overseen
oversleep	overslept	overslept
overtake	overtook	overtaken
overthrow	overthrew	overthrown

pay	paid	paid
prove	proved	proven / proved
put	put	put
quit	quit	quit
read	read	read
ride	rode	ridden
ring	rang	rung
rise	rose	risen
run	ran	run
say	said	said
see	saw	seen
seek	sought	sought
sell	sold	sold
send	sent	sent
set	set	set
sew	sewed	sewn / sewed
shake	shook	shaken
shed	shed	shed
shoot	shot	shot
show	showed	shown / showed
shrink	shrank	shrunk
shut	shut	shut
sing	sang	sung
sit	sat	sat
sleep	slept	slept
slide	slid	slid
sling	slung	slung
slit	slit	slit
speak	spoke	spoken
speed	sped	sped
spend	spent	spent
spin	spun	spun
split	split	split
spread	spread	spread
stand	stood	stood
steal	stole	stolen
stick	stuck	stuck
stink	stank / stunk	stunk
strike	struck	struck / stricken
string	strung	strung
swear	swore	sworn
sweep	swept	swept
swell	swelled	swollen
swim	swam	swum
swing	swung	swung

take	took	taken
teach	taught	taught
tear	tore	torn
tell	told	told
think	thought	thought
throw	threw	thrown
thrust	thrust	thrust
understand	understood	understood
undertake	undertook	undertaken
undo	undid	undone
uphold	upheld	upheld
upset	upset	upset
wake	woke	woken
wear	wore	worn
weave	wove	woven
weep	wept	wept
wet	wet	wet
win	won	won
wind	wound	wound
withdraw	withdrew	withdrawn
write	wrote	written